A Road to Sacred Creation

A ROAD TO SACRED CREATION

Rudolf Steiner's Perspectives on Technology

A Compendium, Volume 1

Edited by
Gary Lamb

Research Associates:
Virginia Hermann, Martin Miller

Illustrated by
Michael Howard

SteinerBooks | 2021

STEINERBOOKS
Anthroposophic Press, Inc.
402 Union Street, No. 58
Hudson, NY 12534
www.steinerbooks.org

Cover drawing: Michael Howard
Book design: William Jens Jensen

LIBRARY OF CONGRESS CONTROL NUMBER: 2021939440
ISBN: 978-1-62148-261-1 (paperback)

Printed in the United States of America

Contents

Preface

How I Came to Edit this Compendium

There are two specific incidents that propelled me to take on the task of creating a compendium of Rudolf Steiner's perspectives on technology. The first is related to an illustration I first saw several years ago, referred to as the "Future Education Map," which was created by an international organization, Global Education Futures (globaledufutures.org). This map provided an imagination of what education would look like by the year 2035. It was not simply about traditional pre-kindergarten education through graduate work; rather, it extolled "personalized learning trajectories [that would] support individual learners from early childhood until their great age" and "integrate formal and informal education, career, volunteering and hobbies, leisure, entertainment, and community." In other words, it portrayed technology as the primary vehicle for educating children and adults in every aspect of cultural life. The map highlighted such things as biometric monitoring, digital reputation badges, social learning platforms, the internet of things, and big data.

This imagination of education shook me to the core. I had been closely following, writing on, and speaking about government education reform efforts in the United States and Europe beginning in the early 1980s. These reforms were guided by representatives of federal and state governments, big business, and major philanthropic organizations. I had known that technology was envisioned to play a central role in education reforms, but now it became clear that formal education was merely a part of what was ultimately a vision of technology being implemented wherever and whenever learning occurred from birth to death. This map further underscored the reality that the primary purpose of education, at least in the West, has been, and continues to be, maximizing economic growth.

The other experience that inspired me to work on this compendium occurred during a series of three technology retreats I helped organize shortly after my encounter with the work of Global Education Futures. As preparation for each retreat, the coordinators proposed certain readings based on the work of Rudolf Steiner. The reading material used for the third retreat was *Machines and the Human Spirit* by Paul Emberson. Emberson had already published a two-volume set about the evolution of technology, *From Gondishapur to Silicon Valley*. For me, Emberson engaged with the issue of technology based on Rudolf Steiner's perspective in a profound way. He was also the first person I came across who wrote about possible new forms of technology that would be created in the future as indicated by Steiner, such as a morally-based technology that could be developed and operated only through the power of selfless love. However, one of the challenges the retreat participants encountered with Emberson's book *Machines and the Human Spirit,* especially with regards to some of the more startling and prophetic proscriptions about the effects of technology, was a sense of ambiguity as to whether Emberson was expressing Steiner's views or his own. This uncertainty left a number of us with the feeling that a comprehensive overview of Steiner's indications on technology was urgently needed in the face of the enormous advances that technology companies were making, seemingly void of ethical standards or moral striving. This situation is made worse because our legal system seems to be at a loss as to how to hold the technology industry accountable for its unethical actions and the harmful effects of the products they make.

Research Methods

Rudolf Steiner's collected works entails about 340 volumes, including about six thousand lectures and approximately forty volumes of written works. Even though he wrote no books on technology nor gave any lecture cycles on the subject, references to technology were identified in about a third of his collected works. Over one hundred such references are included in this volume.

Because Steiner wrote and spoke in German, I began by exploring German anthroposophical books and articles addressing the topic of technology. Even without being fluent in German, it was relatively straightforward to search through the references listed in various works, and secure titles, lecture dates, and collected works numbers. With this information, my research assistants and I could search through corresponding writings and lectures translated into English. We are fortunate to be located close to the Rudolf Steiner Library, in Hudson, New York, which has the largest selection of Steiner's works in English in North America. In addition to hard copies, the library has online search vehicles that we used for topic-related searches.

We employed a spreadsheet format to keep track of Steiner-related references that filled more than thirty-five pages of listings. In the process, we identified and numbered 173 possible topics that were related to technology, and each passage we found was then assigned one or more of the topic numbers. Some of the initial passages were separated into two or more sections according to topic or theme. At a certain point, due to the vast amount of material being gathered, it became clear that at least two volumes would be needed.

Once we had assembled and transcribed the bulk of potential passages, the next task was to sort the references by their assigned topics into groupings under broader themes. This process of collating passages required a significant trimming down of each individual excerpt in order to focus in on essential ideas. Such "pruning" of Steiner's thoughts was painful at times. However, through essentializing, the ideas themselves began to find new connections and contexts. This does not mean there were not seemingly contradictory or inscrutable passages. In such cases, every effort was made to present a multiplicity of perspectives to enable readers to resolve apparent riddles. But to understand and work with Rudolf Steiner's perspectives on technology, especially those of a prophetic nature, ultimately requires a meditative approach.

Editor's Note

The intention in creating this compendium is to provide a broad and comprehensive source of Rudolf Steiner's spiritual-scientific perspectives on technology for personal enlightenment and individual and group research. The attempt was continually made to provide a variety of statements on each topic or theme, especially if some appeared to be contradictory. I have tried to present Steiner's views as objectively as possible, allowing readers to establish their own orientation and reach their own conclusions regarding the future of technology.

In volume one, I have for the most part kept my interpretations based on spiritual-scientific perspectives of the state, use, and effects of modern technology peripheral to the main body of text. Therefore, they appear mainly in chapter notes. However, I think such interpretations by qualified people are essential if this compendium is to have any meaningful impact on the course of technology development. But it is a task that is beyond the scope of this compendium.

I have also tried to keep esoteric vernacular and descriptions to a minimum in the first volume in order to make it as accessible as possible for first-time and newly-acquainted readers of spiritual science. These esoteric terms and concepts will increase in breadth and extent in volume two.

Sacred Creation: Why a Road, Not the Road

Rudolf Steiner's perspectives on technology are manifold and prophetic. He not only critiqued the technology of his day but foretold new forms of technology that would inevitably arise, technologies that would be connected to the makers' very attitudes of soul, either the good or bad within them—in other words, their deepest motivations. How we, as evolving human beings, approach technology and its development will be instrumental in determining how ultimately human evolution will turn out. Our future as human beings and the future of technology are intimately connected. Because of this, and the vastness of the spiritual and physical factors that need to be considered, it would be imprudent to suggest that there is only one approach to researching and developing the new forms of technology that will inevitably come. This compendium offers one way, not the only way. Volume one will identify some of the personal knowledge, inner capacities, and social requirements needed to safely engage in developing technology as an act of sacred creation.

Hand-drawn Illustrations

There are two series of illustrations that appear in this volume that were drawn by Michael Howard. One is related to various atomic theories that arose since the late nineteenth century, including three inspired by Rudolf Steiner's indications; these appear in chapters two and three. The other series of images appears at the beginning of each chapter. They are attempts to make visible a particular quality or dynamic found in a key passage or two in the chapters. Both series serve two purposes. One is to provide the reader with an imaginative picture of a natural and/or spiritual-scientific perspective of the preexisting and human-created world in which we live. The other purpose is to begin, in a preliminary way, a process that is essential for the development of morally based technologies in the future—that is, reintegrating science, art, and spiritual-religious ethics and attitudes in humanly creative processes, including developing new forms of technologies. For instance, the renderings of atoms arose from a dialogue and exchange of perspectives on various atomic theories among Michael Howard, an artist, Gopi Krishna Vijaya, a physicist, and Gary Lamb, the editor of this compendium. The images born from this kind of dialogue should be viewed as pointing in a certain direction. As such, they are works in progress that can be continually modified and developed as new thoughts and perspectives arise while proceeding along the road to sacred creation.

Introduction

Many of Rudolf Steiner's statements about technology were prophetic. For example, he maintained that so-called modern technology would, in essence, collapse upon itself in the not-too-distant future. So too, new forms of technology will arise to replace the current ones. Some of these new forms would be based on harnessing vibrations originating in the human soul, including thoughts, feelings, and attitudes. These vibrations could then be transferred, perhaps through hand gestures or tones, picked up and amplified by delicately attuned machines, and then converted to energy in the form of heat, light, or the capability to power other machinery. Yet other energy sources will be developed through harnessing earthly and cosmic rhythms and the life or etheric forces in plant seeds and living creatures.

There is a great moral challenge in the development of all these new, and in many cases, more powerful forms of "harmonious oscillation" technology. It is not a question of whether, or even what kinds of these or other technologies will be created in the future, but *how* and *why* they are created and used. What is the motivation of the people who create them? Are they primarily motivated to serve their personal egotism, with the goal of gaining financial profit and/or power over others? Or will future technologies be created out of altruism, for the good of humanity, based on a spiritualized knowledge of the human being and the great goals of human and Earth evolution?

Steiner speaks of the need in the future for creative work, and eventually all work, to become a sacred activity of a sacramental nature. Ultimately, the driving force for new forms of etheric technology needs to be of the highest moral quality—that is, selfless love. For this reason, people often call this type of technology *moral technology*.

It is important to understand that in the act of sacred creation we are becoming co-creators with the divine, with the gods. And all creation—including industrial, technological production—needs to be brought into harmony with the great goals of human evolution. This transformational process depends upon imbuing human creative activity with empathic altruism.

The path or road to such sacred creation has multiple lanes, including inner development, relationship building, and creating ethical social forms. It is not a path that one can travel as a lone researcher with either efficacy or the timeliness necessary to accomplish what needs to be done. Creating technology of the future will require collaboration, both in the realm of thinking and practical work. And if it is ever to achieve the stage of becoming a sacred activity, working in collaboration will need to take precedence over working in isolation.

To begin with, by considering atoms as the intersection of cosmic forces and the natural world as the intersection of both cosmic and central forces, we gain insight into how to transform lifeless machines into sacred creations that employ moral forces for the good of humanity. This will be a significant advancement beyond contemporary electricity-based technology, which often can have harmful effects.

Steiner initiated efforts to neutralize the harmful effects of electricity, for instance, by working in new ways with stage lighting and electrical heating systems. He apparently had hopes of redeeming the cinema of his time through the portrayal of human destiny in the context of repeated earth lives. Nevertheless, he also took steps to create an alternative to the cinema that would stimulate human imagination in a positive way through a new art form that he called *light-play art.*

By referring to the American inventor John Worrell Keely and the character Dr. Strader in his Mystery Dramas, Rudolf Steiner described various aspects of new forms of technology. Keely is presented as an intuitively gifted inventor who had certain successes in creating energy through harmonious oscillation techniques, which he could activate through sound and gesture. Fortunately, his success was limited, according to Steiner, because he worked instinctively rather than out of conscious knowledge of the forces he was trying to activate. The character Strader was able to have some success at the experimental level in creating a new form of energy that could be activated anywhere, thus eliminating the need for major power grids, but he too was not able to create a production model because his prototype had an inherent flaw.

For a time, Steiner worked with a young scientist, Ehrenfried Pfeiffer, conducting research and experiments on the development of etheric technology. Here, too, the progress was stymied because of unfavorable results. Steiner told Pfeiffer that he should discontinue his experimentation until principles of a threefold social organism and Waldorf education were more prominent, and when the idea that the heart is in effect a pump was deposed.

The principles of social threefolding and Waldorf education are outlined here to enable the reader to understand why Steiner wanted them to be more prominent.

Volume one concludes with chapters on the spiritual being Ahriman, who is intricately linked to modern technology, and Lucifer, who is currently assisting him. The Christ being is then described as the spiritual balance between Ahriman and Lucifer.

The final chapter focuses on thinking as a spiritual activity that is independent of the brain. This fundamental tenant of Steiner's epistemological and physiological lectures and writings is an important reality to grasp in order to be able to develop the appropriate understanding of human consciousness and artificial intelligence, which will be taken up in volume two.

The Evolution of Science

From Natural Science to Spiritual Science
by Way of Goethe

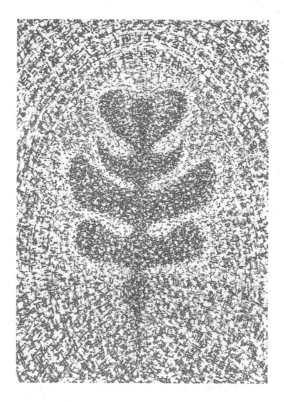

If human beings will only give up looking for anything coarsely material as the basis of nature... they will come to something quite different; they will discover rhythms, rhythmical orderings, everywhere in nature.... In the plants... everything is rhythmically ordered.... The discerning of nature's rhythms, that will be true natural science. (note 35)

The Evolution of Science

From Natural Science to Spiritual Science by Way of Goethe

Introduction

The current forms of technology, their possible applications, and the motivation for creating them are informed by the prevailing materialistic sciences and view of life held by their creators.

This leads to the question: What is the motivation of these innovators to create the inventions they bring about? Is it to make money, to feel the thrill of creation, to gain power over others, or to consciously do good for humanity?

The question of motivation will be an ongoing inquiry in this compendium. In the modern age of technology, the question of motivation is related in some degree to religious beliefs, but more often to the scientific view of life that developers learn, ascribe to, and live by. In this chapter, not only is the significance of natural science upheld but also the current necessity for transitioning to a spiritual science that builds on and extends the findings of natural science. This transition, which begins with the scientific research of Johann Wolfgang von Goethe, is not only necessary for the ethical foundation and moral advancement of technology but also for all human and Earth evolution.

Overview

Western civilization for the most part has gradually lost its inborn connection to the spiritual world over the last four to five hundred years through the pursuit of a natural science that focuses exclusively on the perceptible world. Its focus on mathematics and what can be weighed, measured, and counted in the inanimate world has accelerated this loss. Even so, this type of thinking has been especially useful in mastering the sensible world, and particularly helpful in the development of technology.

Johann Wolfgang von Goethe rejected natural science's exclusive focus on the mineral or physical aspects of the world, the attendant abstract classifications of the organic world of plants and animals into species and genus, and the tendency to accept "weigh, measure, and count" as the only justifiable methodology for gathering information or data.

Instead of these classifications, Goethe wanted to strictly adhere to perceived phenomena by simplifying and grouping what he observed and by recording when and where transformations and metamorphoses occurred. In the process, he also wanted to allow his perception of the growth forces in plants to live in his soul. By focusing on the plant world over many years and "reading" their phenomena, he learned to perceive a spiritual reality that underlies all plant forms, which he called the *archetypal plant.*

Goethe's phenomenological approach to studying the organic realm was a major breakthrough in the evolution of science. Unlike the inanimate world, the sense-perceptible factors in the animate world are not determined solely by other sense-perceptible factors. For instance, when a billiard ball is struck by another ball, the phenomena, both prior to and after the collision, are visible to the naked eye. In the organic or living world, there is a higher unity at play that is not visible. Goethe called this higher, overseeing entity, the *entelechy.*

Goethe was both a scientist and an artist. He maintained that his scientific research and artistic creations were derived from the same source and that they were both equal interpreters of the mysteries of the world.

Rudolf Steiner held Goethe's artistic and scientific works in the highest regard and considered spiritual science to be an extension and expansion of Goethe's accomplishments.

Even though Steiner esteemed Goethe's scientific contributions, he also viewed certain features of natural science as important aids in developing spiritual faculties and conducting spiritual scientific research, including their rigor and exactitude. However, to the degree that natural science focuses exclusively on the inanimate aspects of the world, it is primarily a science of the past, relying on information and data on what already is or has already occurred. Relying exclusively on such quantitative data collected from past events, without including qualitative factors, can have an antisocial, harmful effect, particularly when applied to the social sciences, such as economics.

A science that wants to provide a service to the future development of the social life of humanity must go beyond the sensible to include the spiritual reality that underlies the sensible world. This is a primary goal of spiritual science.

The next great advancement of natural science will be when it goes beyond the sensible to researching and contemplating through imaginative thought forms the metamorphoses and great rhythms within nature and the cosmos, and, ultimately, the spirit itself.

Part 1: A CRITIQUE OF MATERIALISTIC NATURAL SCIENCE UP TO THE EARLY TWENTIETH CENTURY

Cultivation of abstract ideas and intellectualism

Over the last four centuries, abstract rational thinking has become the dominant means of understanding the world and human life. This rational or intellectual thinking is highly spiritual in a certain way, but it lacks the capacity and vitality to go beyond the boundary of the perceptible world.

Let me refer back to earlier lectures and characterize civilized humanity's spiritual evolution over the last four centuries. During this period, intellectual, rational thinking emerged as the primary force in our collective development and our striving for knowledge. As the natural sciences experienced major triumphs and provided an abundance of scientific information on outer realities, our way of relating to the outer world—that is, the inner process of shaping ideas about the natural world and about our life—became thoroughly intellectual.... The most characteristic element of modern soul-spiritual life is its gradual development of abstract, very finely differentiated ideas and concepts, which lack the inherent energy needed to approach anything beyond sense-perceptible reality.[1]

Mathematics and the scientific worldview as death of living thought

Modern science has adopted abstract mathematics as its primary mode of inquiry and analysis. Mathematics is useful for studying the inanimate but provides little foundation for understanding living processes and life itself. It is highly effective in minute analysis and differentiation. But when these differentiated parts are integrated again, all the life that was inherent in them has been lost, eliminated. Nevertheless, we must understand the inanimate or all that is dead in the world since life cannot exist with death.

Modern science set out to master the natural phenomena by means of a mathematics detached from the human being, a mathematics no longer inwardly experienced. By adopting this abstract mathematical view and these concepts divorced from the human being, science arrived at a point where it could examine only the inanimate. Having taken mathematics out of the sphere of living experience, one can only apply it to what is dead. Therefore, owing to this mathematical approach, modern science is directed exclusively to the sphere of death. In the universe,

---

1   Rudolf Steiner, *Freedom of Thought and Societal Forces*, lect. 12/30/1919.

death manifests itself in disintegration, in atomization, in reduction to microscopic parts—putting it simply, in a crumbling into dust. This is the direction taken by the present-day scientific attitude. With a mathematics detached from all living experience, it takes hold of everything in the cosmos that turns to dust, that atomizes. From this moment onward, it becomes possible to dissipate mathematics itself into differentials. We actually kill all living forms of thought.... To differentiate is to kill; to integrate is to piece the dead together again in some kind of framework, to fit the differentials together again into a whole. But they do not thereby become alive again, after having been annihilated....

In earlier times, the coming-into-being, the germinating, had been studied; now, one looked at all that was fading and crumbling into dust. The human being's conception was heading toward atomism, whereas previously it had tended toward the continuous, lasting aspects of things. Since life cannot exist without death and all living things must die, we must look at and understand all that is dead in the world. A science of the inanimate, the dead, had to arise; it was absolutely necessary.[2]

Number, measure, and weight as foundation of reality for modern mechanistic thinking and technical science

Modern science has come to rely on number, weight, and measure as the primary factors in understanding and determining what is real in the physical world. These also created the basis for the development of the technical sciences and technology.[3] Insofar as we live in a technical society, number, weight, and measure are the foundations of modern civilization.

The scales, the measuring rod—to weigh, to count, to measure— these are the ideal of the modern scientist, of the modern technician, whose entire profession has actually developed on the basis

---

2   Rudolf Steiner, *The Origins of Natural Science*, lect. 12/27/1922.

3   Technical sciences mainly focus on the research, development, and use of machines in industry, transportation, and communications.

of external science. We have brought things to such a pass that an important mathematician of our times, in response to the question 'What is the guarantee of existence?' gave the following answer.... "Anything that can be measured is real; anything that cannot be measured is not real." The ideal thing, in this view, is for everything that exists to be brought into the laboratory and weighed, measured, and counted. From the results of this weighing, measuring, and counting, one construes the things that are accepted as science, which then informs technology. Number, measure, and weight are therefore meant to become the foundation of all civilization.[4]

Abstract thinking has enabled technology and human freedom to develop

Because of the focus on number, weight, and measure, materialistic science has limited the possibility of consciously knowing the realm of the living in any depth or profundity. On the positive side, this focus on the material aspects of life has fostered the development of technology and provided for more freedom from outer constraints.

It was both necessary and right for humanity to spend three or four centuries developing the independent intellect. We achieved a certain freedom from natural constraints, but the resulting intellectualism must now be re-imbued with soul and spirit.[5]

People nowadays prefer their concepts to be convenient. However, rigid concepts with sharply defined contours can be applied only to what is dead and does not budge, thus allowing our concepts to remain rigid. Nevertheless, living in rigid concepts that ignore everything living has given us the opportunity to attain an inner awareness of freedom....

Two developments have come about as a result of our concepts having become dead: first, the awareness of freedom, and second, the possibility to apply the rigid concepts, which

---

4   Rudolf Steiner, *Harmony of the Creative Word*, lect. 10/20/1923.
5   Rudolf Steiner, *Freedom of Thought and Societal Forces*, lect. 12/30/1919.

have been developed out of what is dead and can be used only for what is dead, in our magnificent, triumphant technology, which is nothing more than the putting into practice of a rigid system of ideas.[6]

Modern natural science has cut us off from the living aspect of nature. We yearn for the living element in our souls and not to remain in the world of inanimate and lifeless facts.

Ancient peoples naturally perceived life everywhere outside in nature. Modern science's focus on the inanimate is compelling human beings to find the living element in the world through their own inner effort.

We have to understand how human beings, in a sense, have cut themselves off from everything living, that the living has become alien to them. And we also have to understand that when we do not want to remain in the realm of the dead but want to take the impulse of the living into our soul, then we must find this living element on our own.

In very ancient times, people saw life in every cloud formation, every flash of lightning, every roll of thunder, in every living plant, and so on. In a sense, they breathed in life and thus understood it, and without any effort they were in the midst of life. They only had to take in life from the outside. In contrast, in our evolutionary stage, our concepts can grasp only what is dead, and the outer environment can no longer give us what is alive. Therefore, we must bring forth this living element out of the innermost core of our being.[7]

---

6   Rudolf Steiner, *Earthly Knowledge and Heavenly Wisdom*, lect. 2/18/1923.
7   Rudolf Steiner, *Earthly Knowledge and Heavenly Wisdom*, lect. 2/18/1923.

Technology and natural-scientific thinking

Technology is something that we as human beings are able to create, examine, and understand in minute detail. In this sense, materialistic thinking has reached a level of perfection in the technical sciences. The realm of the organic world, however, is quite different from the world of mechanics and technology in that there are many possible variables and unknowns when considering the organic world.

Modern thinking is embodied in mechanics and machinery. And the prevalence of technology in life, in turn, has shaped our modern worldview.

> When we utilize nature's laws in technology, we actually create the phenomena ourselves. . . . What really matters in technology is that which we want to control. And because it is we ourselves who put everything together in the experiments, we can survey every detail. It is just because every detail is surveyable that one can have an immediate feeling of certainty about what is built up technically—for example, in chemistry; whereas, when one turns to nature, there is always the possibility of several interpretations. So, it must be said that a thinking which is truly of our time is to be seen at its most perfect in the technician. Individuals who have no inkling as to how a machine or chemical product is made and works do not yet think in the modern way. They let other people think in them, as it were—namely, people who are in the know, who think technically. The external achievements of technology such as mechanisms, chemistry, and so on have gradually become a basis for a modern view of the world. In the course of time this approach has spread to what is today regarded as a world conception.[8]

8   Rudolf Steiner, *The Human Soul in Relation to World Evolution*, lect. 5/7/1922.

Part 2: GOETHEAN SCIENCE

Basic differences between natural science and Goethean science

When Goethe began his study of natural phenomena, he was troubled by the abstract classifications of species and genera used by natural science in plant and animal research. He was much more concerned with transformation and the metamorphosis of and between phenomena that he perceived by entering into the natural phenomena and trying to understand their inherent movements and rhythms.

> When Goethe began to occupy himself with natural phenomena, he found the classification of natural beings and facts into species and genera highly problematic. He questioned the validity of inducing certain rigid concepts of species and genus from individual concrete beings and concrete facts. Instead, he wanted to pursue the gradual transformation of one phenomenon into another, to follow the transformation of one state of a being into another. What concerned him was not classification into species and genera, but rather the metamorphosis of natural phenomena as well as of individual beings in nature.[9]

Goethe's approach to morphology as the basis for studying organic or living entities

Goethe's contribution to the study of living beings is a major contribution to the evolution of science. There is a fundamental difference in the phenomena of inorganic and organic objects. With inorganic objects, our concepts are derived directly from what we perceive. We succeed in understanding inorganic interactions to the degree that we can associate concepts with what we perceive with our senses. There is nothing in one that is not in the other.

> The great significance of Goethe's morphological works [plant and animal studies] is to be sought in the fact that in them the

---

9   Rudolf Steiner, *The Light Course*, lect. 12/23/1919.

*theoretical basis and method for studying organic entities are established, and this **is a scientific deed of the first order.***

*If one is to do justice to this rightly, one must above all bear in mind the great difference existing between the phenomena of inorganic nature and those of organic nature. A phenomenon of the first kind, for example, is the impact of two elastic balls upon one another. If one ball is at rest and the other ball strikes it from a certain direction and with a certain velocity, then the first ball is likewise given a certain direction and velocity. If it is a matter then of **comprehending** such a phenomenon, this can be achieved only by our transforming into concepts what is directly there for the senses. We would succeed in this to the extent that nothing of a sense-perceptibly real nature remained that we had not permeated conceptually. We see one ball approach and strike the other, which then goes on moving. We have **comprehended** this phenomenon when, from the mass, direction, and velocity of the first ball, and from the mass of the second, we can determine the direction and velocity of the second ball, when we see that under the given conditions this phenomenon must **necessarily** occur. But this means nothing other than: that which offers itself to our senses must appear as a **necessary consequence** of what we have to postulate ideally beforehand. If this is the case, then we can say that concept and phenomenon coincide.*

There is nothing in the concept that is not also in the phenomenon, and nothing in the phenomenon that is not also in the concept.[10]

Things are different when we strive to understand living organisms. The sense-perceptible factors of the various aspects of a living organism are determined not simply by other sense-perceptible factors of the same kind, as in the case of inorganic phenomena. The sense-perceptible factors of what is living are determined by a non-perceptible influence, which is a higher unity that overarches the whole organism. Consequently, the constituent parts of an organism

---

10   Rudolf Steiner, *Goethean Science*, ch. 4.

serve and are served by something higher. Thus, if we want to understand living organisms, we need to go beyond the organism itself. Until Goethe's research findings, the study of living organisms posed an unsolvable riddle for scientists. If we want to understand what unifies the various parts of a plant, we need to go beyond the sense world to the world of concepts. However, there seems to be a division between observation and conceptualization. The object appears in the sense world but seems to be governed by something of another world. Goethe was the first person to address this riddle, as will be described in the section following this one.

> In the case of an organism, sense-perceptible factors appear— form, size, color, warmth conditions of an organ, for example – that are not determined by factors of the same kind. One cannot say of the plant, for example, that the size, form, location, etc. of the roots determine the sense-perceptible factors of the leaf or blossom. A body for which this were the case would not be an organism but rather a machine. It must be admitted that all the sense-perceptible factors of a living being do not manifest as a result of other sense-perceptible factors, as is the case with inorganic nature. On the contrary, in an organism, all sense-perceptible qualities manifest as the result of a factor that is no longer **sense-perceptible**. They manifest as the result of a higher unity hovering over the sense-perceptible processes. It is not the shape of the root which determines that of the trunk, nor the trunk's shape which determines that of the leaf, and so on; rather, all these forms are determined by something standing over them that itself is not again a form observable by the senses; these forms do exist for one another, but not as a result of one another. They do not mutually determine one another, but rather are all determined by something else. Here we cannot trace what we perceive with our senses back to other sense-perceptible factors; we must take up, into the concept of the processes, elements that do not belong to the world of the senses; **we must go out of and beyond the sense world**. Observation no longer suffices; we must grasp **the unity** conceptually if we want to explain the phenomena.

*Because of this, however, a separation occurs between observation and concept; they no longer seem to coincide with each other; the concept hovers over what is observed. It becomes difficult to see the connection. Whereas in inorganic nature, concept and reality were one, here they seem to diverge and actually to belong to two different worlds. The observation that offers itself directly to the senses no longer seems to bear within itself its own basis, its own being. The object does not seem explainable out of itself, but rather from something else. Because the object appears in a way not governed by the laws of the sense world, but is there for the senses, appears nevertheless to the senses, it is then as though we stood here before an insoluble contradiction in nature, as though a chasm existed between inorganic phenomena, which are comprehensible through themselves, and organic beings, in which an intrusion into the laws of nature occurs, **in which universally valid laws seem suddenly to be broken.** Up until Goethe, in fact, science generally considered this chasm to exist; he was the first to succeed in speaking the word that solved the riddle.*[11]

Archetypal phenomena

It is important to understand the principal difference between how Goethe approached nature and how natural science conducts research. Early twentieth-century natural science conducted experiments in the effort to determine the causes behind phenomena. In contrast, Goethe always focused on what is known without worrying at the outset whether various aspects of his perceptions could be weighed, measured, or counted. Rather than putting all his efforts toward determining the unknown that lies behind what is observable, Goethe focused on the observable phenomena, simplifying and grouping them in a way that allows the phenomena reveal their own secrets. He referred to these simplified facts or occurrences as archetypal phenomena.

The way that all of post-Goethean natural science has gone into so-called natural causes was also not at all to Goethe's

---

11 *Goethean Science*, ch. 4.

way of thinking. Concerning this point especially it is of great importance to become acquainted with the principal difference between the method of current natural science and the way Goethe approached nature. Current natural science conducts experiments. It investigates phenomena, attempts to elaborate them conceptually, and seeks to form notions of the so-called causes behind the phenomena—for example, the objective wave movement in the ether as the cause behind the subjective light and color phenomenon.

Goethe does not employ any of this style of scientific thinking. In his research he does not go from the so-called known into the so-called unknown at all. Instead, he always wants to stay with the known, without at first worrying about whether the known is merely subjective—an effect on our senses, our nerves, our soul—or objective. Concepts such as subjective color phenomena or objective wave movement out there in space do not figure with Goethe at all. Instead, what he sees revealed in space and taking place in time is something completely undivided whose subjectivity and objectivity he does not question. He does not employ the thinking and methods used in the natural sciences to induce the unknown from the known. Rather, he employs all his thinking and all his methods to putting the phenomena themselves together, so that, by juxtaposing them, he finally arrives at phenomena he calls archetypal phenomena, which in turn, without consideration of their subjectivity or objectivity, express what he wants to make the basis of his study of nature and of the world. Therefore, Goethe stays within the sequence of the phenomena; he merely simplifies them and then regards the simple phenomena that can be comprehended in this way as the archetypal phenomenon [das Urphänomen].[12]

Goethe placed little value on what natural science refers to as the laws of nature. More important to him were the facts that emerged from a coherent description of what is being observed.

---

12   Rudolf Steiner, *The Light Course*, lect. 12/23/1919.

Goethe regards the whole of what we can call the scientific method only as a tool for grouping the phenomena within the phenomenal sphere itself so that they reveal their own secrets. Nowhere does Goethe attempt to take refuge from a so-called known in any unknown. Therefore, for him there is also nothing that we can call a natural law.

You have a natural law if I say that in their orbits around the Sun the planets make certain motions that describe such and such paths. For Goethe it was not important to arrive at such laws. What he expresses as the basis of his research are facts—for example, the fact of how light and matter placed in its path affect each other. He expresses the effect in words; it is not a law, but a fact. And he attempts to base his study of nature on such facts. He does not want to ascend from the known to the unknown. He also does not want to have laws. What he actually wants is a kind of rational description of nature. Only, for him, there is a difference between the initial description of the phenomenon, which is unmediated and complex, and the description gained by uncovering the simplest elements. Goethe uses these simple elements as the basis of his study of nature, in the same way that otherwise the unknown or the purely conceptually posited framework of laws is used.[13]

Spiritually appropriate way to perceive the world

Goethe made an intensive study of plants and animals for several years using the phenomenological approach previously described. Through this process he gained an understanding of the spiritually perceptible reality that underlies all plant forms, which he called the archetypal plant. To gain such an understanding, he utilized his senses, his intelligence, and the spiritual aspect of his being. He searched for simple elements of the perceptible world and their inherent connections. This type of cognition and inquiry submerges itself in the essence of living things to such a degree that the creative energy

---

13 Ibid.

and growth of plants merges with the creative energy that forges connecting ideas in the soul.

Goethe, who was aware of the growth forces in plants, sought to allow them to live in his soul and come alive in his thoughts. He focused on phenomena as they were perceived and did not try to connect them to anything that might be behind these phenomena.

> You may recall that Goethe undertook an exhaustive study of plants and animals after assuming his responsibilities in Weimar. In the mid-1780s, after years of observation and experimentation in Weimar and Jena, he traveled to Italy, where his ideas on the relationship between plants and the earth coalesced. In letters to friends at home in Weimar, he wrote that he was very close to fully understanding the archetypal plant, the motif—perceptible only in spirit—that unites and underlies all individual plant forms....
>
> His statement tells us that he was attempting to develop a "spiritually appropriate" (as he put it) way of perceiving the natural world—a means of acquiring knowledge that engages not only the senses and human intelligence but also the entire spiritual aspect of the human being. This type of cognition submerges itself in the essence of living things, becoming one with them to such an extent that the creative energy manifesting in plant growth in the outer world and the living energy at work in creating the corresponding "ideas" in the human soul are experienced as being one and the same.
>
> Goethe was clearly aware of the growth-force active in plants as they develop leaf by leaf, node by node, flower by flower. He wanted to connect with that creative force, to allow it to live in his own soul. His intention was to allow the forces inherent in outer objects to come alive in his conceptions of them.
>
> This approach to knowledge aspires to an extremely intimate sharing of experience with outer living things.[14]

---

14   Rudolf Steiner, *Freedom of Thought and Societal Forces*, lect. 12/30/1919.

The Goethean approach to reading phenomena

Goethe's "original or archetypal plant" is not one specific plant visible to the human eye but an image that arises internally when we take in the phenomena of the plant from many different perspectives. Even so, this image is outwardly confirmed everywhere in nature.

Ultimately, this all comes down to staying with the phenomena and learning to read and interpret their meaning.

> It is completely wrong to insist...that with his "original plant," Goethe meant an actual specific plant.... Goethe was talking about an image that could be created internally but nevertheless be verified anywhere in the external world....
>
> This is what made Goethe say to Schiller: "In that case, I see my ideas with my eyes." He saw them with his eyes because he could find them everywhere, in all phenomena. He did not quite understand why some things are perceived only as **ideas**, because when he was producing ideas, he was in complete harmony with experience, exactly as the mathematician feels that he is in harmony with experience when producing mathematical ideas. However, I have to say that consequently, through an internal logic, this led Goethe to a mere phenomenology. In other words, he was not looking for anything else beyond experience, and most important, he was not trying to create a rationalistic world of atoms....
>
> Goethe focuses primarily on the purely sensory phenomena and on the unique elements of sensory facts, without drawing a connection to anything behind them. What he searches for are simply elements in the phenomenal world that are related to each other, and he tries to find the connections between them....
>
> To summarize: from Goethe's perspective, this is all about the fact that we should stay within the realm of phenomena....
>
> Hence, this is all about accepting the realm of the phenomenal and about learning to read its own internal meaning. Such an approach will bring us to a kind of natural science

that will contain nothing rationalistically constructed beyond phenomena.[15]

Self-determining entelechy in organisms

The interaction of various parts in the inorganic world can be studied and understood by observing how one part interacts with and determines another. As has just been described, in the organic world, this is not the case. Rather, an embracing, self-determining whole oversees each part. Goethe refers to this inherent self-determining entity as "entelechy."

A sense-perceptible organism is unique in that it is self-determined from within, yet is also affected by outside factors. In thought, a person can grasp the "idea" of this self-determining entelechy free from outside influences. Thus the archetypal plant manifests in types or variations of plants.

> *What prevails in the inorganic world is the interaction of the parts of a series of phenomena; it is their reciprocal determining of each other. This is not the case in the organic world. There, one part of an entity does not determine the other, but rather the whole (the idea), out of itself and in accordance with its own being, determines each individual part. One can follow Goethe in calling this self-determining whole an "**entelechy**." An entelechy is therefore a power that, out of itself, calls itself into existence. What comes into manifestation also has a sense-perceptible existence, but this is determined by that entelechial principle. From this also arises the seeming contradiction. An organism determines itself out of itself, fashions its characteristics in accordance with a presupposed principle, and yet it is sense-perceptibly real. It has therefore arrived at its sense-perceptible reality in a completely different way than the other objects of the sense world; thus it seems to have arisen in an unnatural way. But it is also entirely explainable that an organism, in its externality, is just as susceptible to the influences of the sense world as is any other body. The stone falling from a roof can strike a living entity just as well as an inorganic object. An organism*

---

15 Rudolf Steiner, *Reimagining Academic Studies*, lect. 3/6/1922.

*is connected with the outer world through its intake of nourishment, etc.; all the physical circumstances of the outer world affect it. Of course, this can also occur only insofar as the organism is an object of the sense world, a spatial-temporal object. This object of the outer world then, this entelechial principle that has come into existence, is the outer manifestation of the organism. But since the organism is subject not only to its own laws of development but also to the conditions of the outer world, since it is not only what it should be in accordance with the being of the self-determining entelechial principle, but also is what other dependencies and influences have made it, therefore the organism never seems, as it were, to accord fully with itself, never seems obedient merely to its own being. Here human reason enters and forms for itself, **in idea**, an organism that is not in accordance with the influences of the outer world, but rather corresponds only to that entelechial principle. Every coincidental influence that has nothing to do with the organism **as such** falls away entirely here. This idea, now, that corresponds purely to what is organic in the organism is the idea of the archetypal organism; it is Goethe's **typus**. From this one can also see the great justification for this idea of the **typus**. This idea is not merely an **intellectual concept**; it is what is truly organic in every organism, without which an organism would not be one. This idea is, in fact, more real than any individual real organism, because it manifests itself in **every** organism. It also expresses the essential nature of an organism **more fully, more purely** than any individual, **particular** organism. It is acquired in an essentially different way than the concept of an inorganic process. This latter is drawn from, abstracted from, reality; it is not at work within reality; the idea of the organism, however, is active, is at work as entelechy within the organism; it is, in the form grasped by our reason, only the being of the entelechy itself. This idea does not draw the experience together; **it brings about** what is to be experienced. Goethe expresses this in the following words: "Concept is **summation**, idea is **result** of experience; to find the sum requires intellect; to grasp the result requires reason" (**Aphorisms in Prose**). This explains that kind of reality which belongs to the Goethean archetypal organism (archetypal plant or archetypal animal). This*

Goethean method is clearly the only possible one by which to penetrate into the essential nature of the world of organisms.[16]

Art and science from one source

It is common to view science as being based on objective facts, while art is sullied by subjective interpretations. Goethe took exception to this characterization of art. He maintained that his scientific and artistic works were derived from one and the same spiritual source, and, consequently, they are both objective interpreters of the mysteries of the natural world and the driving forces of reality, only in a different sense. The aim of science is to objectively grasp something in the realm of ideas, and art at its highest level raises the sense-perceptible into a form in which it more fully reveals its ideal nature or entelechy.[17]

Our age believes itself correct in keeping art and science as far apart as possible. They are supposed to be two completely opposing poles in the cultural evolution of humankind. Science, one thinks, is supposed to sketch for us the most objective picture of the world possible; it is supposed to show us reality in a mirror; or, in other words, it is supposed to hold fast purely to the given, renouncing all subjective arbitrariness. The objective world determines the laws of science; science must subject itself to this world. Science should take the yardstick for what is true and false entirely from the objects of experience.

The situation is supposedly quite different in the case of artistic creations. Their law is given them by the self-creative power of the human spirit. For science, any interference of human subjectivity would be a falsifying of reality, a going beyond experience; art, on the other hand, grows upon the field of the subjectivity of a genius. Its creations are the productions of human imagination, not mirror images of the outer world.

---

16   Rudolf Steiner, *Goethean Science*, ch. 4.

17   The idea that science and art have a common source and equally important missions is an important concept to take hold of when considering the development of morally based technology, which will be a primary focus in Volume 2 of this technology compendium.

Outside of us, in objective existence, lies the source of scientific laws; within us, in our individuality, lies the source of aesthetic laws. The latter, therefore, have not the slightest value for knowledge; they create illusions without the slightest element of reality.

Whoever grasps the matter in this way will never become clear about the relationship of Goethean poetry to Goethean science. He will only misunderstand both. Goethe's world-historic significance lies, indeed, precisely in the fact that his art flows directly from the primal source of all existence, that there is nothing illusory or subjective about it, that, on the contrary, his art appears as the herald of that lawfulness that the poet has grasped by listening to the world spirit within the depths of nature's working. At this level, art becomes the interpreter of the mysteries of the world just as science is also, in a different sense.[18]

Both science and art are revelations of the primary laws and powers of the world. Science expresses them in the form of thoughts or ideas. Artists strive to imbue their works of art with them.

[Art] was for [Goethe] **one** *of the revelations of the primal law of the world; science was for him the* **other** *one. For him art and science sprang from* **one** *source. Whereas the researcher delves down into the depths of reality in order then to express their driving powers in the form of thoughts, the artist seeks to imbue his medium with these same driving powers. "I think that one could call science the knowledge of the general, abstracted knowing; art, on the other hand, would be science turned into action; science would be reason, and art its mechanism; therefore one could also call art practical science. And finally, then science could be called the theorem and art the problem." What science states as idea (theorem) is what art has to imprint into matter, becomes art's problem. "In the works of human beings, as in those of nature, it is the intentions that are primarily worthy of note," says Goethe. He everywhere seeks not only what is given to the senses in the*

---

18   Rudolf Steiner, *Goethean Science*, ch. 8.

*outer world but also the tendency through which it has come into being. To grasp **this** scientifically and to give it artistic form is his mission. In its own formations, nature gets itself, "in its specific forms, into a cul-de-sac"; one must go back to what ought to have come about if the tendency could have unfolded unhindered, just as the mathematician always keeps his eye not upon this or that particular triangle but always upon that lawfulness which underlies every possible triangle. The point is not **what** nature has created but rather the principle by which nature has created it. Then this principle is to be developed in the way that accords with its own nature, and not in the way this has occurred in each particular entity of nature in accordance with thousands of chance factors. The artist has "to evolve the noble out of the common and the beautiful out of the unformed."[19]*

Part 3: SPIRITUAL SCIENCE

Spiritual science as an extension of Goetheanism

The aim of spiritual science is to create a new Goetheanism by taking up Goethe's thoughts and research methods and expanding them further to include a full view of life that includes the inner spirit of the human being.

Our spiritual science...intends to be "Goethean"—not in the sense of compiling anthologies of what Goethe said or wrote on scientific subjects, but by taking up and developing Goethe's initial, elementary efforts so that they may become increasingly fruitful.... Goetheanism in 1919 [when this lecture was given] does not need to rehash Goethe's literal words, but it must continue to work in the same spirit. This can best be done by expanding Goethe's efforts—which were limited to the field of botany and, to a lesser extent, zoology—into the impulse behind a comprehensive worldview that, above all else, includes the human

---

19   *Goethean Science*, ch. 8

being. This new Goetheanism will transform the worldview that is emerging from our culture's most respected (that is, scientific) methods of acquiring knowledge.[20]

[Spiritual science] wishes to expand what Goethe introduced fruitfully into the world of external natural phenomena (so he could find the spirit in nature) to soul phenomena as well. Thus, these soul phenomena themselves are directly stimulated to vigorous life and reveal the inner spirit that lives in the human individual as the eternal, immortal core of one's being.[21]

Natural-scientific discipline as an aid to pursuing spiritual science

Even though Steiner considered spiritual science as a continuation of Goethe's scientific approach, he was emphatic that natural science and the worldview it inspires should be viewed as a necessity in human evolution. What is important is to uncover to what degree natural science is right and when it is misplaced, too restricted, one-sided, or incomplete. Mastering the discipline of modern scientific research is a prerequisite for spiritual-scientific research.

The scientific worldview must be taken seriously, and for this reason I was never an opponent of it; on the contrary, I regarded it as something that of necessity belongs to our time.[22]

We must begin by acquiring the discipline that modern science can teach us. We must school ourselves in this way and then, taking the strict methodology, the scientific discipline we have learned from modern natural science, transcend it, so that we use the same exacting approach to rise into higher regions, thereby extending this methodology to the investigation of entirely different realms as well. [23]

---

20   Rudolf Steiner, *Freedom of Thought and Societal Forces*, lect. 12/30/1919.

21   Rudolf Steiner, CW 67, lect. 2/21/1918, as found in John Michael Barnes, *The Third Culture*, from the chapter "Anthroposophy."

22   Rudolf Steiner, *The Origins of Natural* Science, lect. 12/27/1922.

23   Rudolf Steiner, *The Boundaries of Natural Science*, lect. 9/29/1920.

As I have often emphasised, spiritual science is not hostile toward natural science in its present form, but it realizes that this natural science does not give the whole truth about nature.... The useful thing is to discover how far they are right.[24]

Modern scientific thinking and mechanical ideas as preparation for understanding spiritual realities

Modern scientific thinking and mechanical ideas have enabled people to think more clearly and sharply about the world in the past. From now on, a fundamental task of humanity is to comprehend the spiritual worlds with the same clarity as that evoked by the natural-scientific method of study and research. In this way, the study of modern materialistic science can be an important aid for anyone seeking knowledge about the spiritual laws, forces, and beings through spiritual science. Such a detailed understanding of spiritual realities will be necessary for humanity to meet the challenges of present and future life on earth.[25]

Our powers of soul must be equipped with the ideas that live in modern scientific thought and altogether in modern thought. This is the necessary task of modern times.... The ideas of former times always had vaguer outlines.... These one-sided, mechanical ideas are exceedingly poor in world-content; for at bottom they contain no more than what is dead. Yet they are a remarkable means of education, and this, indeed, we can observe in our time. The truth is that nowadays, only those can think in really sharp outlines who have made certain ideas of natural science their own. All other people think more or less vaguely.

Thus, humankind has passed through a certain education in sharply outlined thinking. But from this point onward, it is necessary to turn to the new revelation of the spirit and to conceive the spiritual worlds with the same clarity with which we have grown accustomed to conceiving the world of natural science.

---

24 Rudolf Steiner, *Three Streams in Human Evolution*, lect. 10/12/1918.

25 More specifically, such a detailed knowledge will be necessary for the future development of new forms of moral technology mentioned in chapter 5, "Keely, Strader, and the Further Development of Resonance Technology."

This is what the modern intellectual conscience requires, nor will humanity be able to dispense with this. Without this, humanity will never be able to solve the all-important questions that will arise in the present and in the near future. Clear and sharp thinking trained in the modern, scientific ideas and then applied to the spiritual world as it reveals itself anew—such is the configuration, fundamentally speaking, of anthroposophical spiritual science. Such is the character which anthroposophical spiritual science wants to have; therefore it reckons with the most necessary requirements of our time.[26]

The application of the scientific method in researching spiritual realities

The critical factor in the natural-scientific method of research is not the object of study, but rather the method and soul attitude employed. It is unreasonable and arbitrary to think that the scientific method can only be applied to sense-perceptible reality. Spiritual or esoteric scientific researchers strive to use scientific methods of research consistent with and as rigorous as those employed in natural science. However, spiritual science includes not only the natural world but also the hidden spiritual reality that underlies it.

The study and practice of the scientific method as applied to the spiritual world helps develop latent capacities that are seldom activated when the focus of attention is exclusively on the material world. The development of these latent capacities can enable the researcher to experience the spiritual reality underlying the physical world.[27]

The definitive factor in the birth of a science is not the object that is studied but the type of human soul activity that takes place during the scientific quest. The activity and attitude of the soul involved in the study of science is what we need to look at. If

---

26 Rudolf Steiner, "The Fundamental Social Demand of Our Time" (Hudson, NY, Rudolf Steiner Library unpublished manuscript), CW 186, lect. 12/20/1918.

27 For more on developing spiritual perception and cognition, see chapter 9, "Thinking as a Spiritual Activity."

we acquire the habit of exercising activity of this sort only when dealing with what the senses disclose, we may easily succumb to the opinion that the sense perception is the essential factor. In that case, we fail to look at the fact that specific activities and attitudes of the human soul have been applied, but instead look only at what is sense-perceptible. However, it is possible to transcend this arbitrary, self-imposed limitation and look at the character of scientific activity itself without regard to its specific application.

This is the basis for speaking of knowledge of the non-sensory content of the world as "scientific." The human power of cognition tries to become involved with this content in the same way it would otherwise become involved with the world's natural-scientific content. It is the intent of spiritual science to free the method and attitudes of scientific research from the particular application to the relationships and processes of sensory facts while preserving their way of thinking and other attributes. Spiritual science attempts to speak about non-sensory things in the same way that the natural sciences speak about sense-perceptible things. While natural-scientific methods of research and ways of thinking stop short at the sensory world, esoteric science views the soul's work in the natural world as a means of self-education and attempts to apply the faculties that develop in this way to non-sensory domains. Instead of attempting to speak about sensory phenomena as such, esoteric science speaks about non-sensory contents of the world in the same way that scientists speak about its sense-perceptible contents. In this process, it retains the inner attitude of the scientific method, which is what makes the study of nature a science in the first place. This permits esoteric science to call itself a science....

The whole of esoteric science must spring from two thoughts that can take root in each human being. For the esoteric scientist, as the term is used in this book, these two thoughts express facts that can be experienced if we apply the right means....The first of these thoughts is that behind the visible world there is an invisible one, a world that is temporarily concealed, at least as far as our senses and sense-bound capacities are concerned.[28] *The second is that by developing human capacities that lie dormant in us, it is possible to enter this hidden world.*[29]

Need for healthy discussion about anthroposophy and science

It is important that within the anthroposophical movement a healthy discussion should take place about the relation between spiritual and natural science. Otherwise, anthroposophy will suffer great harm.

> On this occasion let me state emphatically that I do not wish to be regarded as in any way an opponent of the scientific approach. I would consider it detrimental to all our anthroposophical endeavors if a false opposition were to arise between what anthroposophy seeks by way of spiritual research and what science seeks—and must of necessity seek in its field—out of the modern attitude.
>
> I say this expressly, my dear friends, because a healthy discussion concerning the relationship between anthroposophy and science must come to pass within our movement. Anything that goes wrong in this respect can only do grave harm to anthroposophy and should be avoided.[30]

Natural science applies mathematics to everything

Materialistic natural science tends to develop its concepts from its investigations of the inanimate world. The problem arises when these concepts and methods of research, which are so useful with material objects, are also applied to the world of the living, the organic world. Anthroposophy respects the use of mathematical thinking and

---

28   The reader should not confuse this invisible spiritual reality behind the physical world with theories about atoms, which maintain that there is an invisible material world of atoms behind or underlying the visible material world.

29   Rudolf Steiner, *An Outline of Esoteric Science*, ch. 1, "The Character of Esoteric Science."

30   Rudolf Steiner, *The Origins of Natural Science*, lect. 12/27/1922.

mechanics in relation to the inorganic but objects to its singular use for every other aspect of earthly life.

> It is understandable that contemporary humanity has estab-
> lished its concepts of natural science primarily on the basis of
> inorganic nature. The reason is that inorganic natural phenom-
> ena are relatively simple. In addition, there are processes of the
> inanimate world that certainly continue to act when we move up
> into the realm of organic matter. When we move from the king-
> dom of minerals to the vegetable kingdom, we cannot say that
> there are no inanimate processes in the plant; they are included
> in a higher principle, but they persist in the plant. We are right
> to explore physical and chemical processes in the plant organism
> as we would explore them in inorganic nature.... Scientists are
> tempted, however, to follow only those processes that originate in
> the kingdom of minerals and extend to plants and animals, while
> failing to consider what else is happening in the higher natural
> kingdoms....
>
> We can certainly admit that this mechanical explanation of
> the world is completely plausible—no objections; but it makes
> a difference whether we declare a mechanical explanation to be
> reasonable in certain areas, or whether we want to present it as
> the only possible system of concepts, using it to explain every sin-
> gle thing in the world....
>
> The goal of anthroposophy is certainly not to deny what nat-
> ural science asserts. The question is whether it is legitimate to try
> to explain the entire world of phenomena through mathematical
> thinking.[31]

A social science for the future

During the ancient Greek and Roman civilizations, there was a type of science that looked into the future in a way that embraced social life. In contrast, modern natural science, which focuses exclusively on outer, sensible reality, is a science based on the past, and therefore affects social life negatively.

---

31 Rudolf Steiner, *Reimagining Academic Studies*, lect. 3/6/1922.

There is an important law of the universe that can be described as follows: the degree to which science relies on sense-perceptible reality is the degree to which it focuses on the past. As such, it can be described as focusing on all that is dead, a corpse of the past. Yet, laws that embody dead thoughts from the past continue into the future, including into social life. For a science to embrace socially beneficial guiding thoughts for the future, it needs not only to embrace outer sensible reality but spiritual reality as well.

People must gradually come to the realization that everything has two sides. Modern people are so clever, are they not?—infinitely clever; and these clever modern people say the following: In the fourth post-Atlantean age, in the time of ancient Greece and Rome, people superstitiously believed that the future could be told from the way birds would be flying, from the entrails of animals, and all kinds of other things. They were silly old fools, of course. The fact is that none of these scornful modern people actually know how the predictions were made....

Yet conditions were such in the fourth post-Atlantean age [ancient Greece and Rome, 747 BC—1413 AD] that there really was a science which considered the future. Then, people would not have been able to think that the kind of principles which are applied today would achieve anything in a developing social life. They could not have gained the great perspectives of a social nature, which went far beyond their own time, if they had not had a 'science,' as it were, of the future. Believe me, everything people achieve today in the field of social life and politics is actually still based on the fruits of that old science of the future. This, however, cannot be gained by observing the things that present themselves to the senses. It can never be gained by using the modern scientific approach; for anything we observe in the outside world with the senses makes a science of the past. Let me tell you a most important law of the universe: If you merely consider the world as it presents itself to the senses, which is the modern scientific approach, you observe past laws which are still continuing.

You are really only observing the corpse of a past world. Science is looking at life that has died....

The situation with the world is just like the situation you get with a plant. The true plant is not the plant we see today; something is mysteriously inside it which cannot yet be seen and will only be visible to the eyes in the following year—the primitive germ. It is present in the plant, but it is invisible. In the same way, the world which presents itself to our eyes holds the whole future in it, though this is not visible. It also holds the past, but this has withered and dried up and is now a corpse. Everything naturalists look at is merely the image of a corpse, of something past and gone. It is also true, of course, that this past aspect would be missing if we considered the spiritual aspect only. However, the invisible element must be included if we are to have the complete reality.[32]

Intellectual knowledge is most effective when it is applied to technology, much less so when applied to improving social conditions. The worst scenario for public life is when intellectual knowledge is employed in social renewal efforts, as was the case with Leninism and Trotskyism. Meaningful change in social conditions requires spiritual cognition and knowledge.

By cultivating an all-embracing Goethean approach, anthroposophical spiritual science aspires to a form of spirit cognition that can serve as the foundation for energetic human action. That is the only way to help our world. Although intellectual knowledge is also acquired through inner effort, it applies at best only to technology, that is, to the non-human world. Impulses derived from spiritual knowledge, however, can guide our public life, which has grown so difficult, in the direction of true recovery. Perhaps these claims of spiritual science deserve greater consideration in view of the infinite suffering cause by failed so-called social movements such as Leninism, Trotskyism, and the like, which are nothing more than intellectual poison. For four

---

32   Rudolf Steiner, *The Fall of the Spirits of Darkness*, lect. 10/20/1917.

hundred years, intellectualism helped to free human beings to be individuals, but it served this useful purpose only as long as it did not attach to old social forms. As soon as pure intellectualism seeks to transform society, its horrendous toxic effects become increasingly evident. It is a terrible illusion to believe that we can afford to look on world events dispassionately. These toxic effects are still in their early stages. And recovery can come only from spirit. Spirit cognition must become the basis of social renewal.[33]

True natural science

An important step in the evolution of natural science will be when scientists are able to extend their studies and research beyond the material world. What they will discover everywhere are the rhythmical orderings within nature. The discovery and understanding of nature's rhythms will be the basis for a true natural science in the future.[34]

If human beings will only give up looking for anything coarsely material as the basis of nature—and this they will do before the fourth millennium—they will come to something quite different; they will discover rhythms, rhythmical orderings, everywhere in nature.... This rhythmical order is there in the whole of nature. In the plants one leaf follows another in rhythmical growth; the petals of the blossoms are ordered rhythmically; everything is rhythmically ordered. Fever takes a rhythmical course in sickness; the whole of life is rhythmical. The discerning of nature's rhythms—that will be true natural science.[35]

The eventual merger of natural science with spiritual science

Natural science will become a foundation for spiritual science through certain advancements, and eventually the two will merge. One of the most significant advancements will be when natural science

---

33 Rudolf Steiner, *Freedom of Thought and Societal Forces*, lect. 12/30/1919.

34 The rhythmical orderings in the human soul and the cosmos are an important field of study in the future development of etheric resonance technology. For more on this topic, see chapter 5.

35 Rudolf Steiner, *Three Streams in Human Evolution*, lect. 10/12/1918.

recognizes that the formation of the human sense organs originates in what is being sensed. This will enable people to understand that all matter is born from the spirit.

> It will be a while before it will be commonly understood that light formed the eyes and not vice versa, and that the sounds that we hear formed the ears. Then one will see that all matter is born from the spirit. True natural-scientific facts will flow over into spiritual science without any logical interruption. Natural-scientific facts will provide the best foundation for spiritual science.... Eventually, natural science will merge with spiritual science. Today, they stand at a crossroads.... The day will come when there will be a wonderful harmony between natural-scientific facts and the insights of spiritual science.[36]

---

36 Rudolf Steiner, *Natural Science at the Crossroads*, CW 56, lect. 10/17/1907.

Atoms and Atomic Theories

Atoms, or what are so-called, are crossing points of lines of force. (note 22)

Atoms are to be regarded as ideal contents of space. The contents are the results of force-directions meeting each other. (note 24)

The truth is that the minutest molecule [and hence, the atom] is acted upon by the whole starry heavens. Suppose here [are the planets]. Then there are the fixed stars, which imbue the molecule with their forces. All these lines of force intersect each other in various ways. (note 25)

TWO

Atoms and Atomic Theories

Chapter introduction

In this chapter the reader will encounter several different perspectives by Rudolf Steiner concerning atoms and atomic theories. These include:

> *A fabricated idea from the nineteenth century: A natural world consisting of an invisibly thin ether atoms interspersed with invisible substance atoms.*
>
> *A bridge from matter or physical reality to a spiritual reality: Atoms as consisting of frozen of condensed electricity according to early twentieth-century science.*
>
> *A spiritual reality: Atoms as crossing or focal points of invisible cosmic forces according to spiritual science.*

It is important to note when reading passages by Steiner that are critical of various atomic theories that he is not denying the existence of atoms altogether. Rather, he views atoms to be of a nonmaterial, spiritual nature consisting of intersecting cosmic forces. Modern pictures of atomic and molecular systems derived from electron microscopy may be sufficient proof for some people that material atoms do exist, and that Steiner's view that atoms are of a spiritual nature, the result of the intersection of cosmic forces, is erroneous.

In response, the reader is asked to consider images derived from electron microscopy not as representing material atoms but as a visual plotting of electrical patterns. It is just as if one would plot the electrical sparks generated by a battery and then treat the images formed

Figure 2.1: After an electron microscope photograph of an atom

as the battery itself. Such images are not a picturing of individual material atoms but rather images of specific patterns in an electrical configuration.

Steiner's portrayal of atoms in this and the following chapter in relation to electricity are important concepts that we will return to in volume two when we explore the nature of sacred creation and the development of moral technology.

Chapter overview

As a graduate of the Vienna Institute of Technology and a spiritual scientist, Rudolf Steiner closely followed the atomic theories of the nineteenth and early twentieth centuries. He was highly critical, as were many contemporary scientists of his time, of the prevalent theory of the nineteenth century that portrayed the outer world as consisting of an infinitely thin ether space with ever moving and colliding invisible atoms and molecules that underlie the material world.[1] He not only considered this speculative view of reality inherently illogical, but more importantly, it obviates the possibility of recognizing a spiritual reality behind the material world. Such a spiritual reality was a direct experience for Steiner, and he made it his life's task to illumine the spiritual foundations of reality in objective scientific terms.

He was pleased that natural science was making positive steps forward in the early twentieth century, particularly in relation to electricity, atoms, and human thought. This included describing atoms as "condensed" or "congealed" electricity. For him, this was a step toward the idea that all matter is condensed spirit.

Steiner highly appreciated the scientific works of Johann Wolfgang von Goethe. As we learned in chapter one, Goethe worked from a phenomenological approach by limiting himself to simple elements of what he could perceive and their obvious interconnections. This was part of a deep, intensive process through which he entered the life element of plants, for instance. He allowed their creative growth forces to energize and guide his thoughts. Thus, Goethe focused on and worked with perceived phenomena rather than speculating about an invisible material world that lies behind the visible world. He did, however, point to an invisible spiritual world when referring to entelechy and archetypal phenomena in the organic realm.

Steiner went further and presented ideas about atoms that support the premise that there is a spiritual foundation for the material world. One is that atoms are crossing points where cosmic forces converge. Another is that atoms, when perceived with imaginative cognition are hollow spaces where electric and magnetic forces of a spiritual (ahrimanic) nature can be found. Regarding the future, he maintained that when we come to know the cosmic, spiritual nature of the atom and

---

1   It was more a philosophical than a scientific perspective at the time.

work with this inherent nature, it will be our responsibility to create the world anew.

Part 1: CRITIQUE OF A NINETEENTH-CENTURY ATOMIC THEORY

Ether atoms and substance atoms

Rudolf Steiner gave his first critique of the prevalent atomic theory in 1890, when he was but twenty-nine years old. At that time, the world of space was portrayed scientifically as consisting of an infinitely thin substance called ether, which in turn contained invisibly small particles called atoms. These atoms were in a constant oscillation.

According to this perspective, all sense-perceptible qualities of substances were attributed to the motion of oscillating ether atoms that impinge upon our nervous system with impulses ultimately transmitted to our brain. This implied that our sense world has no objective reality, and by default, neither do our own bodies. Rather, we experience the world subjectively through the ether atoms interacting with our nervous system.

Current (1890) natural science thinks of the world-space as filled with an infinitely thin substance called ether. This substance consists of infinitely small particles, the ether atoms. This ether does not merely exist where there are no bodies but also in the pores (pertaining) to bodies. The physicist imagines that each body consists of an infinite number of immeasurable small parts, like atoms. They are not in contact with each other, but they are separated by small interstices. They, in their turn, unite to larger forms, the molecules, which still cannot be discerned by the eye. Only when an infinite number of molecules unite, we get what our senses perceived as bodies....

We also see by this that for modern physics each substance (fluid, solid, and gaseous) consists of parts between which there exist empty spaces (pores).

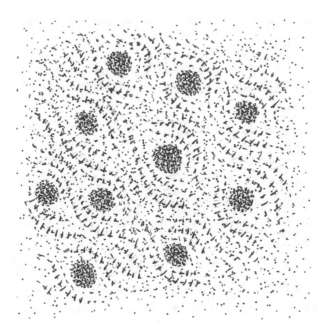

Figure 2.2: Invisible atoms in infinitely thin ether space

Into these pores, there enter the ether atoms which fill the whole cosmos....

Now we have to imagine that both the substance-atoms and the ether-atoms are in a state of constant motion.[2] The motion is oscillating. We must think that each atom is moving back and forth like the pendulum of a clock....

The [nineteenth-century] physicist says: in reality, nothing exists except oscillating, moving atoms [and molecules]; everything else is merely a creation of my brain, formed by it when it is touched by the movement in the outer world....

If there is nothing in the real world except oscillating atoms, then there cannot be any true objective ideas and ideals. For when I conceive an idea, I can ask myself, what does it mean

---

2   Substance atoms in this case consist of two or more types of atoms that combine and form a molecule. For example, two hydrogen atoms and one oxygen atom form a water molecule.

outside of my consciousness? Nothing more than a movement of my brain molecules. Because my brain molecules at that moment vibrate one way or another, my brain gives me the illusion of some idea. All reality in the world then is considered as movement, everything else is empty fog....

If this way of thinking were correct, then I would have to tell myself: the human being is nothing more than a mass of vibrating molecules. That is the only thing in the human being that has reality. If I have a great idea and pursue it to its origin, I will find some kind of movement. Let us say I plan a good deed. I only can do that if a mass of molecules in my brain feels like executing a certain movement.[3]

Warmth created by colliding atoms: A critique

Seventeen years later, Rudolf Steiner again critiqued the prevailing atom theory of the nineteenth century that portrays warmth as being the result of so-called colliding atoms. All our sensory experiences, including warmth, from this materialistic perspective are subjective and the result of moving atoms. The degree of warmth was supposedly determined by the degree and strength of impact of colliding atoms.

Those of us who are forty or fifty years old and have our school education behind us can vividly remember when the warmth theory ruled supreme. The great discoveries in the realm of thermodynamics had developed so that one imagined that gases consisted of millions of small atoms and molecules that move in extremely complicated ways, and that collide and bounce off each other to create the phenomena of heat. What is heat? It is nothing but the play of moving and colliding atoms in space. Then one said matter-of-factly: what you feel as warmth is nothing but the movement that the smallest parts of a body carry out, and the degree of heat depends upon the intensity of the movement. Thus, for the theory of heat there was nothing out in the world but atoms whirling around each other. And what one meant by the word "warmth" was a subjective sensation, an

---

3   Rudolf Steiner, "Atomism and Its Refutation," 9/23/1890.

effect on the human organism or the brain that was purely tangible in nature.[4]

Atoms as superstition

This imagined world of material atoms of the nineteenth century is a superstition. What stands behind the visible world is in fact spirit, a spiritual world. Remaining true to facts will lead natural science to a crossroads, one that would eventually lead it to spiritual science.

> *The belief in material atoms behind our percepts is superstition. Some say that one could see atoms if one had the right instruments. There is nothing behind what we perceive except spirit and the spiritual world into which we penetrate. That is what we look for behind phenomena. We look for the world of the spirit in the world of sensory phenomena, and not for a world of atoms that surge through it. One who thinks that he is finding another material world behind outer phenomena is on the wrong track. Those who continue to fabricate such mental constructs to this day must be countered. This fantastic superstition will someday be recognized as such, and much of what is considered superstition today will be proven to be correct.*
>
> *The true principles of natural science are based on facts. When its theories do not align with facts, natural science brings itself to a crossroad. Where the facts do not agree with them, the theories crumble into nothing. Atoms and the elements that were looked upon as the firmest foundation of science, and from which one tried to explain spirit and consciousness, in the end, fall away. What we want is certainty, and we will only find it when we perceive the spirit working in us.*
>
> *Eventually, natural science will merge with spiritual science.... The day will come when there will be a wonderful harmony between natural-scientific facts and the insights of spiritual science.*[5]

---

4   Rudolf Steiner, *Natural Science at the Crossroads*, CW 56, lect. 10/17/1907.
5   Ibid.

Human nervous system

There is, however, something in the human makeup that appears to support an atomic theory of invisibly small particles. It consists in centers within the body that cause a sensation of minute pricks, or, electrical shocks. It is the human nervous system, which reaches out and senses the world, but also mirrors it back from many specific points through the nerve endings. But when people wake up to this experience, they realize there is nothing that lies on the other side of these prickly sensations, just as nothing is to be found behind a mirror that relates to the reflected image on the visible side of the mirror.[6]

> *I once knew an interesting man who had become conscious of this in an abnormal way. He was a distinguished mathematician, conversant with the whole range of higher mathematics at that time. He was also, of course, much occupied with the differential and integral calculus. The "differential" in mathematics is the atomic, the very smallest unit that can be conceived—I cannot say more about it today. Although it was not a fully conscious experience, this man had the sensation of being pricked all over when he was engrossed in the study of the differential calculus. Now if this experience is not lifted into consciousness in the proper way—by such exercises as are given in the book* Knowledge of the Higher Worlds—*very strange things may occur. This man believed that he was feeling the differentials all over him. "I am crammed full of differentials," he said. "I have nothing integral in me." And moreover, he demonstrated in a very ingenious way that he was full of differentials!*
>
> *Now try to envisage these "pricks" vividly. What does a person do with them if they do not reach his consciousness? He projects them into space, fills space with them—and they are then the* **atoms**. *That, in truth, is the origin of atomism. If there is a mirror in front of you and you have no idea that it is a mirror,*

---

6   Even with advanced microscopes today, it is predominantly electrical forces that come into play when trying to "map the atomic system." In a way, the microscope creates extensions of the nerve endings through its structure and method of sensing miniscule electrical changes on a surface using a needle-like sensor.

*you will certainly believe that **there**, **outside**, is another collection of people. In the same way, human beings conceive that the whole space is filled with what they themselves project into it. The entire nerve-process is reflected back into the human being, owing to the fact that they come up against it (as a kind of barrier). But they are not conscious of this, and so they conceive of the whole of surrounding space as being filled with atoms: the atoms are ostensibly the pricks made by their nerve endings. Nature herself nowhere obliges us to assume the existence of atoms, but the human constitution **does**. At the moment of waking, the human being dives down into its own being and becomes inwardly aware of an infinite number of spatial points. At this moment they are in exactly the same position as when they walk up to a mirror, knock up against it—and realize then that they cannot get behind it. Similarly, at the moment of waking, they come up against their nerve endings and know that they cannot get beyond them. The whole atomic picture is like a reflecting-screen. The moment people realize that they cannot get behind it, they know how things are.[7]*

Part 2: THE NEED FOR
A SPIRITUAL-SCIENTIFIC PERSPECTIVE

Atoms as convenient units of calculation

It is not enough that a few people in the early twentieth century said that materialism had been overcome and that the atomic view of the world was simply a convenient and harmless basis for scientific calculations. What really matters is our orientation of soul, and whether we can give explanations of phenomena that are not based on a materialistic atomic theory. This requires a spiritual-scientific view of the world.

We are assured today that the materialism of the middle and last third of the nineteenth century has been overcome, but this statement is not very convincing to those who really know the

---

7   Rudolf Steiner, *The Occult Movement in the Nineteenth Century and Its Relation to Modern Culture*, lect. 10/16/1915.

nature of materialism and its opposite. The most one can say is that materialism has been overcome by a few people here and there who realize that the facts of [early twentieth-century] science no longer justify the general explanation that everything in existence is merely a mechanical, physical, or chemical process taking place in matter.

*The fact that a few people here or there have come to this conclusion, however, does not mean that materialism has been overcome, for usually when it comes to a concrete explanation or forming a view of something concrete, even these people—and the others as a matter of course—still reveal a materialistic tendency in their way of thinking. True, it is said that atoms and molecules are merely harmless, convenient units of calculation about which nothing more is asserted than that they are abstractions; nevertheless, the considerations are atomistic and molecular in character. We are then explaining world phenomena out of the behavior or interactions of atomic and molecular processes, and the point is not whether we picture that a thought, feeling, or any other process is connected only with material processes of atoms and molecules; the point is the orientation of the entire attitude of our soul and spirit when our explanation is based only on atomic theory, the theory of smallest entities. The point is not whether verbally or in thought a person is convinced that there is something more than the influence of atoms, the material action of atoms, but whether he is able to give explanations other than those based on the atomic theory of phenomena. In short, not **what** we believe is essential but **how** we explain, how we orient our souls within. Here I must say that only a true, anthroposophically oriented spiritual science can help eliminate the defect of which I have spoken.[8]*

To think of atoms in materialistic terms is both erroneous and unhealthy

Even more problematic than simply thinking of atoms in materialistic terms is employing that belief in how we think about the world in

---

8   Rudolf Steiner, *Health Care as a Social Issue*, lect. 4/7/1920.

general. Thinking like this is not merely a matter of right and wrong; it is a matter of health and illness. Thinking in terms of materialistic atoms affects the human organism in an unhealthy way.

> *What is important...is not whether one thinks of [atoms] as small pellets, sources of energy, or mathematical fiction, but whether one thinks of the external world in atomistic terms. This is what is important. For a spiritual scientist, however, it is not merely wrong to think atomistically. The kind of concept determining rightness or wrongness may be sound logic, but it is abstract, and spiritual science has to do with realities. I urge you to take it very seriously when I say that spiritual science has to do with realities!*
>
> *This is why certain concepts that have become merely logical categories for today's abstract worldview must be replaced by something real. This is why, in spiritual science, we not only say that one who seeks atoms or molecules in the external world thinks in the wrong way; we must consider this manner of thinking an unhealthy, sick thinking. We must replace the merely logical concept of wrongness with the realistic concept of sickness, of unhealthiness. We must point to a definite sickness of soul— regardless of how many people it has seized—which expresses itself in atomistic thinking.... To have been able to refute something is considered an accomplishment. Yet, in a spiritual-scientific sense, no final conclusion has been reached by refutation; it is important to refer to the healthy or unhealthy soul life, to actual processes expressed in man's whole physical, soul and spiritual being. To think atomistically is to think unhealthily, not merely erroneously. An actual unhealthy process takes place in the human organism when we think atomistically.*[9]

---

9   Rudolf Steiner, *Spiritual Science as a Foundation for Social Forms*, lect. 8/6/1920.

Part 3: TAKING A PHENOMENOLOGICAL APPROACH TO ATOMIC THEORIES

Observation of phenomena instead of theorizing

To arrive at a truthful picture of reality, we need to limit ourselves to observation and descriptions in the manner of Goethe and to avoid speculation and theorizing.[10] For example, consider a solid ball is passed through a ring without a problem. The ball is then warmed, and unable to pass through the ring until it is cooled down again. We begin to theorize why this is so, and in so doing leave the realm of what is observable and enter the realm of speculation. Compare this passage with the following passage, "Adhering to Phenomenalism."

> *The observable, however, is something that needs only to be described. I can do the following, for instance, and it calls simply for a description. Here is a ball that I will pass through this opening. I will now warm the ball slightly. Now you see it does not go through. It will go through only when it has cooled sufficiently. As soon as I cool it by pouring cold water on it, the ball goes through the opening again. This is an observation, and I need only describe it. Let us suppose, however, that I begin to theorize. I will do this in a sketchy way in order simply to introduce the matter.*
>
> *Here is a ball, which consists of a certain number of small parts—molecules, atoms—as you like. This is not simply observation but something added to observation in theory. At this moment I have left what has been observed, and in doing so I assume an extremely tragic role. Only those in a position to have insight into these things can realize the tragedy....*
>
> *When you theorize about a sphere, however, speculating about how its atoms and molecules are arranged, you abandon the possibility of observation; you cannot in such a case look into the matter and investigate it—you can only theorize.... That is, you carry the whole incompleteness of your logic into your thinking about something that cannot be made the object*

---

10   See chapter 1 for more on Goethe's scientific approach.

of observation. This is the tragedy. We build explanation upon explanation, at the same time abandoning observation, and we think we have explained things simply because we have erected hypotheses and theories. And the consequence of this forced reliance on our mere thinking is that this same thinking fails us the moment we are able to observe. It no longer agrees with the observation.[11]

Adhering to phenomenalism

We can achieve much through the clear concepts we gain by focusing on the external world, but when we try to carry forward these concepts to what stands behind nature, we fabricate an illusionary world of atoms and molecules. Goethe, as described in chapter one, sought to work with simple phenomena that enabled him to withhold from carrying forward, through mental inertia, sense-related thinking processes and fabricating a theoretical and nonexistent world. In other words, he was able to hold back what one usually "projects out" into the world, and instead focused on what the phenomena themselves revealed in terms of ideas. In this way, the speculative element is removed and a direct interaction with the ideas embodied in reality becomes the way forward.

Yesterday we arrived at an indication of what happens when we begin to correlate our consciousness to an external natural world of the senses. Our consciousness awakens to clear concepts but loses itself. It loses itself to the extent that one can only posit empty concepts such as "matter," concepts that then become enigmatic. Only by thus losing ourselves, however, can we achieve the clear conceptual thinking we need to become fully human. In a certain sense we must first lose ourselves in order to find ourselves again out of ourselves. Yet now the time has come when we should learn something from these phenomena. And what can one learn from these phenomena? One can learn that, although clarity of conceptual thinking and perspicuity of

---

11   Rudolf Steiner, *Warmth Course*, lect. 3/1/1920.

mental representation can be won by man in his interaction with the world of sense, this clarity of conceptual thinking becomes useless the moment we strive scientifically for something more than a mere empiricism. It becomes useless the moment we try to proceed toward the kind of phenomenalism that Goethe the scientist cultivated, the moment we want something more than natural science—namely, Goetheanism.

What does this imply? In establishing a correlation between our inner life and the external physical world of the senses, we can use the concepts we form in interaction with nature in such a way that we try not to remain within the natural phenomena but to think on beyond them.... We are doing this if we do not simply interrelate the phenomena with the help of our concepts but seek instead, as it were, to pierce the veil of the senses and construct something more behind it with the aid of our concepts. We are doing this if we say: out of the clear concepts I have achieved I shall construct atoms, molecules—all the movements of matter that are supposed to exist behind natural phenomena. Thereby something extraordinary happens. What happens is that when I as a human being confront the world of nature, I use my concepts not only to create for myself a conceptual order within the realm of the senses but also to break through the boundary of sense and construct behind it atoms and the like.... I have a certain inertia, and I roll with my concepts on beyond the realm of the senses to construct there a world the existence of which I can begin to doubt when I notice that my thinking has been borne along only by inertia.... Goethe rebelled against this law of inertia. He did not want to roll onward thus with his thinking but rather... to apply concepts within the realm of the senses....

What was it that Goethe was actually seeking to do? Goethe wanted to find simple phenomena within the complex, but above all such phenomena as allowed him to remain within this limit... by means of which he did not roll on into a realm that one reaches only through a certain mental inertia. Goethe wanted to adhere to a strict phenomenalism.[12]

---

12   Rudolf Steiner, *The Boundaries of Natural Science*, lect. 9/28/1920.

Part 4: ATOMS, ELECTRICITY, AND THOUGHT

Perspectives on atoms in the early twentieth century

In the early twentieth century, there was a growing recognition of the relation of atoms to electricity and human thought, something that had been discussed by the esotericist Helena Blavatsky (1831–1891). Atoms have the same relationship to the force of electricity (as a non-material phenomena) as a lump of ice has to water. Just as there is a relation between atoms and electricity, so too is there a connection between electricity and human thought. Thus, electricity is a bridge between atoms and human thought.[13] It will be necessary to gain a true perspective of atoms and all external matter, to go further and view them as condensed and formed spirit. All matter is born out of spirit. Understanding the relation between thought, electricity, and the atom will be extremely important for the future of human development.

> If you read Blavatsky's The Secret Doctrine, *you will find there a passage relating to electricity, which expresses word for word what physicists are now gradually arriving at. What is written there is, however, only a hint at what is actually involved. It is the physical atom which is in question.... Nowadays, one is beginning to recognize that this physical atom bears the same relationship to the force of electricity that a lump of ice bears to the water from which it has been frozen. If you conceive of water becoming frozen to ice, so is the ice also water, and in like manner the atom of physics is nothing else but frozen electricity. If you can grasp this point completely and were to go through the statements about the atom contained in all the scientific journals until a year or two ago, and were to regard them as rubbish, you will have more or less the right idea. It is only very recently that science has been able to form a conception of what the atom is....*

---

13 See chapter 9, "Thinking as a Spiritual Activity" for more on the nature of thinking, thought, and electricity within the human organism.

Now one is beginning to realize that the physical atom is condensed electricity. But there is still a second thing to be considered: what electricity itself is. That is still unknown. They are ignorant of one thing: namely, where the real nature of electricity must be sought. This nature of electricity cannot be discovered by means of any outer experiments or through outer observation. The secret which will be discovered is that electricity—when one learns to view it from a particular level—is exactly the same as what human thought is. Human thought is the same thing as electricity, viewed one time from the inside, another time from the outside.

Whoever is now aware of what electricity is, knows that there is something living within them which, in a frozen state, forms the atom. Here is the bridge from human thought to the atom. One will learn to know the building stones of the physical world; they are tiny, condensed monads, condensed electricity. In that moment when human beings realize this elementary occult truth about thought, electricity and the atom, in that same moment they will have understood something which is of the utmost importance for the future and for the whole of the sixth post-Atlantean epoch.[14] They will have learned how to build with atoms through the power of thinking.[15]

We are going forward to an age when, as I recently indicated, understanding will reach right into the atom. It will be realized—by the popular mind, too—that the atom is nothing else than congealed electricity. Thought itself is composed of the same substance.

Before the end of our present cultural epoch, one will in fact have come so far that people will be able to penetrate into the atom itself. When one is able to grasp the materiality between

---

14   See Appendix A, figure A-3 for the position of the sixth post-Atlantean age in Earth evolution.

15   Rudolf Steiner, *The Temple Legend*, lect. 12/16/1904. See chapter 9, for more on the nature of thinking as a spiritual activity

the thought and the atom, then one will soon be able to understand how to penetrate the atom.[16]

Matter as condensed spirit

It is important to show the connection between matter and spirit in the right way. We are used to speaking of condensation or freezing in connection with ordinary matter, where solids are sometimes frozen liquids. What Steiner maintains is that this idea has a wider applicability than is conventionally assumed, and that what we call matter is actually condensed or "frozen" spirit. There is no material world behind the matter that we can observe. Disintegrated matter is in reality spirit. Spirit stands behind all matter.

> *What the English Prime Minister Balfour (1848–1930) nicely expressed: If we imagine atoms today, then we can only say that something like a fluid is flowing through the world, and atoms are like pieces of ice in water.*
>
> *That is a nice idea, but where does it lead? Just try to follow it further. What it leads to is that natural science is on the verge of realizing that what previously was mere appearance is the actual reality. It was a strange belief to think that color, and what we call red, only exists in my head—and that only small particles exist that knock and press into each other to produce sensations of light, color, and sound. These ideas will soon have to disappear through the power of facts. It will become clear that what we see and hear is real, and that it was a wild, fantastic idea to imagine a material world behind this one. This material world will disperse and disintegrate. Our understanding of what is behind the material world will be based on what we can experience. We will come to realize that an atom is nothing else than frozen electricity, frozen heat, frozen light. Then we will go even further and come to the point of seeing everything material as condensed spirit. There is no matter. Matter is related to spirit as ice is to water. If one melts ice, one gets water. If you disintegrate*

---

16   Rudolf Steiner, *The Temple Legend*, 12/23/1904.

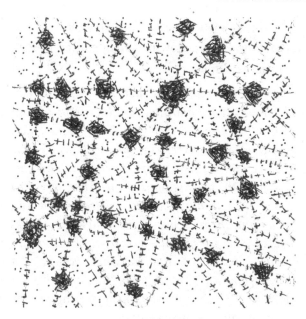

Figure 2.3: Atoms as condensed or frozen electricity

matter, it disappears and becomes spirit. Matter is the external manifestation of the spirit.[17]

Part 5: COSMIC AND TERRESTRIAL EFFECTS

The sun as negative space and forces of suction

Just as we are led astray when we disregard observation and fabricate a world of atoms and electrons, so, too, we abandon reality if we try to create concepts about the sun based on what we observe on the earth.

The sun is not a ball of rarified, glowing gases that radiate out into space, but a negative space, a negation of matter that creates a suction effect.[18] Early twentieth-century science confirms that the sun is cooler at its surface than at a distance from its surface. It shows enormous

---

17   Rudolf Steiner, *Natural Science at the Crossroads*, lect. 10/17/1907.

18   We will return to the important concepts of pressure and suction as these manifest in the human brain in chapter 9.

temperatures in the upper corona. This behavior is the opposite of the typical idea that the sun is a glowing ball of matter, which must get hotter the closer one gets to it.

> People will come to realize the fact that it is simply impossible for people to apply to conditions on the sun or to cosmic space notions that have been derived from heat phenomena available to observation in the terrestrial sphere. It will be understood that the sun's corona and similar phenomena have antecedents not included in the observations made under terrestrial conditions. Just as our thinking leads us astray when we abandon observation and theorize our way through the world of atoms and molecules, so we fall into error when we go out into the macrocosm and apply to the sun what we have determined from observations under earthly conditions. Such a method has led to the belief that the sun is a kind of glowing gas ball, but the sun is by no means a glowing ball of gas.
>
> Consider a moment—we have matter here on earth. All earthly matter has a certain degree of intensity in its action. This may be measured in one way or another, by density or the like—in any way you wish—it has a certain intensity in its action. This may become zero. In other words, we may have apparently empty space. But this is not yet the end, inasmuch as there is an end. I can illustrate to you that empty space is not the ultimate condition: assume that you had a son and that you said to yourself, "He is a fool. I made over a small property to him, but he has begun to squander it. At least he can't end up with less than nothing. He may finally have nothing, but I comfort myself with the thought that he cannot go any further once he has nothing!" But you may now be disillusioned as the fellow begins to go into debt. Then he does not stop at nothing, he ends up with less than nothing. This has a very real meaning....
>
> The same sort of thing applies to conditions on the sun. It is not usually considered as empty space, but it is considered in terms of the greatest possible rarefaction; it is postulated that the sun consists of rarefied, glowing gas. What we must actually do, though, in considering the sun is to go first to a condition of

emptiness, to zero, and then to go beyond this.... At the place where the sun is, we would find a hole going into empty space. There is less there than empty space. Therefore, all the effects to be observed on the sun must be considered as suction effects, not as pressure effects or the like. The sun's corona, for instance, must not be thought of as it is considered by the [early twentieth-century] physicist. It must be considered in such a way that we become conscious not of forces radiating outward, as appearances would indicate, but of suction effects from the hole in space, from the negation of matter. Here our logic fails us. Here our thinking is unable to grasp the macrocosmic, as it is unable to grasp the microcosmic. In the case I have cited we can only theorize about atomic particles.[19]

What happens on Earth is influenced by both the suction forces caused by negative space and pressure from space filled with matter. Primal suction forces are cosmic and are based in the planets and stars, while forces of pressure are terrestrial in nature. The mutual interaction of both find expression in what natural science calls molecules and atoms.

It must become possible for human beings to picture that an emptying of space is possible. Furthermore, what happens on the earth is indeed influenced not only by what happens from one side but by effects from all sides....

We must find the transition from a space filled with matter to one emptied of matter. This condition of space emptied of matter, in so far as it acts on our earth, we must think of as localized in the planets surrounding the earth.[20] *Thus at every point where earthly events can take place, there is a mutual interaction between the earthly and the cosmic; and this is due to the fact that from the spaces emptied of matter a suction-like effect is active, while in what is active here through the formative forces there are effects of pressure.*

---

19   Rudolf Steiner, *Warmth Course*, lect. 3/1/1920.

20   Apparently, Rudolf Steiner is making an extraordinary point here—that the planets are emptied of matter!

This mutual interaction meets us in those configurations of earthly events ordinarily sought for in molecular forces and attractions.... What the stars, like giants, do in presenting their many-sided relationships in earthly processes is given expression by the dwarves of atoms and molecules. Indeed, what is necessary is for us to know that when we represent a material, earthly process or perform calculations on it, we are dealing with nothing other than an image of extraterrestrial, of cosmic interactions.[21]

Part 6: CENTRAL AND COSMIC FORCES

Atoms as the intersection of cosmic forces

We will now consider passages that point to the spiritual rather than material nature of atoms. This is done in terms of the intersection of cosmic or peripheral forces and centric forces: centric forces that radiate outward from a center, and peripheral forces that radiate inward from the cosmos or the periphery.

Rudolf Steiner succinctly describes atoms as the intersection or the meeting of forces.

Atoms, or what are so-called, are crossing points of lines of force.[22]

Atoms are to be regarded as ideal contents of space.[23] *The contents are the results of force-directions meeting each other—for example, directions of force.*

---

21   Rudolf Steiner, *Warmth Course*, lect. 3/14/1920. Elsewhere, Steiner speaks of the necessity of taking into consideration extraterrestrial cosmic forces in practical life, for instance, in the realm farming. See, for instance, *The Spiritual Foundations for the Renewal of Agriculture*, lect. 6/7/1924 and lect. 6/10/1924.

22   Rudolf Steiner, *The Schiller File*, as quoted by Dr. Oskar Schmiedel, following a conversation with Rudolf Steiner on Feb. 16, 1920 (folio 17).

23   "Ideal" as in conceptual, rather than physical.

Figure 2.4: Atoms as crossing points of macrocosmic lines of forces or force rays

Force is the revelation of spirit viewed in a one-sided way.... Matter consists merely in the arrangements of force-rays when they meet.[24]

Given that atoms and molecules are focal points or intersections of cosmic forces, we need to turn our attention away from microscopic analysis of atoms and molecules to considering the starry heavens if we want to understand their structure and internal processes. In other words, to understand the infinitely small, we need to look to the infinitely great. Molecules (clusters of atoms) are a focus of cosmic forces.

Of course, the great fault of the [early twentieth-century] outlook is that we never take the macrocosm into consideration,

24 Rudolf Steiner, "Atomism and Its Refutation," article originally published in 1890. This passage is in an appendix to the article, "Dr. Rudolf Steiner's Answers to Six Questions about Some Basic Concepts of Natural Science" (1919).

*and therefore never become conscious of the origin of the forces whose effect we observe. I must once again remind you of the following. The [early twentieth-century] physicist or chemist says that there are molecules which are composed of atoms, that the atoms possess forces by means of which they act upon each other. Now this is a conception which simply does not accord with reality. The truth is that the minutest molecule is acted upon by **the whole starry heavens**. Suppose here is a planet, here another, here another, and so on. Then there are the fixed stars, which imbue the molecule with their forces. All these lines of force intersect each other in various ways. The planets also transmit their forces in the same way, and we come to realize that the molecule is nothing but **a focus of macrocosmic forces**. It is the ardent desire of [early twentieth-century] science to bring microscopy far enough to enable the atoms to be seen within the molecule. This way of looking at things must cease. Instead of wishing to examine the structure of the molecule microscopically, we must turn our gaze outward to the starry heavens, we must look at the constellations and see copper in one, tin in another! It is out there in the macrocosm that we need to behold the structure of the molecule that is only **reflected** in the molecule. Instead of passing into the infinitely small, we must turn our gaze outward to the infinitely great, for it is there we have to look for the reality of what lives in minuscule processes.*

This materialistic conception of things also affects other domains of thought. People who consider themselves capable of giving an opinion on the progress of human knowledge may say: Nineteenth-century materialism is now overcome! But it isn't! It is not overcome so long as people still think atomistically, so long as they fail to search in the wider universe for the form and configuration of the small. Neither is the materialism relating to humanity overcome, so long as we continue to ignore the connection of the human being, the microcosm, with the macrocosm.[25]

---

25   Rudolf Steiner, *Mystery of the Universe*, lect. 4/24/1920.

Measurable central forces vs. immeasurable cosmic forces

Materialistic physical science includes identifying points or centers from which forces emanate. The measurement of these forces that can affect the surroundings are referred to as their potential or potential force.

From a Goethean perspective, organic sciences or the sciences of the living should not be limited to the potential of central forces. When life is involved, we must also take into consideration incalculable peripheral or cosmic forces. Indeed, from a certain perspective all aspects of nature, even the mineral, have some degree of inherent life and therefore are affected to some degree by universal forces.[26] There is only one aspect of earthly life where incalculable forces are not at work: human-made machinery or mechanical devices.[27]

> We have to understand that in a given point or a given space, forces are concentrated that can act upon their surroundings. That is actually what we always find when we speak of the world in physical terms. All physical research consists of pursuing the central forces to their centers, of attempting to penetrate to the points from which effects can emanate. Thus, we have to assume that there are centers for such natural effects that are charged, so to speak, with possible effects in certain directions. Indeed, we can measure these possible effects by all sorts of procedures, and we can also express in measurements how strongly such a point can act. In general, when forces that can act when we fulfill certain conditions are concentrated in a given point, we call the measurement of the forces concentrated there the potential, the potential force. Thus, we can also say that when we study natural effects, we are intent on pursuing the potentials of central forces.

26 This leads to the question: How should we view so-called atoms or molecules? If an atom is a physical thing, then it should be subject to both central and cosmic forces according to Steiner. However, he maintains that what we call atoms are nonphysical, spiritual entities that are focal points of cosmic forces only. One could say that atoms and molecules exist as spiritual entities but do not manifest materially.

27 This refers to technology in its present form. In volume 2, we will explore forms of etheric technology that have both central and cosmic forces.

Figure 2.5: Nature as the result of central and cosmic forces

We go toward certain middle points in order to study them as the point of origin of potential forces.

This is basically the path taken by the particular direction of natural science that would like to transform everything into mechanics. It searches for the central forces, or better, the potentials of the central forces. But taking the important step into nature itself is a question of clearly realizing that you cannot understand a phenomenon in which life plays a role if you proceed only according to this method, if you only search for the potentials of central forces. . . . It will be the dawn of a new worldview in this discipline when we arrive at the realization that the pursuit of such central forces will not work to study phenomena in which life plays a role. And why not? Well, let us imagine for the sake of simplicity that we wanted to study natural processes by physical experimentation. We go to the centers and study the possible effects that can emanate from such centers. We find the effect. Thus, when I calculate the potentials of the three points **a, b, c,** *I find that* **a** *can affect* **A, B, C,** *likewise* **c** *can affect* **A¹, B¹, C¹,** *etc. I would then get an idea of how the effects of a given* *sphere play out under the influence of the potentials of certain central forces. Using this method, however, I will never be able to explain anything in which life plays a role. Why? Because the forces that are involved in life do not have potentials and are not central forces.*

*Thus, if you were to try in this case to find in **d** the physical effects under the influence of **a, b, c,** you would be able to go back to the central forces. If you wanted to study the effects of life, however, you could never say this, because there are no centers **a, b, c** for life effects. Instead, you can understand the situation correctly only if you say, "in **d** I have life." Now I look for the forces that have an effect on life. I cannot find them in **a, b, c,** and not even if I go further, but only if I go more or less to the end of the universe, in fact, to its entire surroundings. In other words, starting from **d,** I would have to go to the end of the world and conceive that forces are acting inward from every point in the sphere, coinciding in such a way that they all come together in point **d.** Thus, it is the complete opposite of central forces, which have a potential. How could I calculate a potential for something that acts from all sides from the infinity of space! It would have to be calculated by dividing the forces. I would have to divide a total force into smaller and smaller parts as I came closer to the edge of the world. The force would fragment. Every calculation would fragment too, because in this case universal forces, not central forces, are at work. That is where calculations cease. And that is once again the leap from lifeless nature into living nature.*

We can find our way to a real study of nature only when we understand first the leap from kinematics to mechanics, and when in turn we understand the leap from outer nature to something that can no longer be arrived at through calculations because every calculation fragments and every potential disintegrates. By this second leap we pass from outer, inorganic nature to living nature, However, in order to grasp what life is, we must be clear how all calculations come to an end.

Now I have neatly separated out for you everything that can be traced from potential and central forces from that which leads to universal forces. However, out there in nature it is not separated in this way. You could pose the question, where is there a situation where only central forces act according to potentials, and where is there the other situation, where universal forces are at work that are not calculable according to potentials? There is an answer to this question, but it immediately indicates what important considerations have to be taken into account. We can say that in everything that people produce in the way of machines, which are put together from natural elements, we find purely abstract central forces according to their potential.

Figure 2.6: Machines as the result of central forces only

Whatever is found in nature, however, even inorganic things, cannot be studied solely according to central forces. That does not exist. That does not add up. Rather, in every case, where we have to do with things that are not artificially produced by people, what we are dealing with is a confluence that takes place between the effects of central forces and the effects of universal forces. In the entire realm of so-called nature, we find nothing that is lifeless in the true meaning of the word, with the exception of what people produce artificially—their machines, their mechanical products.[28]

---

28   Rudolf Steiner, *The Light Course*, Lect. 12/23/1919.

Differing views of Goethe and Newton on central and peripheral forces

It is important to understand the difference between Goethe's and Newton's approaches to research.[29] Newton and those who thought like him focused exclusively on centric forces and potentials in nature. Goethe rejected this approach because nature was thereby reduced to a lifeless abstraction. For him, the reality of the perceived world could only be understood if both centric and peripheral universal forces were taken into consideration.

> *In a deeply instinctual way this was something that was both clear and unclear for Goethe, for it was an instinct on which he based his entire view of nature. And the contrast between Goethe and the natural scientist as represented by Newton actually derives from this fact—[in the early twentieth century] the natural scientist has studied only this one thing: the observation of outer nature solely for the purpose of tracing it back to the central forces and for driving out of nature everything that could not be determined by central forces and potentials. Goethe did not accept the validity of such an approach, for to him what was called nature was only a lifeless abstraction under the influence of this approach. For him there was something real only when, in addition to central forces, forces from the periphery, universal forces, come into play.[30]*

Part 7: IMAGINATIVE COGNITION AND THE ULTIMATE TRANSFORMATION OF THE MINERAL WORLD

Employing imaginative cognition: atoms as bubbles

Through imaginative or pictorial cognition, we can gain another insight into the nature of so-called atoms. From this perspective, they are bubbles that consist of something different from their surroundings.

---

29   Johann Wolfgang von Goethe (1749–1832) and Isaac Newton (1643–1727).
30   Rudolf Steiner, *The Light Course*, lect. 12/23/1919.

This something is made up of a specific kind of spiritual substance—ahrimanic spiritual substance.[31]

> *To imaginative cognition, atoms are revealed as bubbles, and the reality is where the empty space is supposed to be. Atoms are blown up bubbles. In other words, in contrast to what surrounds them they are nothing. You know that where bubbles are seen in soda-water there is no water. Atoms are bubbles in that sense; where they are the space is hollow, nothing is there. And yet it is possible to push against it; impact occurs precisely because, in pushing against hollowness, an effect is produced. How can nothing produce an effect? Take the case of the space, practically empty of air, within an air-pump; there you see how air streams into nothingness. A wrong interpretation might imagine the empty space in the bulb of the air pump as containing a substance that forced in the air. That is exactly the illusion prevailing in regard to the atom. The opposite is true: atoms are empty—yet again not empty. There is after all something within these bubbles. And what is it?—This is also something about which I have already spoken—what exists within the atom bubbles is ahrimanic substance. Ahriman is there. The whole system of atoms consists of ahrimanic substantiality. As you see, this is a considerable metamorphosis of the ideas entertained by those who theorize about matter. Where in space they see something material, we see the presence of Ahriman.[32]*

Reforming the mineral world

Our task in the present age is to transform the physical or mineral world through our actions as spiritual beings. Whatever we build or create, we are fashioning with our spirit. When we build a machine, not

---

31 The electric and magnetic fields of early twentieth-century science approach the nature of this substance, with the important distinction made by Rudolf Steiner that these fields are not something physical, but spiritual or etheric in nature. The electric and magnetic fields form the spiritual substance of Ahriman. See chapter 8 for more on the being of Ahriman and ahrimanic forces. Also, volume 2 will have more on the etheric world and etheric forces.

32 Rudolf Steiner, *The Karma of Materialism*, lect. 8/7/1917.

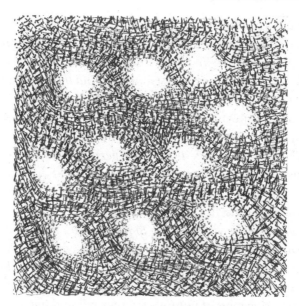

Figure 2.7: Atoms as bubbles of Ahrimanic substance

only the machine but everything that it changes will be permeated by our creative spirit.

What we make of the mineral world now is what humanity will be in the future. It will become possible for human beings to elevate the spiritual nature of the kingdoms of nature through its activities. This theme will be taken up again in relation to sacred creation in volume two.

We are living now in the epoch of evolution that may be called the mineral epoch; and our task is to permeate this mineral world through and through with our own spirit. Grasp exactly what this means. You are building a house. You fetch the stones from some quarry. You hew them into the shapes needed for the house, and so on. With what are you joining this raw material, obtained from the mineral kingdom? You are joining raw material with human spirit. When you make a machine, you have introduced your spirit into that machine. The actual machine does, of course, perish and become dust; it will be broken up. Not a trace of it will survive. But what it has done does not vanish without a trace but passes into the very atoms. Every atom bears a trace of your spirit and will carry this trace with it. It is not a matter of indifference whether or not an atom has at some time been in a machine. The atom itself has undergone change as a result of having once been in a machine, and this change that you have wrought in the atom will never again be lost to it. . . .

But what we ourselves create in the world—that is what will, through ourselves, constitute our future being.

The mineral world, as such, we perceive; what we make out of it we will, in the future, **be.** *What we make of the plant world, of the animal world, and of the world of human beings, that too we will* **be** *in the future. If you found a charitable institution or have contributed something to it, what you have contributed, you will be. If individuals do nothing which they can draw back in this way into their souls from outside, they will remain empty. It must be possible for them to spiritualize as much as they can of the three kingdoms of nature—four, for humankind also belongs thereto. . . .*

We are going forward to an age when, as I recently indicated, understanding will reach right into the atom. It will be realized—by the popular mind too—that the atom is nothing else than congealed electricity. Thought itself is composed of the same substance.

Before the end of our present cultural epoch, one will in fact have come so far that people will be able to penetrate into the atom itself. When one is able to grasp the materiality between the thought and the atom, then one will soon be able to understand how to penetrate the atom.[33]

---

33   Rudolf Steiner, *The Temple Legend,* 12/23/1904,

Electricity and the Challenge of Evil

[The human being] must understand sub-nature for what it really is. This we can only do if we rise, in spiritual knowledge, at least as far into the extra-earthly super-nature as we have descended, in technical sciences, into sub-nature....

Electricity... celebrated since its discovery as the very soul of nature's existence, must be recognized in its true character—in its peculiar power of leading down from nature to sub-nature.

(note 34)

THREE

Electricity and the Challenge of Evil

Introduction

With the current push to make internet and cell phone service accessible over the entire earth, and efforts to replace fossil fuel–based energy sources with ones that are based primarily on electricity, it is imperative that humanity becomes more conscious of the nature of electricity and its effects on the human being and the planet. This grows in importance when taking into consideration the connection of electricity with the forces of evil as revealed in this chapter, and the role that electricity plays in human and Earth evolution. There will be further indications about electricity in volume two.

Chapter overview

The discovery and development of electricity radically changed human culture and our way of viewing life and the world. The pervasiveness of electricity has made it difficult to retain a connection to the spirit. It has the power to lead the human being from nature into sub-nature. To the degree that we are drawn down into sub-nature we need to rise in spirit above nature through conscious, willed activity.

This includes inner development exercises and gaining a greater understanding of the nature of the human being and human and earthly evolution.

Electricity-based technology is dominated by ahrimanic beings who oppose the further spiritual development of human and Earth evolution.[1] One of the goals of anthroposophy is to develop a realm of

---

1   For more on Ahriman and ahrimanic beings, refer to chapter 8.

knowledge to which these highly intelligent beings have no access, and by which human beings can counterbalance their retarding influences.

As described in the previous chapter on atoms and atomic theories, Rudolf Steiner considered the perspective that arose in the early twentieth century—namely, that atoms are congealed or frozen electricity—as a positive step forward. He thought that such a perspective at least provided a bridge to the idea that all matter is condensed spirit.

Electricity is not simply a force of nature; it is a moral force as well.[2] To gain an objective and truthful understanding of electricity, we must develop the courage to speak about it in terms of moral and anti-moral concepts. With the increased exploitation of electrical energy in the future, it will become possible to spread evil over the earth. In addition, evil will be spread over the earth directly out of the power of electricity itself. Even so, the evil associated with electricity is not something to be simply avoided but countered through the development of powerful forces of moral goodness. Indeed, human evolution progresses through the interplay between good and evil. When scientists ascribe electricity to atoms, they are unwittingly associating atoms with evil.

The origin of electricity took place long ago, when the sun and Earth were still united. In spiritual-scientific terms, the essence of electricity is an ancient, hidden sun force. In modern times, electricity can be characterized as decayed sunlight. The insertion of electricity and magnetism into the human being took place in the Lemurian age.[3] On one hand, electricity residing in the human body absorbs immoral forces while, on the other, natural light taken into the body conserves moral forces.

Electric cables that surround us also induce currents in us. One effect of such radiant electricity is that it diminishes a person's ability to

---

2   The term "moral" as used here refers to the realm of morality, which includes both good and evil, rather than referring solely to the quality of goodness. It is important to be clear which connotation Steiner means to convey wherever the word appears in this chapter.

3   See Appendix A, figure A-2, for the position of Lemuria in Earth evolution.

comprehend the information that is being rapidly transmitted through it. Spiritual science is not only meant to strengthen our relation to the spirit but also to help us overcome the negative effects of exposure to radiant electricity.

Electricity and magnetism can be useful in countering certain illnesses of the rhythmic system and metabolism within the human being. The topic of magnetism will be taken up more fully in relation to geographic forces in volume two.

Part 1: THE HUMAN SPIRIT, CULTURAL LIFE, AND THINKING

Electric forces and the challenge to the human spirit

Our current age of electricity and materialism presents a challenge to human beings to seek spiritual deepening. We need to counterbalance the invisible forces of electricity in the outer world with powerful spiritual forces that are ready to be awakened within us. It would have been hard to imagine that the discoveries of Galvani (1737–1798) and Volta (1745–1827) regarding electricity would lead to such immense changes to the outer world. So, too, it is hard to imagine that spiritual science can elicit moral and social changes in the world to a similar degree. But such thoughts can prepare the ground for necessary progress.

> *Anyone who understands the spiritual evolution of the world must at the same time regard the age of electricity as a challenge to seek a genuine spiritual deepening.... To the [electrical] power that remains outside us, unknown to our sensory observation, there must be added... the spiritual power which lies as deeply hidden within us as do the electrical forces that have yet to be awakened. Just think how mysterious electric power is! It took Galvani and Volta to draw it out of its hidden realm. What sits in human souls and is investigated by spiritual science is just as hidden. The two are inherently attracted to each other like the north and south poles. And as truly as electric power is drawn*

up as the force concealed in nature, just as truly will the power that belongs to it rise up, the power sought by spiritual science as the power concealed within the soul. This is the case even though many people are standing in front of what spiritual science wants to accomplish as someone would have stood in front of Galvani and Volta in the days when they prepared their frogs and studied the twitching of their hind legs, seeing that a force was working in these legs to make them twitch. Did science know then that in the hind leg of this frog everything about contact electricity was already contained, everything that is known today about electricity? Just imagine Galvani in his simple laboratory, hanging his frog legs on a hook in the window and watching them begin to twitch. Do you suppose that when Galvani first noticed this he could have predicted that someday the energy making his frog legs twitch could be used to drive railroad trains over the earth and send thoughts around the world?... Anyone who at that time had had grand visions of all that would eventually result from this would surely have been regarded as a fool. In the same way it has happened that someone who has the task of laying the foundations of a spiritual science today is also regarded as a fool. But a time will come when what comes out of spiritual science will be just as significant for the world—only it will be the moral, soul-spiritual world—as what has come out of Galvani's frog legs has been for the material world and material civilization. This is how progress is made in human evolution.[4]

Discovery of electricity and its effects on thinking and our worldview

The discovery and development of electricity has not only made profound changes in outer life but also has changed the way we view the world. It pervades our thinking and cultural life. Even modern atomic theories have incorporated electricity and electrons in their descriptions of the atom. The pervasiveness of electricity has made it nearly impossible to retain a connection to anything spiritual. In addition, the

---

4   Rudolf Steiner, *Goethe's* Faust *in the Light of Anthroposophy*, lect. 9/30/1916.

purity of light that pervades the universe is being devalued and compromised when it is described as being similar to artificial light.

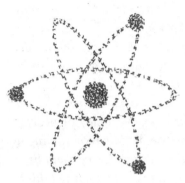

Figure 3.1: Atoms as tiny suns with orbiting electrons

Across from the moral order stands the natural order, which has brought about our awe-inspiring modern natural science. The thrust of the natural sciences now affects every aspect of human culture. Farmers today know more about modern science than they know about a spiritual worldview. Under what circumstances have the newer natural sciences developed? We can make this clear by using the example of electricity, a discovery that was quickly followed by its practical application.... But it is not just a matter of producing changes in daily life. The very substance of scientific explanations also changed very rapidly. When people born in the third quarter of the nineteenth century were going to school and studying physics, no one thought of describing atoms as anything other than tiny, inelastic balls that bumped up against one another. Physicists even calculated the force necessary to produce the impact between atoms. It had not yet occurred to anyone that an atom would be described as an electron, as if it were an entity that consists entirely of electricity. But the latter is what is taught in schools today.

The extent to which human thinking has become saturated with electricity is a fairly recent development. Now we speak about atoms as if they were tiny suns surrounded by orbiting electrons. When we look around us at the forces within the universe, we presume that electricity is everywhere. This permeates our entire culture, including our manner of thinking. If we did not ride trains so frequently, we might not have associated atoms so quickly with electricity.

> *If we were to look at the ideas that humanity had before the age of electricity, we could see that at one time an observer of nature still had the freedom to recognize the spiritual aspect of nature, at least to the point of thinking about it abstractly.... But electricity is so pervasive in the lives of modern human beings that it gets on our nerves. Our sensitivity to electricity made it impossible to maintain a connection to the spiritual.*
>
> *The effects of this go even further. The true light that floods the space of our universe is increasingly compromised in its purity, and even suffers the degradation of being seen as something similar to artificially generated light. When we begin to speak openly about these things, anyone who is completely committed to the value of the electrical culture thinks that we are out of our senses.*[5]

Effect of radiant electricity on reaching the spirit

There was a profound difference between the state of the world in the early 1800s and in the early 1900s regarding the prevalence of electrical wires and telephone cables.[6] This has an effect on the bodily and soul aspects of the human being. To simply be human requires much more spiritual effort. But we must not reject or flee from using electrical devices. Spiritual science provides a means to strengthen our connection to the spirit when contending with the forces of electricity.[7]

> *In some areas of the world, we are finally reaching a point in which there is a difference between now and a century ago. One speaks of Goethe, how he lived in, let us say, 1823, without emphasizing something that they are beginning to realize over there in America, where it is much more evident than it is in Europe. Consider that in the Weimar that Goethe went about in—or wherever*

---

5 Rudolf Steiner, *Awake! For the Sake of the Future*, lect. 1/28/1923.

6 Today, there is dramatically more wireless transmission.

7 It is important today to ask how much exposure to radiant electricity the adult human being can counterbalance with spiritual science, given the immense increase of such radiation through cell phone use. Its effect on children who are not mature enough to counterbalance such forces is an obvious additional concern.

Goethe went—he was not surrounded by telegraph wires, there were no telephone cables, etc. There the air was not crisscrossed by telegraph cables and electricity cables. Now consider just for once how subtle the instruments are wherever we send out the effect of electricity. But people are surrounded by such equipment. People in America are realizing that having electrical cables etc., buzzing around them everywhere has an effect on the physical human being. Goethe travelled around without his body having induction currents. Nowadays we can travel somewhere far away—but we cannot get so far away that the electrical cables do not follow us. They constantly induce currents in us. Goethe was not exposed to such currents. Humanity absorbs all of that in the physical body, making the physical such that the soul does not enter it. We should be clear about this: in the times when there were no electric currents, when the air did not have electric cables whizzing through it, it was easier to be human. Because then these ahrimanic forces were not constantly present which take one's body away even when awake. Then it was unnecessary for people to work so hard to reach the spirit. For, only when we enter into ourselves do we really reach the spirit. Therefore, to be a human being at all, it is necessary today to expend a much greater spiritual effort than it was a century ago.

I would not dream of being reactionary and saying for instance: get rid of all that stuff, all those products of modern culture. That is not my intention. But people today need the immediate devotion to the spirit that spiritual science gives them, so that, through its stronger experiencing of the spirit, they can in fact also be strengthened vis-à-vis precisely those forces that arise with modern culture hardening our physical bodies and taking them from us. Otherwise, it will turn out that human beings will lose their connection in the evolution of humanity.[8]

Compare the world today with the one of a hundred years ago. There are a multitude of differences, but one could say that

8   Rudolf Steiner, *The Human Soul in Connection with Divine-Spiritual Individuals* (CW 224), lect. 7/11/1923, as found in "Rudolf Steiner on Technology: A Review," *Jupiter* (Dornach, Switzerland, Verlag am Goetheanum, April 2012).

*one of the greatest differences is that today our atmosphere is
crisscrossed either with telegraph or telephone wires.... Eventually one will sense that people are not immune to the activity
buzzing through telephone wires in the air, making people into
actual induction apparatuses.*[9]

Part 2: ELECTRICITY, CONSCIOUSNESS, AND MORALITY

Electrical and magnetic forces in the human being

It is widely recognized that the human body is permeated with
magnetic and electrical forces. These forces entered the human organism in the distant past, in the Lemurian epoch.[10] In biblical terminology, this was the time when the Fall of Adam and Eve occurred.

Evolution does not proceed continuously in a linear fashion. Rather,
it proceeds in rhythmical cycles in that it repeatedly turns back and
shifts again to the future, like moving along a lemniscate.[11] The time
when electricity entered the human being is the crossing point. At the
end of the eighteenth and the beginning of the nineteenth century, a
reconnection with the ancient epoch occurred in such a way that several scientists of the time opened up the science of electricity, for example, Galvani (1737–1798) and also Faraday (1791–1867).

*Let us look back for a moment to an event of the Lemurian
epoch. We find there a certain moment in evolution—it lies
thousands and thousands of years back—when humankind on
earth was quite different from what it is now. You will know from
the descriptions I have given of human evolution on the earth in
Esoteric Science that the various impulses entered only gradually into the human being. There was a moment in evolution
when what we today call magnetic and electric forces established
themselves within the human being. For magnetic and electric*

---

9   Rudolf Steiner, *Course for the Priests of the Christian Community*, CW 345, lect.
7/11/1923.

10   See Appendix A, figure A-2, for the position of Lemuria in Earth evolution.

11   Imagine a figure eight in a horizontal position like the symbol for infinity.

forces live in us in a mysterious manner. Before this time, human beings lived on earth without the magnetic and electric forces that have developed ever since on a spiritual level between the workings of the nerves and the blood. They were incorporated into the human being at that time. The forces of magnetism we will leave out of consideration, also some forms of the forces of electricity. But the forces which I will distinguish as the electric forces in galvanism, voltaism, etc., forces that have taken deep hold in the culture and civilization of our time, these forces entered the human organism in that far-off time and combined with human life; and this very fact made it possible for them to remain for a long time unknown to human consciousness....

After humankind had passed the moment in the Lemurian age when it had implanted into it the forces that pass through the wire today as electricity and work in an invisible manner in the human being himself, after this time had passed, electricity existed inside the human being. Evolution never proceeds in the simple straightforward way in which people are inclined to picture it. They imagine that time goes ever forward on and on to infinity. That is an altogether abstract conception. The truth is that time moves and turns in such a way that evolution is constantly reversed and runs back on itself. It is not only in space that we find movements in curves, such as in lemniscates, but also in time.

During the Lemurian epoch human beings were at the crossing point of the lemniscate and that was the time when they implanted into themselves the principle of electrical force. They traversed the return path in the Atlantean period and, in respect of certain forces, in the post-Atlantean period, and at about the end of the eighteenth and beginning of the nineteenth century arrived exactly at the point in the evolution of the cosmos at which they were in the old Lemurian age when they implanted into themselves from the cosmos the principle of electricity. There you have the explanation of how it came about that Galvani discovered electricity at that particular time. Human beings always go back again in later times to what they experienced at an earlier stage. Life takes its course in cycles, in rhythms. In the middle of the materialistic age which had been developing since the fourteenth and fifteenth centuries, humankind was standing at that point in the cosmos through which it had passed long ago in the Lemurian epoch. And humankind as a whole at that point remembered the entry of electricity into the human being and as a result of this memory endowed the whole of civilization with electricity. The soul and spirit in the human being rediscovered what it had once experienced long ago.

Truths like this must be clearly seen again, for it is only with truths like this that we shall escape decadence in the future.[12]

Electrical and magnetic forces, thoughts, and mechanical forces

Human consciousness is linked to the death forces within the nervous system, which are in turn related to electricity and magnetism.[13] In the future, people will learn to transform their thoughts and intentions into mechanical forces via electrical and magnetic forces.[14]

Recently I have often very deliberately pointed out, also in public lectures, that human consciousness is linked with the forces of destruction. Twice in public lectures in Basel [sic] I have said: "We die into our nervous system." These forces, these forces of death will grow ever stronger and stronger. Connections will be created between the human being's forces of death—which are related to electrical, to magnetic forces, and to external mechanical forces. People will be able in a certain way to steer their intentions and their thoughts into the mechanical forces. Yet undiscovered forces in the human being will be discovered, forces that work on external electrical and magnetic forces.[15]

---

12 Rudolf Steiner, *The Knights Templar*, lect. 10/2/1916.

13 For more information on death forces and the human nervous system, see chapter 9.

14 This appears to be a foretelling of twenty-first century artificial intelligence.

15 Rudolf Steiner, *Secret Brotherhoods*, lect. 11/25/1917.

Part 3: INSTINCTS, MORALITY, AND EVIL

The necessity of conquering lower instincts
before directly perceiving electricity and magnetism

Humanity is not ready for the direct perception of electricity and magnetism. Such a capacity in people would engender certain powers that would cause harm to others if lower instincts were not sufficiently mastered. The guiding wisdom of human evolution provides for the necessity of mastering lower instincts and powers before advancing to the attainment of higher spiritual powers.

Let us consider asking the question, "What would it be like if instead of eyes people really had these organs for direct perception of electricity and magnesium, if this idea put forward naively by someone were to be brought to realization for us human beings?" We would then find our way in the realm of electricity and magnetism but not in the realm of light and sound. But there would be a consequence. If people had an organ for the direct perception of electricity and magnetism, they would have not only this organ, which would be an organ of perception, but also the power to kill any other person or to make them sick. Such an organ would directly confer that power.

So, this is what can be said about William Crookes' idea from the point of view of spiritual science, for we know that forces related to magnetic and electrical forces are present in human beings here on earth. The question now has a very different meaning, and we really see the naivety of simply setting up such an idea. Someone who does not possess higher vision sets up the idea of looking into electrical and magnetic forces, but for the spiritual scientist this leads directly to what has just been said. If we bring that to mind, we begin to see clearly that we must not stay on the surface but truly seek to go deeply into the wisdom that lies behind the world order and understand it. For the spiritual scientist's insight shows that it is a very good thing for human beings not to have the electrical and magnetic organs, for in this way they will not be able to damage others with them.

*Their lower instincts and desires thus also cannot run free ini-
tially, causing disaster to them and to others. Human beings have
a world around them which teaches them slowly and gradually
to conquer these lower powers and only then progress to higher
powers.... They would not be able to do this if in the course of
Earth evolution, they had developed organs that let them have
direct perception of electricity and magnetism. If they had, the
temptation would have been too great to kill people whom for
some reason or another they did not like and allow only those
who suited them to remain on earth.*[16]

The development of higher levels of morality

Since the beginning of the nineteenth century, electricity has played
a major role in the advancement of external life. It not only powers the
economy but is also a dominant cultural force and will be more so in
the future. Indirectly, electricity can play a positive role in the moral
development of humanity by providing human beings with the challenge of encountering and overcoming the increased egotism and harm
made possible by electricity as a cultural force. Through meeting and
overcoming these challenges, human beings can evolve to a higher level
of morality than would otherwise be the case.

*In the nineteenth century, the age in which materialism reached
a certain height, as I explained to you a week ago, a particular force of nature came to the fore. The peculiar nature of this
force is characterized by the fact that today everyone is saying:
"We have this force of nature, but no one can understand it; it is
hidden from science." You know that of all the forces of nature,
electricity was precisely the one that came into human use. Now
electrical energy is of such a nature that as a general rule, human
beings cannot experience it internally; it remains something
external. The nineteenth century achieved a certain greatness,
which became even greater than is generally believed, through the
rise of electricity. It would be easy to show how infinitely much*

16   Rudolf Steiner, *How the Spiritual World Projects into Physical Existence*, lect.
6/10/1913.

our present civilization owes to electric power, and how much more it will depend on it in the future, when electric power will be used as it is today without being experienced inwardly. Even more! But it is precisely the power of electricity that has replaced the old, familiar power in the cultural development of humanity, and it is the one through which human beings are intended to mature to a higher level with respect to their moral development. No one using electricity today thinks of it as having any connection with morality. But there is wisdom in the ongoing historical evolution of humanity. People will mature by virtue of the fact that for a time they will be able to bring about even greater harm in the bearer of their lower "I"—their depraved, dissolute egoism—than is already present there in sufficient quantity, as every day now shows us.... Electric power, as a cultural force in modern civilization, is the very power that makes this possible. In a certain way, steam can do this too, but not to the same extent.[17]

The moral and immoral aspects of electricity

To imaginative cognition, electricity is not simply a part of nature like sound and light. It also has a moral component associated with it. Human beings can sense this moral element when experiencing an electrical shock coursing through their bodies. Additionally, the electricity that naturally occurs in the human body is a region where moral impulses of a certain nature originate. Whoever experiences the totality of electricity in nature can also experience a moral aspect of nature.

When physicists characterize atoms as electrical in nature, they unwittingly associate them with a moral nature, a moral impulse. Electricity has all kinds of moral impulses streaming through it. These impulses include an instinctively evil, immoral aspect. Humanity must overcome these evil impulses with the help of higher spiritual powers.

The greatest contrast to electricity is natural light. When we use electric lights, we are mixing good and evil forces.

---

17   Rudolf Steiner, *Goethe's* Faust *in the Light of Anthroposophy*, lect. 9/30/1916.

For, you see, with electricity one enters a realm that presents itself to imaginative beholding differently than other natural realms. As long as one remained in light, in the world of tones—that is, in optics and acoustics—there was no need to judge morally what a stone, plant, or animal brought to expression in light as colors or in the auditory world as sounds, because one had an echo, albeit a weak one, of the reality of concepts and ideas. But electricity drives out this echo. And if, on the one hand, one is today unable to find reality in relation to the world of moral impulses, then, on the other hand, one is certainly not in a position to find the moral element in the field of what is today considered the most important ingredient of nature [i.e., electricity].

If today someone ascribes real effectiveness to moral impulses so that they are seen as containing the power, like the seed of a plant, to later become sensory reality, then he is considered a partial fool. But if someone were to come today and attribute moral impulses to the workings of nature, then he would be considered a complete fool. And yet, whoever has once, with real spiritual beholding, consciously felt the electric current going through their nervous system knows that electricity is not just a natural force; rather, they know that electricity in its nature is at the same time a moral force, and that at the moment in which we enter the realm of the electric, we simultaneously enter the realm of the moral. For if you stick your finger into a closed current [of electricity], then you will immediately feel that you are expanding your inner life into a realm of the inner human being where the moral element simultaneously emerges. You cannot look for the intrinsic electricity that lies in human beings in any other realm than the one where the moral impulses simultaneously emerge. Whoever experiences the totality of the electric element simultaneously experiences the natural-moral element. And, unknowingly, modern physicists have actually made a strange hocus-pocus. They have pictured the atom as electric, and, out of the general consciousness of our time, they have forgotten that when they picture the atom as electric, they thereby ascribe to this atom, to every atom, a moral impulse, and thus make it into a moral being. But I am speaking incorrectly now. For, in reality, in making the atom an electron, one does not thereby make it into a moral being but rather an immoral being. In electricity, the moral impulses, the natural impulses, are indeed swimming— but these are the immoral ones, these are the instincts of evil that must be overcome by the upper world.

And the greatest contrast to electricity is light. And it is a mixing up of good and evil when one sees light as electricity. One loses the real perception of evil in the natural order if one is not aware that by electrifying the atoms, one actually makes them into the bearers of evil—not only, as I explained in the last course, into the bearers of death but into the bearers of evil. They are made into the bearers of death by virtue of the fact that one allows them to be atoms at all, by virtue of the fact that one pictures matter atomistically. The moment one electrifies this part of matter, one pictures nature as evil. For electric atoms are evil, they are little demons.

With this, quite a lot is actually said. For it is thereby said that the modern explanation of nature is on the path of actually joining itself with evil. These peculiar people at the end of the Middle Ages who were so afraid of [Heinrich Cornelius] Agrippa von Nettesheim, [Johannes] Trithemius of Sponheim, and all the others, and who perceived them as going around with the evil poodle of Faust[18]—they indeed brought it all to expression clumsily. But even if their concepts were wrong, their feeling was not entirely wrong.[19] For when we see the physicist of today unknow-

---

18 Translator's note: In Goethe's work *Faust* (1808), Mephistopheles, the evil spirit to whom Faust sold his soul, first appears as a black poodle. This notion of an evil spirit appearing in the form of a dog has its roots in earlier Faustian legends, which were based on the historical Johann Georg Faust (c. 1480–1540). Heinrich Agrippa von Nettesheim (1486–1535) had a black dog, which some of his contemporaries, apparently drawing a parallel with the legends of Faust, believed to be a demonic being in disguise.

19 Translator's note: It is not entirely clear what Rudolf Steiner intends to say with this whole passage about those who were afraid of Agrippa and Trithemius. One possibility is that he is saying that these people, while wrong in their concepts—which were rather superstitious—were still partly correct in their feeling, insofar as the work of Agrippa and Trithemius contributed to the development of analytic modern science, which in turn would provide the basis for the materialistic view of the atom that Rudolf Steiner is here characterizing.

ingly declare that nature consists of electrons, he is actually declaring that nature consists of tiny demons of evil. And insofar as one then only recognizes this nature, evil is declared to be the God of the world. If we would be modern people and not proceed according to traditional concepts but according to reality, then we would indeed come to the conclusion that, just as the moral impulses have life, have natural life, through which they realize themselves as a subsequent, sensorially real world, so, too, does the electric element in nature have morality. That is, if the moral element has a natural reality in the future, the electric had a moral reality in the past. And if we look at it [i.e. electricity] today, we see the images of a former moral reality, which have, however, turned into evil.[20]

Contending with evil in the current epoch due to the widespread use of electricity

The widespread use of electricity and electrical energy will create the possibility of spreading evil over the earth. Through the mastery of the forces of nature, evil impulses will enter the world, but they will also enter directly from the power of electricity itself. Humanity will need to summon the opposing forces of good to meet these challenges.

We humans will have to struggle with evil.... In particular, it will be through the mastery of various forces of nature that the drives and impulses for evil will work their way into the world with colossal magnificence. And it will be in the resistance people will have to summon up out of subterranean depths that the opposing forces, the forces of good, will have to grow. It will be especially during the fifth epoch that through the exploitation of electrical energy, which will assume quite other dimensions than it has hitherto, it will become possible for humanity to spread evil all over the earth, but evil will also come over the earth directly out of the power of electricity itself.[21]

---

20 Rudolf Steiner, *Awake! For the Sake of the Future*, lect. 1/28/1923. (The translation of this passage has been revised. See Bibliography, *Lebendiges Naturerkennen, Intellektueller Sündenfall, und Spirituelle Sündenerhebung*.)

21 Rudolf Steiner, *Goethe's* Faust *in the Light of Anthroposophy*, lect. 11/4/1917.

Confronting evil as an opportunity for progress

Even though the exploitation of electricity and electricity itself have the potential to spread evil all over the earth, they are not to be avoided; confronting them is necessary for human progress. Counter forces of good in opposition to evil need to be created. This is only possible if humanity can understand the Christ principle.[22]

> Anyone who understands spiritual science will realize quite clearly that [electricity] should not be done away with, that we cannot be reactionary or conservative in the sense that we must be opposed to progress. Indeed, the [proliferation of technology] signifies progress, and the earth will continue to make more and more progress. Developments in the world soon will make it possible to produce immense effects ranging outward into the universe. Doing away with these things or condemning them is not what we are after because they are obviously justified. But what must be borne in mind is that since they must appear on the one side in the course of human progress, counter forces must be created on the other to reestablish a balance. Counter forces must be created. They must bring about a balance that can be created only if humanity again comes to understand the Christ principle.[23]

Electricity and evil:
World progress through the interaction of good and evil

The world progresses through the interplay of good and evil forces. Goethe portrays this artistically in his play *Faust*. He gives the devil his due, but also directs the "Sons of God" to bestow enduring thoughts of the eternal spirit upon humanity to counterbalance materialism and the insertion of electricity into the human being and civilization. The task of spiritual science is to assist in this process.

---

22 The themes of overcoming evil and the mission of Christ will be addressed more fully in volume 2.

23 Rudolf Steiner, *The Karma of Vocation*, 11/26/1916.

The whole of evolution, as we said, progresses not just through the work of good forces but others also. And a man like Goethe expressed in Faust, *even though in part unconsciously but nevertheless through inspiration, notable and great truths. When the Lord is conversing with Mephistopheles in the "Prologue in Heaven," he says finally to Mephistopheles that he has no objection to his work and influence. He recognizes and allows him his place in the evolution of the cosmos. It is owing to him that there are such things as temptations and influences that create evil. But then the Lord turns and directs his Word to the true and genuine sons of the gods who create progress in normal evolution and with whose work the work of the other stream is combined. And what does he say to these true sons of the gods?*

> *But ye, true Sons of Heaven, it is your duty*
> *To take your joy in the living wealth of beauty.*
> *The changing Essence which ever works and lives*
> *Wall you around with love, serene, secure!*
> *And that which floats in flickering appearance*
> *Fix ye it firm in thoughts that must endure.*
>
> (Tr. Louis Macneice, Faber 1951)

The Lord gives to his sons the direct command to fix enduring thoughts in the places of the cosmos. Such an enduring thought was placed into the world when the principle of electricity was implanted into the human being and the human being was led back again to the enduring thought when he discovered the principle of electricity and implanted it into his materialistic civilization.

The thought expressed in the following lines is of immeasurable depth:

> *The changing Essence which ever works and lives*
> *Wall you around with love, serene, secure!*
> *And that which floats in flickering appearance*
> *Fix ye it firm in thoughts that must endure.*

And it represents a deep experience for the soul to feel the mystery of the "thoughts that must endure." For then we feel how in the world here and there the eternal stands at rest in the form of an enduring thought and we who belong to the world of movement are passing through what is being placed into "that which floats in flickering appearance" as thoughts that must endure, as the beauty that weaves and works everlastingly and reveals itself in order that we may comprehend it when the right moment comes.

May a right moment also come for humankind in the near future, even as it is predestined to come if humankind is not to fall into decadence. May the human being understand that he has to pass through the next point which reverses materialism into its opposite, the point where the great thoughts of the spiritual world can ray into humankind. Preparation is now being made for this in those whose karma has allowed them to encounter spiritual science. And it will be the continually recurring task of spiritual science to turn its work in this direction. For to the materialistic age that has found the enduring thought which in its newest form Ahriman-Mephistopheles has placed into modern evolution must be added what can be experienced in passing through a spiritual enduring thought. Spiritual science must see to it that humankind does not fail to grasp this spiritual thought. Therefore, we must also not cease in warning people repeatedly so that the moment of time for the comprehension of spiritual science does not slip by and is not lost.[24]

Living in the presence of evil and the being of Ahriman

Even though we can understand the relation between electricity and the forces of evil, we should not rail against electricity, or the being Ahriman who inspires its use. We need to learn to find the right way to live in the presence of Ahriman and his cohort Lucifer and not be overpowered by them. This means knowing when and how they are

---

24 Rudolf Steiner, *The Knights Templar*, lect. 10/2/1916.

present, and, most importantly, knowing the significance of electricity and its relation to evil.

> *If anthroposophy were either fanatical or ascetic, a great storm would be brought to bear against the culture of electricity. Of course, that would be absurd, for the only people who would talk this way have a worldview that does not take reality into account.... You cannot avoid the fact that you have to learn to live with Ahriman. But you must find the right way to live with him; for you cannot allow yourself to be overpowered by him.*
>
> *If you turn to the final scene of my first mystery drama,* The Portal of Initiation, *you can see the effect of unconsciousness in this matter. Read this scene again and you will understand the difference between being in Ahriman's presence unconsciously and confronting him in full consciousness. Ahriman and Lucifer have their greatest power over human beings when we are unconscious of being in their presence; for then we can be manipulated by these beings without even being aware of it. This is pointed out in the last scene of* The Portal of Initiation. *Thus, the power of the ahrimanic aspect of electricity over human beings in our culture can hold sway only so long as we are unconscious and unaware of the significance of the electrification of the atom, and blindly assume that electricity is harmless. Thus, we would remain unprotected from the fact that nature bound up with electricity produces a nature made up of tiny* **demons** *connected to evil. It is frightening to witness the extent to which today's scientific research is* **demon-idolatry**, *a worship or veneration of* **demons**. *We must become aware of this, for by awakening our inner consciousness we also become aware that we are living in the time of the consciousness soul.*[25]

Courage and understanding are needed

Courage is required to recognize and understand human morality, moral deeds, and the moral and anti-moral order of nature that is

---

25   Rudolf Steiner, *Awake! For the Sake of the Future*, lect. 1/28/1923.

permeated with electricity. A true understanding of the human being is necessary also.[26]

The electricity that resides in the human being absorbs the immoral impulses in us, just as outer light taken into our bodies conserves good moral impulses. We must have the courage to speak about electricity in terms of moral and immoral ideas.

Courage is the key:
- *to recognize the reality that stands behind moral deeds.*
- *to see the moral idealism in nature in its proper perspective.*
- *to understand that moral impulses are the seeds for a natural order that may be attained in the future.*
- *to acknowledge that nature's order today, with its electricity, is a moral order as well as an anti-moral order connected to evil.*

We must have courage to see moral qualities in nature in the right way.

In addition to courage, a true understanding of the human being is absolutely necessary. If an individual recognized an immoral impulse that would damage his or her physical body· and tried to understand this impulse from the perspective of today's physiology and biology, it would be foolish to expect helpful insights from conventional science. We would learn about the function of the circulatory and nervous systems, but there would be no mention of morality. Likewise, scientists talk about electricity and even recognize the presence of electricity within the human being, but they have nothing to say about the fact that the electricity within the human being can absorb immoral impulses. Today we talk about the absorption of oxygen and many other examples of absorption in a material sense. But you never hear that the electricity within the human being absorbs the immoral impulses within us, and that this phenomenon is a natural law like other natural laws. Nor is it ever mentioned that the light

---

26 The full import of this section on morality will become clearer in volume 2 when etheric technology will be considered more deeply.

that we take into our bodies from the outer world keeps the absorption of good, moral impulses. We need to bring spiritual knowledge into the science of physiology.

We shall be able to achieve this only when we free ourselves from the ideas and theories espoused in the past that irritate and suffocate us....

I asked you to imagine a complete transformation of thinking [umdenken] *and a complete transformation of empathetic understanding* [umempfinden]. *That is, I encouraged you to turn your thinking and knowing inside out and to fundamentally renew the way you think and understand the forces of your heart. We have to do more than observe from the outside in order to come to a different way of imagining or picturing the cosmos. We have to muster our courage, so that when we speak about electricity, we can use moral and anti-moral concepts in our discussions. Human beings in the modern era shudder at thoughts like these. We find it unpleasant to realize that when we enter an electric tram we have to sit in Ahriman's seat. Many of us would rather ignore this and prefer to organize sectarian gatherings where people can talk about how to protect themselves from Ahriman's influence. But, in fact, the most important task we have is to know that, from now on, the development of earthly existence calls for the integration of natural forces into cultural life. That means that the active influence of Ahriman must be taken into account as a reality. We have to be fully conscious of this in order to put ourselves in the right relationship to it.*[27]

---

27 Rudolf Steiner, *Awake! For the Sake of the Future*, lect. 1/28/1923.

Part 4: SUN FORCES, DECAYED LIGHT, SUBNATURE, AND ELECTROMAGNETIC FORCES

Electricity, an "old Sun" force

From a spiritual-scientific perspective, there was a time when Earth and the Sun were still a united body during old Saturn and old Sun.[28] It is there that time that we can find the origin of electricity. With electricity, we have a hidden Sun force in the Earth.

> We know that once earth and sun were one body. Of course, this is long ago, during the Saturn and Sun periods. Then there was also a short repetition of those periods during the Earth period. But something remains behind which still belongs there. And this we bring forth again today. And we bring it forth from the repetitious condition on earth not only by heating our rooms with coal, but we bring it forth by using electricity. For, what remains from those times after old Saturn and old Sun, when the sun and earth were one, that provided the basis for what we have today on earth as electricity. We have in electricity a force which is sun force, long connected with the earth, a hidden sun force in the earth.[29]

Decaying light and electricity

Light is a result of the previously mentioned sun force. It was continually evolving until the time of Atlantis, which preceded our post-Atlantean times. We are now in the fifth post-Atlantean age.[30] Light is now in a stage of decline. Decayed or fallen light is what we call electricity.

> Light is destroying itself in our post-Atlantean, earthly process. Until the time of Atlantis, earthly processes had been progressive, but since then they have been in a process of decay. What is light?

---

28   See Rudolf Steiner, *An Outline of Esoteric Science*, for an overview of the evolution of the earth and our solar system. Also, see Appendix A, figure A-1.

29   Rudolf Steiner, *St. John's Tide*, lect. 6/24/1923.

30   See Appendix A, figure A-3, for the position of the fifth post-Atlantean age in Earth evolution.

*Light decays, and the decaying light is electricity. What we know
as electricity is really light that is destroying itself within matter.
The chemical force that is transformed in the process of earthly
evolution is magnetism.*[31]

Condensed light as the essence of material existence

The whole of our material world comes into being through a condensation process. All matter is in essence condensed or compressed light.

*Spiritual science [can enable one to observe] how, in the spaces
between our substances, there is always a uniform substance
everywhere which represents the extreme limit to which matter
is reducible.... Every singly substance... is there seen to be a condensation of this fundamental substance, which is really no longer matter. There is a fundamental essence of our material earth
existence out of which all matter only comes into being by a con-
densing process, and to the question: "What is this fundamental
substance of our earth existence," a spiritual science gives the
answer: "Every substance on the earth is condensed light." There
is nothing in material existence in any form whatever which is
anything but condensed light.... Light cannot be traced back to
anything else in our material existence. Whenever you reach out
and touch a substance, there you have condensed, compressed
light. All matter is, in essence, light.... In as much as human
beings are material beings, they are composed of light.*[32]

*Electricity is light in the sub-physical state where it is com-
pressed to the greatest degree. An inner quality must also be
ascribed to light.*[33]

Electricity and the realm of sub-nature or the sub-physical

The human being must not be dragged down from nature to sub-
nature. This was not an issue when early technical development was
still united with nature and the divine. The spirit as it manifested in

31 Rudolf Steiner, *The Reappearance of Christ in the Etheric*, lect. 10/1/1911.
32 Rudolf Steiner, *Manifestations of Karma*, lect. 5/27/1910.
33 Rudolf Steiner, *The Reappearance of Christ in the Etheric*, lect. 10/1/1911.

earlier times can no longer be found in the world of technology. Now it is dominated by spiritual beings of an ahrimanic nature. It is the goal of modern spiritual science to develop a realm of knowledge in which the ahrimanic element has been removed, thus enabling humanity to develop the strength to meet these beings with courage.

> [The human being] must understand sub-nature for what it really is. This we can only do if we rise, in spiritual knowledge, at least as far into the extra-earthly super-nature as we have descended, in technical sciences, into sub-nature....
>
> There are a very few as yet who even feel the greatness of the spiritual tasks approaching man in this direction. Electricity, for instance, celebrated since its discovery as the very soul of nature's existence, must be recognized in its true character—in its peculiar power of leading down from nature to sub-nature. Only human beings themselves must beware lest they slide downward with it.
>
> In the age when there was not yet a technical industry independent of true nature, human beings found the spirit **within** their view of nature. But the technical processes, emancipating themselves from nature, caused human beings to stare more and more fixedly at the mechanical material, which now became for them the really scientific realm. In this mechanical-material domain, all the divine-spiritual being connected with the origin of human evolution, is completely absent. The purely ahrimanic dominates this sphere.
>
> In the science of the spirit, we now create another sphere in which there is no ahrimanic element. It is just by receiving in knowledge this spirituality to which the ahrimanic powers have no access, that humanity is strengthened to confront Ahriman **within the world.**
>
> In the age of natural science, since about the middle of the nineteenth century, the civilized activities of humanity are gradually sliding downward, not only into the lowest regions of Nature, but even **beneath nature.** Technical science and industry become sub-nature....

*This makes it urgent for human beings to find in conscious experience a knowledge of the Spirit, wherein they will rise as high above nature as in their sub-natural technical activities they sink beneath her. They will thus create within themselves the inner strength **not to go under**....*

A past conception of nature still bore within it the spirit with which the source of all human evolution is connected. By degrees, this spirit vanished altogether from man's theory of nature. The purely ahrimanic spirit has entered in its place and passed from theory of nature into the technical civilization of humankind.[34]

Severing the connection of plants to the cosmos with artificial lighting

The reliance of plants on cosmic forces, including sunlight, has been circumvented by creating artificially lit greenhouse environments. The European Blood Beech was one exception until 1914 because it continued to go through its normal winter rest even in an artificial environment. In 1914, the researcher Klebs was successful in overcoming this obstacle. Spiritual science distinguishes between natural sunlight and electrical lighting, which is ancient sunlight within the earth. Through proper research, such as testing the sap from trees growing in natural sunlight and trees growing under electric light, it is possible to compare the effects of artificial light and natural sunlight on the life of the Blood Beech tree.

> *When using a microscope one is used to having everything limited to a narrow view. Everything takes place in the small enclosure. It must be possible to look at a plant by itself, not in connection to the whole cosmos!*
>
> *And look how at the turn of the nineteenth to the twentieth century the scientists succeeded to an extraordinary degree in this region. It was known, of course, from some plants in hothouses, greenhouses, that the mere summer and winter aspects of the plant could be overcome. But on the whole, not enough could be discovered about the plant needing a certain winter rest....*

34 Rudolf Steiner, *Anthroposophical Leading Thoughts*, March 1925.

But the most interesting and grandiose experiments in this direction were made exactly at the turn of the nineteenth to the twentieth century, when one succeeded in driving the stubbornness... from the plant. It was possible to do this in plants known as annuals by creating certain conditions. In the case of most of the trees growing in the temperate zone, conditions could be established which caused them to remain green all year round, to give up their winter sleep. This then provided the basis for certain materialistic explanations. In this way really magnificent accomplishments were achieved.

It was discovered that the cosmic element could be driven out of trees if they were brought into enclosed spaces, given enough nourishing minerals, making it possible that plants in wintertime, when the soil is poor in minerals, can find this nourishment. If enough moisture, warmth, and light is supplied, the trees will grow. However, one tree in Central Europe was defiant: the Blood Beech. It was approached from all sides to give up its independence and subjected to isolation in a prison. It was provided everything necessary, but remained stubborn and demanded nevertheless its winter rest. But it was the only one that still resisted.

And now we must record that in the twentieth century, in 1914, at the beginning of the war, another great historical event occurred: the immense, mighty accomplishment of the most capable researcher Klebs, who was able to compel the Blood Beech to give up its independence. He simply was able to bring it into an enclosed space, provide the necessary nutrients, warmth, and light, which could be measured, and the Blood Beech submitted to the demands of research....

Why should not the stubborn Blood Beech, when approached forcefully enough, be induced to use not the sun that radiates from the cosmos, but to use the sun force retained within the earth... electricity?...

When our attention is called to such brilliant results of materialistic science as those discovered by Klebs, that even the stubborn Blood Beech can be compelled to grow with electric light, this will lead us, without spiritual science, to the point where we will shatter everything into pieces and have a very narrow view. The Blood Beech will stand before us, growing in electric light, and we will know nothing except what this very narrow picture tells us.

With spiritual science, however, we can say something else: Klebs took the sunlight from the Blood Beech. He then had to give her electric light, which is actually ancient sun light. . . .

But what about cosmic connections? Let us free ourselves of such a worldview. Let us become clear that the stubborn Blood Beech no longer needs the sun. If we imprison her and give her enough electricity, she will grow without the sun. No! She will in fact not grow without the sun. But we need to seek the sun in the right way when we do something like that. And we must be clear that it is different when the Blood Beech grows in the sunlight or when ahrimanic sunlight, originating from long-past, is forced upon her. . . .

With an adequately wide view of these things, we will not admire our brilliance at having overcome the stubbornness of the beech but go much further. We will progress on to the sap of the beech and investigate its effect on the human organism, investigate both the beech we permitted to be stubborn and the one which we treated with electric light, and we might discover something very special about the healing forces of one as opposed to the other. But we must do this by considering the spiritual![35]

Northern lights

The electric and magnetic forces that the earth gives out are destroyed by sunlight when it enters the atmosphere, especially at the equator where sunlight is at its maximum. When the sun forces are diminished as they are in the polar regions, moon forces prevail. The moon forces then encounter the electrical and magnetic forces of the earth, and therefore the phenomena of northern and southern lights arise.

We realize that wherever the sun shines life arises—dissolving, evaporating, ever-spreading life! And wherever the moon works,

---

35   Rudolf Steiner, *St. John's Tide*, lect. 6/24/1923.

there arise forms, pictures.... In the north, where chiefly the moon is active and sun loses its power... the atmosphere becomes such that it gives out something always contained up here in the earth—namely, magnetism and electricity. They are contained everywhere in the earth. The earth is simply full of them.... But when the sun shines on the earth, as on the equator in the torrid zone, electricity is destroyed as soon as it tries to reach the air. The force of sunlight extinguishes electricity; but where sun activity is weak, electricity rises and is seen hovering in the atmosphere above the earth. Northern lights are electric forces of the earth that stream forth under influence of the moon forces. For this reason, such lights are rarely seen in our parts of continental Europe, but are often, if not always, present in northern regions.

Here again is a point beyond which science cannot go. Of course, contemporary science knows the earth is full of electricity. Science keeps observing the northern lights, but if you look for their explanation in books, you find these people always believe that they stream down to earth from the universe. This, however, is all nonsense; nothing streams in, it streams out!...

In hot countries, however, sunlight seizes upon this at once with the result that it is extinguished. In northern districts, moonlight activity predominates, and when not shining, its aftereffects remain, so out-raying electricity becomes visible as northern lights. Now the lights are strong in these parts, as the moon forces are especially powerful. Some northern lights are really present everywhere, only, being feeble, they are invisible. In our own regions [continental Europe] northern lights—in other words, out-raying electricity—are feeble too.[36]

Part 5: ELECTRICITY, HEALTH AND ILLNESS, AND HEALING

Electricity reduces comprehension

Electrical currents and radiations influence the entire human being in an unconscious way. They strongly affect the head organism of both

---

36 Rudolf Steiner, *Man and the Earth in Northern and Southern Regions*, lect. 10/13/1923.

humans and animals. Constantly defending itself against electricity will have a sclerotic effect on a living organism. Radiant electricity can affect a person's ability to comprehend things, including the news that is transmitted ever more quickly. Nothing good can come from applying electricity to a living being.[37]

> *Here, of course, the role of electricity in nature needs to be considered. It is of some comfort to know that at least in America, where people are developing a better gift of observation than here in Europe, voices can be heard saying that human beings will no longer be able to grow and develop as they used to, now that the whole atmosphere has electric currents and radiations running through it. This has an effect on the entire development of the human being. It even makes a difference whether the trains in a given area have steam engines or are electrified. The effects of steam can be recognized, but electricity has a terribly unconscious way of working—people simply cannot tell where certain things are coming from. Nowadays both radiant and conducted electricity are being used above ground to carry news as quickly as possible from one place to another. The effect of the radiant electricity on the people living in the midst of it will be that they will no longer be able to comprehend the news that is transmitted so quickly. Electricity gradually wipes out comprehension. This effect is already noticeable today; you can already see that people have a harder time comprehending things that come toward them than they did a few decades ago....*
>
> *You mustn't forget that electricity always works most strongly on the head-organization of humans and animals (and correspondingly on the root-organization of plants). If you preserve fodder by passing electricity through it, the animals that eat it will eventually become sclerotic. This is a slow process; you won't notice it right away.... Electricity is really not something that can*

37 The following quotation is a response by Rudolf Steiner, after a lecture on agriculture, to the question: "Is it permissible to preserve bulk fodder by means of electric currents?" Steiner appears to contradict himself here as he does give examples of using electricity in certain types of illnesses as described in examples that appear later in this chapter.

work on living things and do them any good. You see, electricity lies one level below the living, and the higher a given form of life is, the more it tries to ward off the electricity. If you constantly make an organism defend itself unnecessarily, it gradually gets nervous and fidgety and sclerotic.[38]

Electrotherapy:
Helpful for ahrimanic but not luciferic types of illnesses

In contrast to the previous passage, that no good can come from using electricity on a living organism, Steiner has suggested elsewhere that electricity and magnetism can be useful with certain illnesses. In general, it can be helpful for ahrimanic forms of illnesses, but not luciferic ones.[39]

Today external forces are used for the purposes of healing in a way which betrays a certain want of judgment—forces such as electrotherapy, the cold-water treatment, and so on. Much light could be thrown by spiritual science on the suitability of one method or another if it were first decided whether a luciferic or ahrimanic illness is being treated. For example, electrotherapy ought not to be used in illnesses which originate from luciferic causes, but only in ahrimanic forms of illnesses. For electricity, which has no connection whatever with the activities of Lucifer, is useless in treating luciferic forms of disease; it belongs to the sphere of the ahrimanic beings, although, of course, other beings beside the ahrimanic make use of the forces of electricity. On the other hand, heat and cold belong to the sphere of Lucifer.[40]

Electric and magnetic fields: illness and therapy indications

One such example is that electrical and magnetic fields could be used beneficially for countering arrhythmia within the human organism.

---

38   Rudolf Steiner, "Fourth Discussion," as found in *Spiritual Foundations for the Renewal of Agriculture*, lect. 6/16/1924.

39   Ahrimanic forms of illnesses tend to have cold, hardening effects, (i.e., tumors), and luciferic forms are usually of an inflammatory nature, such as asthma.

40   Rudolf Steiner, *Manifestations of Karma*, lect. 5/19/1910.

Phenomena involving electricity and magnetism encompass a process on earth or a sum of processes on earth which are inwardly connected with what we must call both earthly and non-earthly. The field of electricity and magnetism is one that really ought to be studied more deeply in relation to human health and illness. Here, though, we should feel our way very carefully due to the following: if you picture the surface of the earth to yourself schematically—here the interior of the earth, and here, what is above it—then phenomena of electricity and magnetism have a close connection to what is intrinsically earthly in nature.

You know of course that electricity conducts itself from one earth conductor to another, say from one Morse telegraph station to the next: there is only ever one wire connection and the circuit is completed underground. Here we see the electrical field which the earth has already appropriated. We can say that electricity and magnetism are basically constituted by something that is both outside of the earth and within it. But the earth appropriates electricity and contains electrical effects that really originate outside of the earth. In fact, the electrical and also magnetic effects can be held back in the earth's atmospheric periphery without being appropriated by the earth. These are all the electrical and magnetic effects which we find in our electrical and magnetic fields.

If we magnetize iron, in relation to the earth this means we turn the magnet into a little thief. We endow it with the capacity to rob the earth and retain what the latter wishes to absorb from the cosmos, before it can do so. Thus, we make the magnet into a little robber. It appropriates what the earth wants and has the inward strength to retain it for itself. All electrical and magnetic fields we have created on the earth are really stolen from the earth for our own use; and thus we inveigle nature into stealing, teach it to keep beyond the earth's reach what comes from outside the earth. And here we have something eminently extraterrestrial, which we cunningly retain above the earth although the earth seeks with all its strength to draw it inside itself, in order to let it stream out from itself again. But we do not allow it to do so, holding it back instead from this activity. And this is why we must regard electrical and magnetic fields as excellent opponents of arrhythmic processes in us. Thus, a form of therapy should be developed which specifically addresses severe arrhythmia or any other severe or mild disorders of the rhythmic system—in mild cases it works even better—by holding a strong magnet close to the human organism, not actually touching the body, at a distance that would need to be determined experimentally. You would have to try this out to get the right distance.[41]

Healing with electricity: Lung ailments

Lung ailments, in particular tuberculosis, can be treated by things that are external to the human being, such as a change of climate or altitude, light, and electrical and magnetic fields. Metabolic ailments can also be treated with electrical fields in certain situations. Here, the distinction is made between passing electricity directly through the human being and enabling an electric field to influence one from the outside. This sheds additional light on the contradiction mentioned in the previous section between the harmful and the healing aspects of electricity.

One might investigate what happens by applying a strong magnet to the back of someone, say, with incipient tuberculosis—thus allowing such a person to be irradiated by a magnetic field, and enhancing this action by moving the magnet, held crosswise, from above downward and from below upward. In this way the whole chest organism would gradually be suffused by the magnetic field. In applying this magnetic field, one does not need a light field too, at the same time, for this would only disrupt the effect.... You will find that this has a range of extremely beneficial effects for combating disorders such as those implicated in tuberculosis of the lungs.

At the same time, such things demonstrate the great importance of remembering the principle that we really only have effects in the human chest; and that therefore, when we wish to

---

41 Rudolf Steiner, *Illness and Therapy: Spiritual-Scientific Aspects of Healing*, lect. 4/13/1921.

bring about a cure, we must turn to our surroundings and use something that belongs to the world external to us; light, climatic influences, taking a patient to a higher altitude and every aspect of the magnetic field. This is true too of the electric field, but here we must give special consideration to the mode of treatment involved. Placing an electrical pole directly on the human organism and allowing electricity to pass through it is quite a different matter from first creating an electrical field and placing a person into this field without a circuit passing directly through him or her from one pole to the other. It will be necessary to experiment with such things, which are extraordinarily important. Under certain circumstances one can also obtain beneficial effects by allowing the circuit to pass between two poles through a person. But the action in this case will only be one that works over from the metabolic into the rhythmic system. When I conduct electricity through a person, passing it from one pole to the other and as it were including the person in the electrical circuit, only the metabolic system is affected. If, on the other hand, I place a person into an electrical field, ... I will find that I can treat patients by this means, even those whose digestion and so forth is well regulated but who show tuberculosis-related disorders. This is particularly relevant for disorders that arise in this area.[42]

Caution about healing with electricity

The fact that electricity can be used for some specific states of illness can lead to it being seen unjustifiably as a cure-all.

Now, as often happens, when something new appears on the scene, it is soon used for healing. But then it also is taken advantage of by the "prophets." When something first appears, it is strange how things that are a matter for clairvoyance are reduced to a mundane level. People come along and make all kinds of wild prophesies about the healing power of electricity, even though earlier it would not have occurred to them at all. Things come into fashion this way. As long as it had not been

---

42 Ibid.

discovered, it was impossible to think of healing by means of electricity. Now all of a sudden, it's a method of healing, not just because it is available, but because it has become fashionable. Radiant electricity is sometimes not much more of a remedy than if you were to take tiny, thin needles and poke the patient with them. Any healing that occurs is not due to the electricity but to the shock effect.[43]

Part 6: MEETING AND EMPLOYING ELECTRICITY IN CREATIVE WAYS

The Christian Community in an age of electricity

There is nothing inherent in most religions that can enable people to contend with the effects of technology because they were founded prior to the advent of electricity. The recently developed Movement for Religious Renewal (The Christian Community),[44] which is based on anthroposophy, does offer a spiritual antidote through its service and sermon to what we experience in the modern technological age. In addition, Christian Community priests can help strengthen and fortify an awareness of the influences of technology in modern life.

Compare the world today with one of a hundred years ago. There are a multitude of differences, but one could say that one of the greatest differences is that today our atmosphere is crisscrossed either with telegraph or telephone wires.... Eventually one will sense that people are not immune to the activity buzzing through telephone wires in the air, making people into actual induction apparatuses....

---

43 Rudolf Steiner, *Spiritual Foundations for the Renewal of Agriculture*, lect. 6/16/1924, "Fourth Discussion."

44 Rudolf Steiner created an offering service for children and youth in addition to the Christian Community Church ritual or service for adults. He also spoke about a reverse ritual that entails groups of two or more people meeting together in an elevated spiritual manner, and a cosmic ritual related to the festivals and the cycle of the year. More about the latter two will be considered in volume 2.

When you now look around at how the highest spiritual religious needs are satisfied, you must pose the question: Are there in these gratifications already some impulses inherent which take into account an element which renders these things [effects of electricity] harmless as part of the soul-spiritual experience? That is not so! The satisfaction of religious needs goes back to a time when all of this was not present, which I have illustrated for you. Today there is a gratification of religious needs which is only valid for a few people, which is not alive in the culture we have today. Anthroposophy wants to enter here to introduce newer impulses, impulses capable of making people independent from what they can't be independent of outwardly. What is external must be absorbed inwardly. Yet the polar opposite must be created—that means a strong awareness needs to be created for the importance of your Movement in order to create more and more impulses to come out of your Movement. The most important things must be thought through when you are to answer the question: What shall we do? The correct application of the ritual and sermon already offers the necessary strong impulse because this religious movement is built on the basis of anthroposophy. Yet the awareness that humanity stands amid these influences in the world must be present in every single one of us. Each one of you can contribute much toward fortifying awareness in this direction by raising it up and strengthening it.[45]

Openness to using electromagnetic forces in a productive way

Rudolf Steiner was not a dogmatist regarding the use of electricity: four examples are cited here in which he worked with, or at least was open to, using electricity in a creative, even artistic way.

1. Developing a new art of stage lighting: Rudolf Steiner worked with Ehrenfried Pfeiffer to develop a new art of electrical stage lighting for eurythmy performances.[46]

---

45   Rudolf Steiner, *The Essence of the Active Word: Course for the Priests of the Christian Community,* lect. 7/11/1923.

46   Ehrenfried Pfeiffer, *A Modern Quest for the Spirit,* "Fragments of a Biography."

2. Openness to having his lectures broadcast via radio under certain conditions.[47]

3. Openness to using an electric heating system for the original Goetheanum building if the heating source was in a separate building, and the electricity-generated heat would be transmitted through water.[48]

4. Rudolf Steiner's apparent intention to create films that illustrate reincarnation and karma. (See chapter 4.)

---

47 Paul Eugen Schiller (ed.), *The Schiller File*, folio 10 a-b. The *Schiller File* is a collection of guidelines and practical advice for experimental research given by Rudolf Steiner to some of his colleagues. The indications come from various sources, including lectures, research records, and notes made by people who had conversations with Rudolf Steiner. Sometimes these were written a considerable time after the conversations occurred.

48 Paul Eugen Schiller (ed.), *The Schiller File*, notes from July 2, 1984.

Early Twentieth-Century Technology

Script derived directly from the spirit. Then it grew ever more abstract. . . .

The declining line of development must give way in turn to an ascending one. . . . Script emerged from art originally, and it must return to art. And it must move beyond symbolism to allow the spirit to live directly within it, by becoming again a new kind of hieroglyph. (note 19)

FOUR
Early Twentieth-Century Technology

Introduction

This chapter gathers together some of Rudolf Steiner's comments on Western technology during the transition from the nineteenth to the twentieth centuries and its effects on the soul state of human beings. It was a time when Western humanity was becoming disconnected from traditional religion and the spiritual aspect of life. Technology and technical thinking were fast becoming the foundation for a modern view of the world.

Into this world of swirling materialism, Steiner offers up spiritual perspectives on technology and technical thinking that can enable human beings to ascend again to spiritual realities but in a more conscious way than through traditional religions as they were experienced in the past. In following his thinking about the technological developments of his time, one can sense how Steiner sought to acknowledge the importance of technology as an aid in human advancement while offering perspectives for how to counterbalance any potential harm it may bring about.

Chapter overview

Human beings have devoted a tremendous amount of mental and spiritual forces and energy to the furtherance of technology, primarily to further human needs such as comfort, convenience, and economic efficiency. The time has come, however, when we need to spend more of these forces and energy on spiritual development lest we lose our sense of what is most important and meaningful in life and become overwhelmed by technology itself.

Even so, we should not shun this spiritless environment. Rather, we should find the way to the spirit again in a new way that includes mastering technical thinking. Those who work with technology (which is virtually everyone today) should give priority to their spiritual life. The education of technology students should enable them to find connections between their various fields of study. This would lead to a greater understanding of their subjects and potentially to the spirit itself.

Movies, and the media in general, have been instrumental in pushing people toward materialism and away from the spirit. The cinema has the effect of driving people into the subconscious realm and has a harmful effect on the ether body. Even so, with the appropriate spiritual countermeasures, one can view as many films as one would like without undue harm.[1]

The one aspect of technology Steiner mentioned that cannot be counterbalanced by human beings by themselves was when they developed enthusiasm for the mechanizing of art, as occurred with the gramophone, which was the beginning of recorded music.[2] In this case, we need the assistance of the gods! Even though Steiner knew more than most people about the potential harmful effects of technology, particularly from a spiritual perspective, he took advantage of the many technologies of his day, including various forms of transportation, communication, and architectural and engineering design.

He also initiated research with various colleagues into developing spiritually informed alternatives to stage lighting and the cinema, more so with stage lighting, which has been used to a certain degree for eurythmy and drama performances.

---

1   Of course, this cannot apply to young children, whose sense organs are still developing and who are not able out of their own forces of individuality to initiate counterbalancing measures.

2   This mechanization has proliferated today with the rise of computerized music using digital electronic synthesizers.

Part 1: HARMONIZING TECHNOLOGY AND MACHINES WITH THE HUMAN SPIRIT

Optimal use of spiritual forces

Human beings have a limited amount of spiritual forces at their disposal. An enormous quantity of these forces is being used for technological development, mainly for soul needs and convenience. This has benefited humanity to a large degree in an external sense, but we are now faced with a descent into a spiritual abyss or void. We have come to a moment of decision between descending further into materialism or rising again to the spirit.

> We have now, in fact, reached a point in human evolution—and all that I am saying is in accordance with the apocalyptic presentation [in the Apocalypse of Saint John]—when in a certain way humanity is confronted by the need for a decision. We have already shown that in our age an enormous amount of spiritual energy is used to provide for the lowest needs; we have shown how the telephone, telegraph, railway, steamboat, and other things still to come have absorbed a tremendous amount of spiritual force; they are only used for the mere satisfaction of lower human needs. Human beings, however, have only a certain amount of spiritual force. Now consider the following: Human beings have used an enormous amount of spiritual force in order to invent and construct telephones, railways, steamboats, and airships in order to further external culture. This had to be so. It would have gone badly with humanity if this had not come about. This spiritual power has also been used for many other things. Only consider how all social connections have gradually been spun into an extremely fine intellectual web. What tremendous spiritual force has been expended so that one may now draw a cheque in America and cash it in Japan. An enormous amount of spiritual force has been absorbed in this activity. These forces had, so to speak, to descend below the line of the physical plane that separates the spiritual kingdom from the abyss. For in a certain way humanity has actually already descended into the abyss, and

one who studies the age from the standpoint of spiritual science can see by the most mundane phenomena how this goes on from decade to decade, how a certain point is always reached where the personality can still keep a hold on itself. If at this point it allows itself to sink down, the personality is lost, it is not rescued and lifted into the spiritual worlds.[3]

Immersion in technology and technical thinking

Our lives have become dominated by technology and the technical thinking that creates it. In the process, humanity has become disconnected from the spiritual world. The world that we live in is viewed as a big machine and/or a chemical factory. We should not shun the world of technology and technical thinking, but rather use this technological world, apparently devoid of spirit, to find the spirit again in a way that is more conscious than in the past.

What really matters in technology is that which we want to control. And as it is, we ourselves who put everything together in the experiments, we can survey every detail.

It is just because every detail is surveyable that one can have an immediate feeling of certainty about what is built up technically—for example, in chemistry; whereas, when one turns to nature there is always the possibility of several interpretations. So, it must be said that a thinking which is truly of our time is to be seen at its most perfect in the technician. People with no inkling as to how a machine or chemical product is made and works do not yet think in the modern way. They let other people think in them, as it were; people who are in the know, think technically. The external achievements of technology, such as mechanisms, chemistry, and so on, have gradually become a basis for a modern view of the world. In the course of time this approach has spread to what is today regarded as a world conception....

The age in which we live is completely oriented toward knowledge of a technical nature. There is no choice but to adapt to this

---

3   Rudolf Steiner, *The Apocalypse of St. John*, 6/24/1908.

approach; otherwise, the doctrines derived from the instinctive experience of the world in ancient times, and still preserved in the creeds and so on, will be distorted. No other possibility exists than to make use of concepts which are also applicable to the construction of machinery and so on. We live in a world that is thought of as a huge machine and as a huge chemical plant. If we are to find again what is spiritual in the world, then we must simply break completely with everything that has come down in the form of mysticism from former times. In the mechanical world, devoid of spirit, given us by modern science, there we must find the spirit.[4]

Pathway from machines to the spiritual world

It is essential that humanity begins to consciously understand the connection between the world of technology and the world of spirit. Otherwise, we will degenerate to the level of machines and become their accomplices, if not their servants. For students of technology, the key to this understanding is to take spiritual impulses into their soul. The desire to do this can begin by being taught, and then discovering on our own, the underlying connections between the various aspects of machines and technology. This is only a short step away from understanding the nature of machines and breaking through to the spiritual world. Thus, a rightly conceived and implemented training in the technical sciences can become a path from machines to the spiritual world.

In technology—although it may appear to be furthest away from the spirit—it is above all necessary that bridges should be built to the life of the spirit, out of direct practical life. The fifth post-Atlantean period is the one which is concerned with the development of the material world, and if the human beings are not to degenerate totally into a mere accomplice of machines—which would make them into nothing more than an animal—then a path must be found which leads from these very machines to the life of the spirit. The priority for those working practically with machines is that they take spiritual impulses into their own

---

4   Rudolf Steiner, *The Human Soul in Relation to World Evolution*, lect. 5/7/1922.

soul. This will come about the moment students of technology are taught to think just a little more than is the case at present, the moment they are taught to think in such a way that they see the connections between the different things they learn. As yet, they are unable to do this. They attend lectures on mathematics, on descriptive geometry, even on topology sometimes, on pure mechanics, analytical mechanics, industrial mechanics, and also all the various more practical subjects. But it does not even occur to them to look for a connection between all these different things. As soon as people are obliged to apply their own common sense to things, they will be forced—simply on account of the stage of development these various subjects have reached—to push forward into the nature of these things and then on into the spiritual realm. From machines, in particular, a path will truly have to be found into the spiritual world.[5]

Part 2: TRANSPORTATION: CARS, TRAINS, AND SHIPS

German medical experts on the effects of the first railroads

Health experts were consulted prior to the building of the first railroad in Germany. They advised that the railroad should not be built, or at a minimum, that high barriers should be placed along the railway to protect people from concussions. While this is laughable from a certain perspective, there has been an increase in nervousness since the advent of railroads.

In Germany, the first railroad was built in 1835, from Fürth to Nuremberg. Before this, the Bavarian health authorities were asked whether, from a medical point of view, building such a railroad would be recommended. Before beginning major projects such as this, it was always the custom to seek expert advice. The Bavarian health authorities responded (this is documented) that expert medical opinion could not recommend building railroads because passengers and railroad workers alike would suffer

---

5   Rudolf Steiner, *The Karma of Untruthfulness*, vol. 2, lect. 1/30/1917.

*severe nervous strain by traveling on trains. However, they con-
tinued, if railroads were built despite their warning, all railroad
lines should at least be closed off by high wooden walls to prevent
brain concussions to farmers in nearby fields or others likely to
be near moving trains.*

*These were the findings of medical experts employed by the
Bavarian health authority. Today we can laugh about this and
similar examples. Nevertheless, there are at least two sides to
every problem, and from a certain point of view, one could even
agree with some aspects of this report, which was made not so
long ago—in fact not even a century ago. The fact is, people have
become more nervous since the arrival of rail travel. And if we
made the necessary investigation into the difference between
people in our present age of the train and those who continued
to travel in the old and venerable but rather rough stagecoach,
we would definitely be able to ascertain that the constitutions of
these latter folks were different. Their nervous systems behaved
quite differently. Although the Bavarian health officials made
fools of themselves, from a certain perspective they were not
entirely wrong.*[6]

Effects of early cars on people in northern Wales

In rural areas in the early twentieth century, such as in North
Wales, where people still had a relation to the spiritual through a natural imaginative consciousness, cars had a disrupting effect. However,
we should not view this, or the disturbing effect of trains on the nerves,
as mentioned above, as an excuse to reject such modes of transportation. We can be assured that when technology provides human beings a
good external service, we can cope with such things if we respond with
freedom and spiritual attunement.

*A few days ago, I said that in this region [North Wales], where
imaginations take so firm a hold on the spirit, we get the dis-
turbance of motor cars. I am not speaking against cars, for in*

---

6   Rudolf Steiner, *Soul Economy*, lect. 12/31/1921.

anthroposophy we cannot express reactionary views. I am passionately fond of traveling by car when necessary, for we must not try to turn the clock back. What we have to do is balance what is one-sided by introducing the opposite. There is no harm in motoring, provided that we take it and everything of its kind with a heart attuned to the spiritual world. Then, even when other things follow motor cars, we shall be able to press on through our own strength and freedom, for freedom has to come.[7]

Effects of sleeping in trains and ships on human soul life

People who have developed themselves inwardly and have achieved at least the early stages of spiritual initiation will experience sleeping overnight on trains or ships differently than those who have not done so. To understand this, we need to know that when individuals are asleep, certain higher members of their being—the I and astral body—are temporarily outside, but close to, their physical and etheric bodies.[8] Even though these two higher members are outside the physical body, they are inside the noise and tumult of the train or ship. When the I and astral body return to their physical and etheric bodies, they bring with them, at least temporarily, the disharmony caused by these tumultuous experiences. Nevertheless, this fact should not be an excuse to shun such modern conveniences and seek the protection of "hothouse" cultures.[9] Rather, we should strengthen ourselves to withstand the negative effects of modern life through the soul strengthening benefits of spiritual-scientific research and insights and counterbalancing actions based on them.[10]

---

7   Rudolf Steiner, *The Evolution of Consciousness*, lect. 8/29/1923.

8   See editor's introduction and chapter 7 on education and child development for more about the physical, etheric, and astral bodies, and the I of the human being.

9   One could make the argument today that the trains and ships are quieter and more efficient than in the early twentieth century. However, this advance or refinement in technology can have other side effects, such as increased exposure to radiant electricity.

10   Following up on such indications, adults need think of how to educate the rising generations of children so that they are prepared to meet the ever-increasing

Those who are enabled by the first stages of the life of initiation to experience what modern civilization, in all its aspects, actually does to them will gain deeper insights into the significance it has for human existence than that obtained from an external view of life unsupported by spirituality. People who have taken the first steps in the life of initiation will pass differently through the experience of spending a night in a train or on a steamer, especially if they sleep on the journey. What is different for individuals who are in these first stages of initiation, as opposed to those who have not had any connection with it, is that the experiences become conscious for the former, and they find out what is actually happening to them when they spend a night traveling on a train or a ship, especially if they go to sleep. Of course, the person who has not acquired initiation knowledge of things also undergoes the effects that an experience of that sort has on the whole human organism. With regard to the whole effect on the human being there is, of course, no difference.

If we want to understand what these indications actually mean, we must call to mind a spiritual-scientific truth which you no doubt know—namely, that while we are asleep our I and astral body are outside our physical and ether bodies. Actually, because of certain limitations which cosmic laws impose on us in the natural order of things, our I and astral body remain very close to our physical and ether bodies, so that if we are asleep on a train journey, our I and astral body are right inside all the rattling, rumbling, and braking going on in the wheels and the engine of the train. This is equally the case on a modern steamer. We are inside everything going on around us. We are inside these not exactly musical experiences in our surroundings, and you need only have taken the very first steps in initiation to notice on waking up that when the I returns with the astral body into the physical and ether bodies, they bring with them what they experienced while they were being squeezed by the machinery,

---

challenges of technology. Read more about this in chapter 7 on education and child development.

for they really were inside the moving machinery right up to the moment of waking.

We bring all this disharmonious squeezing and tearing back into our physical and ether bodies, and if you have ever woken up with the after effects of what the engines of a steamer or a train have done to your I and astral body, if you have brought all that into your waking consciousness, you will have noticed how little it synchronizes with what goes on within you in the way the I and the astral body experience the inner harmony of the physical and ether bodies. You bring back with you the wildest confusion, the most frightful din of pulling, screeching, and rattling, and if you are sensitive to it, you will feel that the effect on the ether body really is as though your physical body were being bruised and dismembered in a machine—which is, of course, rather a drastic comparison, but you will not misunderstand it. This is an absolutely unavoidable side effect of modern life, and I want to give a word of warning right at the outset, as the kind of lecture I shall give today can very easily arouse what I would call the veiled high-mindedness of anthroposophists, which flourishes all too well in some quarters.

I am not making a general allusion, of course, let alone a particular allusion, but when one gives a talk on matters like this, one immediately provokes judgements. What I mean by the high-mindedness of anthroposophists is that it can easily happen that people immediately imagine they must take great care not to expose their bodies to these destructive forces, that they must protect themselves from all the influences of modern life, that they must closet themselves in a room containing the right surroundings, with walls of the color recommended by anthroposophy, to make sure that modern life cannot reach them in any way that would be harmful to their bodily organization.

I really don't want my lectures to have this effect. All this withdrawing and protecting oneself from the influences that we necessarily have to encounter, because of world karma, arises out of weakness. Anthroposophy can only strengthen the human being as a whole; it is intended to develop those forces that strengthen and arm us inwardly against these influences. Therefore, within *our spiritual movement there can never be any kind of recom-mendation to cut oneself off from modern life, or to turn spiri-tual life into a kind of hothouse culture. This could never apply in the realm of true spiritual culture. Although it is understandable that weaker natures prefer to withdraw from modern life and go into one or another kind of settlement where they are out of reach of it, the fact remains that this arises not from strength but from weakness of soul. Our task, however, consists in strengthen-ing our soul life by filling ourselves with the impulses of spiritual science and spiritual research so that we are armed against the onslaughts of modern life, and so that our souls can stand any amount of hammering and knocking and are still capable of find-ing their way into the divine spiritual realms right through the hammering and knocking of the ahrimanic spirits.*[11]

Part 3: COMMUNICATIONS: TYPING AND TYPEWRITERS, MECHANICAL STENOGRAPHY, AND WIRELESS TELEGRAPH; ARCHITECTURE AS A NEW COSMIC SCRIPT

From handwriting to the typewriter

An early source for ink was oak galls, which have a long history of medicinal use. The fragrance of such ink had a counterbalancing effect on the physical strain of sitting for long periods of time. Oak gall-based ink was replaced by aniline, a derivative of crude oil, which has a destructive influence on the ether or life body, and ultimately the heart. Switching from handwriting to the typewriter brought new health problems. The "dirt" used to make typewriter ink attacks the ether body, which can lead to heart disease.

Technological progress increases the potential for harm that can be done to the human being. At a minimum, every step of progress should be balanced by increased understanding of its effects on the human being.[12]

---

11   Rudolf Steiner, *Art as Seen in the Light of Mystery Wisdom*, lect. 12/28/1914.

12   One of the major problems with the current modern technology industry is that there is not a sufficient sense of ethics within it nor adequate legal requirements for

People do not usually consider these things from the spiritual point of view, but they need to consider them from that point of view. Just consider this. In the past people would write. Today they work for the typewriter. What is important for health when we write, apart from movement and so on? I would say one of the less obvious things to affect our health when we are writing is the smell of the ink. With the kind of ink manufactured in the past, the smell was not harmful but, in a sense, acted as a corrective. When people had worn themselves down by being in an unnatural position, putting strain on the writing hand, the old-style ink made from oak apples would restore the balance. The smell of substances obtained from oak apples [galls] was such that it actually strengthened the ether body—not much, but a little. When aniline dyes came to be used, so that one no longer drew on nature but made synthetic ink, as chemists call it, the human being was completely closed off. Aniline ink has a smell that has literally the opposite effect from the one the smell of ink used to have. Today many people have changed to using a typewriter. The movements that are required for this and the rattle of the keys— there are typewriters now that write quietly, but that is a very new design—are not the worst part of it. The worst thing is the dirt used to make the ink for the letters. This completely ruins the human ether body, going so far that people develop heart disease from typing, for the heart is mainly activated by the ether body. Civilization is, of course, making progress in this area, but this is never balanced out by the knowledge which people should have about what is really involved. It is a fact that people today are increasingly resisting progress. That should not be so, but there is a certain instinct that makes people notice, though they don't know exactly why, that things are getting increasingly more harmful as advances are made into the future. These things go together. It is how things are.[13]

---

companies to reveal the potential harm of their products to consumers.

13   Rudolf Steiner, *From Beetroot to Buddhism*, lect. 4/26/1924.

Observing the effects of typing with the faculty of imagination

One can become aware through imaginative consciousness of the effects technology has on the heart.[14] Even though typing may be deleterious in certain ways, one should not reject its use but become awake to possible negative consequences and seek ways to compensate for them.[15] Teachers need to be fully informed about changes in the world, including the negative effects on the heart caused by typing at an early age.

> To believe that anthroposophists always rail against new technology is to seriously misunderstand this movement and its contribution to our knowledge of the human being. It is necessary to see the complexities of life from a holistic perspective. For example, I do not object at all to the use of typewriters. Typing is, of course, a far less human activity than writing by hand, but I do not remonstrate against it. Nevertheless, I find it is important to realize its implications, because everything we do in life has repercussions. So you must forgive me if, to illustrate my point, I say something about typewriting from the point of view of anthroposophic spiritual insight. Anyone unwilling to accept it is perfectly free to dismiss this aspect of life's realities as foolish nonsense. But what I have to say does accord with the facts.
>
> You see, if you are aware of spiritual processes, like those in ordinary life, using a typewriter creates a very definite impression. After I have been typing during the day (as you see, I am really not against it, and I'm pleased when I have time for it), it continues to affect me for quite a while afterward. In itself, this does not disturb me, but the effects are noticeable. When I finally reach a state of inner quiet, the activity of typing—seen in

---

14   Spiritual science refers to three levels of higher consciousness that can be achieved through inner development: *imagination, inspiration,* and *intuition.* The path of development that is used to achieve such levels of consciousness can be found in the works of Rudolf Steiner, such as *How to Know Higher Worlds, An Outline of Esoteric Science,* and *Theosophy.*

15   In Steiner's time, typewriting was mechanical, but today, with the advent of smart phones and touch screens, a tiny electrical charge between the finger and the screen has also become a part of the typing experience.

*imaginative consciousness—is transformed into seeing myself. Facing oneself standing there, one is thus able to witness outwardly what is happening inwardly. All this must occur in full consciousness, which enables us to recognize that appearance, as form, as an outer image, is simply a projection of what is or has been taking place, possibly much earlier, as inner organic activity. We can clearly see what is happening inside the human body once we have reached the stage of clairvoyant **imagination**. In objective seeing such as this, every stroke of a typewriter key becomes a flash of lightning. And during the state of **imagination**, what one sees as the human heart is constantly struck and pierced by those lightning flashes. As you know, typewriter keys are not arranged according to any spiritual principle but according to frequency of their use so that we can type more quickly. Consequently, when the fingers hit various keys, the flashes of lightning become completely chaotic. In other words, when seen with spiritual vision, a terrible thunderstorm rages when one is typing.*

Such causes and effects are part of the pattern of life. There is no desire on our part to deride technical innovations, but we should be able to keep our eyes open to what they do to us, and we should find ways to compensate for any harmful effects. Such matters are especially important to teachers, because they have to relate education to ordinary life. What we do at school and with children is not the only thing that matters. The most important thing is that school and everything related to education must relate to life in the fullest sense. This implies that those who choose to be educators must be familiar with events in the larger world; they must know and recognize life in its widest context. What does this mean? It means simply that here we have an explanation of why so many people walk about with weak hearts; they are unable to balance the harmful effects of typing through the appropriate countermeasures. This is especially true of people who started typing when they were too young, when the heart is most susceptible to adverse effects. If typing continues to spread, we will soon see an increase in all sorts of heart complaints.[16]

Wireless telegraph: Beyond ordinary visibility—the world of electricity

With the wireless telegraph, humanity enters a world beyond the senses—the invisible world of electricity.

Today we have a method by which ordinary visibility can be bypassed. Even in lifeless nature we have situations today where visibility with the naked eye—not visibility of a more subtle kind—is done away with. Just think of wireless telegraphy. This is based on an apparatus that generates electricity that is not connected by wires but stands there by itself. Somewhere else, and in no way physically connected to it, is an apparatus with parallel plates that may be set in motion. It is called a coherer. To begin with, there seems to be no visible physical connection, but if you produce an electric current here, the signs move there; and if you link this up with an apparatus, you can receive telegrams, just as you can pick up electricity with wires. We know this is due to electricity spreading, but this is something we cannot see; it spreads without there being any tangible physical link. Here you have a connection in lifeless nature where we may certainly say: the visible sphere has been overcome, at least to some extent....

You can see from all this that it is possible for connections to exist in the world that are not physical. If we go into these more subtle connections, we find that people, too, will sometimes sense something that they have certainly not been able to perceive with the physical senses. Let us take an example. Someone gives a sudden start and sees some kind of image before him—this is only a dream, of course. He shouts: "My friend!" But the friend may be far away. The person may have the experience in Europe when the friend is perhaps in America. "My friend! Something has happened to him!" As it turns out, the friend has died. Such things do certainly occur. It is possible to establish that they happen, though there is no physical link.

---

16 Rudolf Steiner, *Soul Economy: Body, Soul, and Spirit in Waldorf Education*, lect. 12/31/1921.

It has to be said, however, that it is a good thing for humanity that these things are none too common. Just think what it would be like if your head enabled you to perceive all the bad things someone else is thinking or saying about you—that would be a bad business! You know that when one has a telegraph, this has to be set up first, the wire has to be switched on, and then you get a transmission. With wireless telegraphy, too, this part must be functioning properly [pointing to the blackboard] or you will get no transmission. Normal, healthy people are not connected to all the currents that are there; they are switched off. [17]

From mechanical stenography to revelations of the spirit

Handwriting as we know it will become a thing of the past; it will be supplanted by a form of machine writing. In response to the mechanization of external life, the time will come when the human being seeks to receive direct revelations from the spiritual worlds.

Today people still learn how to write. In a near future, human beings will have only a memory that people in earlier centuries once wrote. There will be a kind of mechanical stenography, which will be machine-written to boot. Mechanization of life! I will only indicate it through a symptom: imagine the peak of a culture in which people will excavate the historical truth that once there were human beings who had handwritten manuscripts, just as today we excavate what is found in the Egyptian temples. People will excavate handwritten manuscripts, as we excavate the monuments of the Egyptians. However, a reaction of the soul life against it will also appear. And, as true as it is that our handwriting will be for the future something similar to what hieroglyphics are for us, something that human beings will be amazed at, it is equally true that human souls will also press to receive the direct revelations of the spirit again. External life will become superficial, but the inner life will demand its due. [18]

17   Rudolf Steiner, *From Beetroot to Buddhism*, lect. 3/05/1924.
18   Rudolf Steiner, *Approaching the Mystery of Golgotha*, lect. 10/14/1913.

Architecture as a new form of cosmic script

The written word today has evolved from ancient Egypt and Sanskrit, which consisted of artistic images that were still derived directly from the spirit. In contrast, modern writing has become abstract with no connection to the spirit. Stenography represents an even greater disconnection from the spirit. Script must ascend again to the spirit and be represented through art, and the first Goetheanum was meant to help us do just that as a new kind of world hieroglyph through its artistic forms.

> Look at any book today and you will see these little devils, printed words, as black words on white paper. They have grotesque forms, and in their juxtaposition, they signify the sounds of speech. They can be traced back to other, more expressive forms of writing and script. If we go back a long way we come to forms of writing such as the Egyptians possessed, or ancient Sanskrit, which more or less originated entirely from snakelike forms. Sanskrit symbols are transformed snake shapes, with all sorts of additions. The Egyptian hieroglyphs were still painted or drawn images, picture script; and in their most ancient period were even an imagination of what was portrayed or embodied. Script derived directly from the spirit. Then it grew ever more abstract until it became something that was already bad enough, our own ordinary script, connected with what it signifies only by virtue of our learning its forms.
>
> Then came something still more dire, stenography, which is now the complete death of this whole system that developed out of the old picture script. The declining line of development must give way in turn to an ascending one. We have to return to a trajectory that leads us back from everything that script, especially, drew us down into. And the beginning of an attempt to do so has been made in the form of what stands here on the Dornach hill. Though this building leaves much to be desired, much of it is imperfect, its forms express in a contemporary way the supersensible being toward whom we human beings should look. It is also, I would say, intended as a world hieroglyph. If you really study

its various forms, you will be able to read in them far more than you can absorb through descriptions of the spiritual realm, or at least that is the intention. The intention is to realize a cosmic script in this building. Script emerged from art originally, and it must return to art. And it must move beyond symbolism to allow the spirit to live directly within it, by becoming again a new kind of hieroglyph.

The building that stands here will only be rightly understood if we recognize that there are various demands on humanity today that require an answer. Basically, the words of language are no longer by any means sufficient to give this reply. Such an answer has been attempted with the forms of this building. Much in it is imperfect, but this building has been an attempt to give an answer. And if one looks at it in this light, it will be the right way to look at it.[19]

Part 4: MEDIA: NEWSPAPERS AND THE RADIO

Newspaper-influenced culture

As a primary medium of the early twentieth century, newspapers played a powerful role in shaping the opinions and the worldview of readers. In tongue-in-cheek fashion, Steiner derides the magical effect newspapers have over people, an effect that leads to polarizations. An article on the psychology of newspaper readers is referred to that mentions that most people limit themselves to the view of one paper and consider someone who is attached to the views of another paper as being "insane." Editors on their part are loath to acknowledge fallibility.[20]

We simply cannot do enough to keep making clear to ourselves how dependent human beings are today on judgments which are swarming all around us, on judgments, specifically, which are

---

19 Rudolf Steiner, *Understanding Society through Spiritual–Scientific Knowledge*, lect. 10/23/1919.

20 Much of what is described here can be viewed as a milder version or precursor of internet news services and social media today.

swarming all about because they are recorded in the papers with smudgy ink; and this smudgy ink is an infinitely effective magic potion with regard to all things that people believe in the world. It is interesting, then, to see the occasions when these gentlemen of the press are not quite in agreement among themselves because, you see, there is that which floods all minds, that which is [conjured up on] the dirty paper with smudgy ink and which exercises such an incredible magic on the whole of humanity today. But there are of course always a few who think that we should believe what it says on this dirty paper using smudgy ink in this or that particular way, and others who want to proclaim as irrefutable truth what is magicked on paper in different words written in smudgy ink. They are at odds with one another. And so people could see where the actual error and harm lies. Except that the person who comes from the right in the newspaper office merely says it is the fault of the person who of course finds their belief on the left. And so it is of interest to call up some words before our soul which for example a certain Dr. Eduard Engel has written in the Türmer of 1911. It was headed: "On the Psychology of the Newspaper Reader." I do not want to say too much myself about these things, so I want to show you what people sometimes say when they judge one another among themselves. [On] page 230, it says: "The newspaper reader is a very complex being. But his numerous less important characteristics are overshadowed by two others: he believes everything and he forgets everything. The whole secret of the incredible development of the daily papers is based on these two main characteristics which are present in each newspaper reader. He believes everything and he forgets everything. The papers are one of the essential features of the modern cultured person. The vast majority of readers read only one newspaper and believe what they read. Their view of the world in the evening is the one which they scooped out of their newspaper in the morning. If they meet other people who read another newspaper and hold forth about theirs, that is, their newspaper's view, those people appear insane or at least paradoxical to them. Newspaper editors who have a particularly subtle understanding of the soul of their readers nurse their delicate belief in the papers with anxious attention. A newspaper will never print a correction for the great masses of what it has told its readers. Even in the not infrequent cases in which an erroneous report has presented the opposite of the truth and complete nonsense, they guard against shattering the belief of their readers in the infallibility of newspapers. But now and again they are forced to report the truth a few days later. Here they are assisted by the second indispensable characteristic of the newspaper reader, his forgetfulness.". ...

If we consider the power which the papers have gradually acquired in the nineteenth century and into our day, and the part which the belief in the papers plays in the whole declining part of our culture, it is necessary occasionally to take a look at the whole miserable situation.[21]

Newspapers and the spreading of materialism

Newspapers play a significant role in spreading the materialistic worldview. We absorb this perspective in just about everything we read. This is simply a characterization of the early twentieth century and is equally true today.

Modern cultural life brings up in every field ... objective concepts concerning external nature and has done so for centuries. These concepts about the world fill human being's inner being. Whether it is only a little local paper he reads or one of the Sunday supplements, he is learning, in both, to look at the world according to such concepts. He is not aware that, even from the smallest publication, he absorbs a natural-scientific view of the world, but he does so nonetheless. So, it can be said that the only thing that really occupies people today is the external world. I am not saying this in criticism of individuals. It is more a criticism of the age; or, better said, a characterization of the age, for there is no point in criticizing. The whole situation is simply a necessary outcome of the time.[22]

---

21 Rudolf Steiner, *Unifying Humanity Spiritually*, lect. 1/2/1916.

22 Rudolf Steiner, *The Human Soul in Relation to World Evolution*, lect. 5/7/1922.

Radio transmission and the human voice

The following passages were written by Guenther Wachsmuth, a colleague of Rudolf Steiner. It shows Steiner's flexibility and creativity in relating to technology. While he was willing to accommodate the transmission of the spoken word by way of the radio, he also offered suggestions of how to begin research in demonstrating the more delicate spiritual aspects of speech that are not supported by electrical and magnetic forces of transmission.

At that time, I was permitted to place before Dr. Steiner certain questions in the fields of physics and technology in which we were greatly interested. The radio had at that time reached only a primitive stage of development, but it was then being greatly improved through technical advances and was beginning to enter private homes and to exercise a wide influence on daily life. I had such a very primitive apparatus in my home; and, when I asked Rudolf Steiner whether I might build one for him, he had nothing against this. But we protected his studio from this. The problem with which we were concerned was the fact that this was an apparatus for conveying language, the word, the loftiest, noblest expression of the human being, and it was activated by means of electricity and magnetism, with mechanical forces, which are utterly alien to the most subtle processes of life as these are at work in human speech. In a conversation which I had, together with Dr. von Dechend, with Rudolf Steiner about this, we placed the question before him whether it would not be possible to find a more delicate reagent for the spiritual and physical molding forces of human speech. After brief reflection, he said: There you must work with the sensitive flame. In this and later conversations, he gave us a profound insight into the peculiar place held by the element of warmth in the transition sphere between the psychic and the physical processes in nature, that subtle interweaving of the inner spiritual-psychic processes of the human being with the processes of warmth in the body, the relation between consciousness and temperature in the processes of life, the processes of molding which the speech organs exercise upon the out-breathed warmed air in the process of speaking. He reminded us then of the discovery of Tyndall, who had observed the delicate changes in the gas flame burning in the open caused by noises, tones, and words in the same space, and he advised us to concentrate our thinking and research in this direction.

Out of these suggestions of Rudolf Steiner, comprehensive series of experiments have taken place in the physical laboratory which had been established by the side of the biological research laboratory in Dornach, and these have been brought to valuable results by Paul Eugen Schiller. The first findings have already been published in scientific periodicals. The experiments during a number of years with the sensitive flame brought about the necessity for developing a new and finer research apparatus, and this was produced and patented by Dr. Schiller. Thus, in the field of substances and forces, in physics and technology, new knowledge has grown out of the first suggestions made by Dr. Steiner within the circle of his students, as had already occurred in the field of the living.[23]

Ehrenfried Pfeiffer and Dr. Dechend also provide some additional memories of Steiner's response to whether he would allow his lectures to be broadcast by way of the radio. He said that radio transmission would need to be more refined so that the personal nuances of a speaker's voice were retained, and, in addition, some way needed to be developed so that only designated people could receive the broadcast.

Dr. E. E. Pfeiffer reports on the September 24, 1924. First conversation took place between Dr. Steiner, Dr. Wachsmuth, and Dr. Pfeiffer; Dr. von Dechend arrived soon after and the conversation continued.

Dr. Wachsmuth asked whether it would be possible to broadcast Dr. Steiner's lecture by radio, perhaps with a transmitter at the Goetheanum, in such a way that only the members of the Anthroposophical Society could receive the transmission. Would

---

23 Guenther Wachsmuth, *The Life and Work of Rudolf Steiner: From the Turn of the Century to His Death*, chapter "1922."

Dr. Steiner reject such an idea, or what were the requirements for carrying it out?

Rudolf Steiner: "In the current use of radio the influence of the voice of the person is lost. It must first be made possible that the personal nuances are kept and are not mechanized. This could be achieved by using a flame as a detector. This would be a necessary condition. One must work out a code so that only those could receive it whom one wished to allow."

Dr. von Dechend reports this part of the conversation from memory as follows: Rudolf Steiner said he could only "think of a solution that you take a flame and follow the effect of speech on the flame and express it in curves as it were and then allow different people to speak. Study the differences that appear. And then give the coherer[24] the form that you discover—it is well-named coherer. Then only those who have the coherer can receive the message."[25]

Part 5: THE CINEMA (MOVIES), SLIDES, AND PHOTOGRAPHS

Cinema and spiritual science: Popular entertainment vs. noble pursuit

Some people think that spiritual-scientific perspectives keep people from the pleasures and enjoyment of life. Steiner considered the cinema, at least at the stage of development that it had reached during his time, to be superficial entertainment, and said that higher forms of pleasure arising from working with spiritual-scientific ideas could and should be obtained.[26]

---

24   A radio signal detector used with early radio receivers in wireless telegraphy at the beginning of the twentieth century.

25   Paul Eugene Schiller, *The Schiller File*, folio 10a-b.

26   One may wonder whether Steiner would have a different view regarding the much more evolved modern cinematics or platforms such as YouTube.

One hears people say: "[spiritual science] presents the world in a very nice light, offering great ideals, but it deflects people from life itself, from the true enjoyment of and pleasure in life."…

It is a question, of course, of what we take pleasure in, and the issue must really go deeper. For it is possible to look for better and more noble objects of pleasure and to work with these to take life to a nobler level. We can give life a new content, and there is no need to spoil young people's pleasure in life, for we shall give them new kinds of pleasure and enjoyment. People often find it hard to understand that one may find the things others consider entertaining rather uninteresting—going to the cinema and spending one's time talking about things that have nothing to do with the reality of life. Perhaps a day will come when we speak of today's popular amusements as of a cloud cuckoo land.[27]

Damaging effects of screen images and the cinema on the etheric body

Aside from the entertainment or educational value that the cinema may or may not have as referred to in the previous passage, Steiner considered the cinema of his time to be damaging to a viewer's ether or life body and to arouse sensuality. True art can bring down something from the higher worlds. Inner, wakeful activity is what can give us certainty in life.

Our thinking about the outer world necessarily contains a destructive, reductive element that works back harmfully on the physical body. Sleep heals this harm. Many phenomena of the cultural life of today have a destructive effect, especially screen images—which definitely harm the etheric body. Such images also arouse sensuality. True art can bring down into the sense world what comes from higher worlds. In the science of the spirit, we work together with supersensible powers. Spirit knowledge is the only thing that gives us inner certainty.… Only one's own inner, wakeful activity can give the soul certainty. A spiritual-scientific attitude sustains people and makes them happy, for what the science of the spirit gives offers them

---

27   Rudolf Steiner, *Original Impulses for the Science of the Spirit*, lect. 10/01/1906.

a solid point of reference in their inner lives, as necessary to the soul as daily bread to the body.[28]

Cinema and the spread of materialism

The cinema, which will develop much further, provides a powerful means of driving people toward materialism and away from spiritual realities. It works at a deeper level than normal perception and influences the subconscious in a powerful way. Watching lots of films makes a person "goggle-eyed," giving the human ether body the appearance of the eyes of a seal. This does not mean, however, that we should shun the cinema. Descending below visual perception requires a counterbalancing ascent to spiritual realities. If we do not spiritually counterbalance such things as the cinema through inner effort, we will become cut off from the spiritual world.[29]

> *I have to say that everything is geared toward leading humanity firmly in the direction of materialism. This cannot be prevented; it is part of the nature of the fifth post-Atlantean epoch. But there needs to be some kind of balance. A particularly powerful means of driving people toward materialism is something that has hardly been viewed from this angle at all: the cinematograph. For what one perceives in films is not reality as it is actually seen. Only an age that has so little idea of reality as ours, which worships reality as an idol in the materialistic sense, could believe that the cinematograph represents reality. A different age would consider whether people walk along the street as they do in films, whether... the images that one sees really correspond to reality. Ask yourselves very honestly: is what you have seen on the street closer to a picture painted by an artist, which does not move, or to the ghastly*

---

28   Rudolf Steiner, *Esoteric Christianity and the Mission of Christian Rosenkreutz,* lect. 1/29/1911.

29   It goes without saying that small children do not have the maturity of soul to develop the necessary counterbalancing spiritual faculties. Thus, parents and teachers need to develop the knowledge to determine at what age and how much exposure are appropriate for the growing child.

flickering images of the cinematograph?[30] *If you are really honest, you will say to yourself: what the painter portrays in a state of rest has a much stronger resemblance to what you yourself see on the street. So, when people are sitting in the cinema, what they see there comes to reside within them not through their ordinary faculties of perception but at a deeper material level than is normal for the process of perception. A person becomes etherically goggle-eyed. His eyes begin to look like those of a seal, only much bigger, when he watches lots of films. I mean etherically bigger. This has an effect not only on what lives in his conscious mind, but it has a materializing influence on his subconscious. Do not interpret this as a denunciation of the cinematograph. I should like to make it quite clear that it is perfectly natural that there should be cinematographs; and the art of cinematography or filmmaking will be developed to an ever-increasing degree. This will be the road leading to materialism. But a counterbalance needs to be sought. This can happen only if the addiction for the kind of reality that is being developed through films is connected to something else. Just as with this addiction there develops a tendency to descend below perception by way of the senses, so must there develop an ascent above sensory perception, that is, into spiritual reality. Then it will do no harm to go to the cinema, and one can see such things as often as one wishes. But if no counterbalance is created, people will be led through such things to relate to the earth not in the way that is necessary but to become more and more closely related to it to the point where they are completely cut off from the spiritual world.*[31]

Cinema as external stimulus to passive culture

In our modern intellectual age, a certain passivity has set in and people enjoy the outer stimulation of slide presentations and movies

---

30   Cinematography has improved since Steiner's time, and flickering images are not such an issue as they were back then.

31   Rudolf Steiner, *Building Stones for an Understanding of the Mystery of Golgotha*, lect. 2/27/1917. The question here is whether Rudolf Steiner is referring to inner efforts on the part of individuals, outer initiatives such as developing an alternative to the cinema (Light-Play Art) as described later in this section, or both.

because no significant inner effort is required. In contrast, studying spiritual science and the reasoning capacity it demands requires inner effort. This type of self-development is the basis for the renewal of culture and spiritual life.

> Today people love to attend lectures that present what they are to learn through slides or other perceptible means. People go to movies because they can see something there. They do not value the fact that there are also some words. People want to remain passive: they just want to be people who watch. You will gain nothing from a spiritual-scientific book or lecture if you allow these modern habits to predominate, as spiritual-scientific lectures or books contain nothing of that sort. Everything depends on your working inwardly with what such books or lectures offer as a thread.
>
> It is important that reasoning, which has become passive in our intellectual age, should now become active. Spiritual science is an inner activity to the extent that it concerns the world of ideas and is therefore radically different from what modern people are used to. This inner training of self is extremely important, since that is how we can overcome the abstract spirituality connected with modern reasoning. This self-training will renew the entire spiritual and soul constitution of a human being.[32]

The longing for the outer stimulation of the cinema is connected to the dearth of inner activity in a large part of humanity. In contrast, presenting something of a spiritual-scientific nature is an invitation to inner activity that stimulates inner imaginative thinking rather than appealing to outer stimulation.

> We must be clear about the following characteristic of our age, namely, that if human beings today do not strive out of inner activity for development and maintain it consciously, they will rest with mere intellectualism from their twentieth year on. They will keep themselves going only through stimuli from outside. Do

---

32 Rudolf Steiner, *The Renewal of Education*, lect. 4/23/1920.

you think that if things were not like that people would flock to the cinema so much? This longing for the cinema, this longing to see everything externally, is caused by human beings becoming inwardly inactive, by their no longer wanting inner activity.[33]

Human beings are often preoccupied with external matters, displaying little interest in the nature of the human being. This can lead to an indifference as to whether one is viewing a live person on stage or an image on a movie screen. A feeling for this difference would enable people to have more concern about the part played by the cinema in the decline of civilization.

It can be said that the only thing that really occupies people today is the external world. I am not saying this in criticism of individuals. It is more a criticism of the age; or, better said, a characterization of the age, for there is no point in criticizing. The whole situation is simply a necessary outcome of the time. People today are so little interested in man as such that it has become a matter of indifference whether a living actor is seen on the stage or a specter on the cinema screen. In reality, it naturally does make a considerable difference. But today there is no deep fundamental feeling for this difference. If there were, then there would also be more concern for the considerable part played by the cinema and similar phenomena in the decline of our civilization.[34]

The effort to create an alternative to the cinema

Even though Rudolf Steiner said that people could watch as many films as they wanted without undue harm if they would counterbalance such experiences with spiritual development, he felt it was important that an alternative to the cinema be created as a remedy to its overall effects on the general populace. In 1918, he asked the artist Jan Stuten (1890–1948) to work with him on this task. This alternative art form

---

33 Rudolf Steiner, *Becoming the Archangel Michael's Companions*, lect. 10/12/1922.
34 Rudolf Steiner, *The Human Soul in Relation to World Evolution*, lect. 5/7/1922.

would combine sound, colored lights, colored movements, and colored shadows. Steiner suggested the theme "Metamorphosis of Fear" for the first work of this new art form. Stuten created fifteen colored sketches in response to Rudolf Steiner's suggestion. It would be many years later that Stuten would give a first presentation of his efforts in Dornach, Switzerland. Rudolf Steiner had died in 1925. Therefore, Stuten had to work on the project without the physical presence of Rudolf Steiner.

In 1937, Stuten attended the Paris International Exposition on "Art and Technology in Modern Life" with a stage group from the Goetheanum in Switzerland that performed scenes from Goethe's *Faust*. Walt Disney and several of his staff saw the performance, which included eurythmy. Disney then arranged to meet with Stuten to learn more about the art of eurythmy. During their meeting, Stuten showed Disney and his crew the fifteen sketches. It is ironic that three years later, the animated film *Fantasia* was released by Disney in 1940. The following passages are by David Adams for the "Art Section Newsletter."

In 1918, at the World War I, Rudolf Steiner (1861-1925), the Austrian-born founder of anthroposophy, gave the musician, composer, and scenery designer Jan Stuten (1890-1948) a task. Arising from his concerns about mechanizing, materialistic (or, in anthroposophical terminology, "ahrimanic") influences from watching the inartistic silent films of his day, Steiner had the idea of a new, alternative color art combining sound, colored light, color movement, and colored shadows in a way that would leave the viewer free to interpret what was seen and would keep the spectator inwardly active (as opposed to the passivity of watching films). Steiner said, "It would be an unprecedented, serious, human-pedagogical concern of anthroposophically working artists to forcefully raise this up...to place something in opposition to this pseudo art [film], something that offers itself like a remedy...but creatively formed, not produced through any humanly detached technical device. Thus, a kind of light-play-art of forms and colors moving to music or speech but controlled by the human being." Moreover, he recommended that its approach should be learned from the ancient mystery art of the shadow plays, but renewed in a modern form as a colored light-play-art. The following description of this artistic initiative and its development and offshoots is largely drawn from the primary source of information about it, the 1993 German book Bewegte Bilder *(moving pictures), by Wolfgang Veit....*[35] *Steiner was concerned about how film fascinated viewers, drawing them subconsciously into materialism. He felt that viewers only saw illusory images in a way that deadened the imagination, where the viewer did not ascend to anything higher. [It should be remembered that the kind of early black-and-white-only films Steiner was able to see at the time were still quite rough in technique.]...*

In 1919 Steiner gave Stuten the theme Metamorphoses of Fear for the first work of this new art form, a theme related to people's experiences from the just-ended world war. At that time many people in Central Europe were full of fear, and Steiner hoped this artwork could help them to transform or overcome their fear. Steiner felt that Stuten with his imaginative capacity would be able creatively to picture and realize such a new "light-play-art." In response to Steiner's idea, Stuten drew with chalk on packing-paper fifteen sketches, which would be something like a full-score (or "storyboards") for a new colored light-play, "Metamorphoses of Fear." That which he suggested through the sketches as stage-pictures was intended to move and change itself in relationship to music. A presentation of Stuten's initial efforts was given years later at the Goetheanum in Dornach, Switzerland, and then at the Paris World's Fair in [1937]. The music was improvised on the piano by Stuten.

Walt Disney and his American team at the [Paris Exhibition "Art and Technology in Modern Life"] had seen the dramatic performance of a scene from Goethe's Faust *from the Goetheanum stage group in Dornach—with the music and stage scenery design*

---

35 Wolfgang Veit, *Bewegte Bilder: Der Zyklus "Metamorphosen der Furcht" von Jan Stuten—Entwurf zu einer neuen Licht-Spiel-Kunst nach einer Idee von Rudolf Steiner* (German ed.).

of Jan Stuten. Disney showed an interest above all in eurythmy (Steiner's new movement art of "visible speech and song"), a part of the performance, seeking a conversation with Jan Stuten on this new art of movement created by Steiner. Stuten, who himself at the World's Fair had learned about modern projection and lighting technology in order to pursue further the task given him by Steiner, showed the Americans his fifteen sketches for the new light-play-art work, the "Metamorphoses of Fear." The film people with Disney's studio studied these with great interest. A little later Fantasia *appeared with the Bach Fugue, whose imagery may have been partly inspired by Stuten's sketches (but certainly more so by the work of pioneering experimental filmmakers Jules Engel and Oskar Fischinger, who worked on* Fantasia *for a time; Fischinger also was interested in anthroposophy in the 1920s in Germany). But its execution as a successful Hollywood animation in this film was really opposite to the original intention of Rudolf Steiner to create a counter-impulse against the illusion and materialistic suggestiveness of film. Meanwhile, the concept of Steiner and the sketches of Stuten for a long time remained forgotten.*[36]

Using the cinema to portray reincarnation and karma

The following excerpt is from the recently published book by Reto Andrea Savoldelli, *The Future Art of Cinema: Rudolf Steiner's Vision.*[37] The excerpt is a submission by J. E. Zeylmans van Emmichoven in response to an essay written by the well-known author Michael Ende in the journal *Info3* about the filming of his best-seller fantasy novel, *The Neverending Story* (1979). Van Emmichoven maintained that Rudolf Steiner thought the cinema was a suitable means for portraying reincarnation and karma.

---

36 David Adams, "On the 'New Light-Play Art'" (*Art Section Newsletter,* no. 22, spring/summer 2004 (revised 2012); at http://www.eana.org/wordpress/wp-content/uploads/2014/09/LightPlayArtIntroPublic.pdf.

37 Reto Andrea Savoldelli, *The Future Art of Cinema: Rudolf Steiner's Vision.*

In 1983, readers of the monthly journal Info3 *(based in Frankfurt, Germany) were offered a sequence of articles in several successive issues about the artistic potential of the cinema and its limitations, in response to an essay on this theme by Michael Ende.... Ende was writing here about the filming of his bestseller,* The Neverending Story, *which had left him highly dissatisfied. (Conflict with the film producer reached such a level that he was even barred from the film set.) In his essay he sought dialogue with other authors, and with the readers of a journal regarded as "anthroposophical." In this context, some of the critical remarks by Steiner about the cinema... were aired... by Ende.... At the point when a response to these articles was drying up, a reader's letter from J. E. Zeylmans van Emmichoven was published. He is well known in anthroposophic circles as a priest.... The letter, published in the April 1983 issue of* Info3, *ran as follows: "Michael Ende says that Rudolf Steiner was opposed to the cinema and he even has evidence of comments to that effect by Dr. Steiner. I would therefore like to put it on record that, curiously, I can testify to the opposite. For five years, I was secretary to the Dutch publisher Pieter de Haan, who joined the [Anthroposophical] Society in 1912, and, until 1924, had many conversations with Rudolf Steiner. Thus, he had a very close acquaintance with him. Mr. de Haan often told me that Dr. Steiner wanted us to make films. According to de Haan, Rudolf Steiner said that it was a suitable medium for presenting the laws of destiny in the course of recurring incarnations. It is my belief that Dr. Steiner was a little different from how many nowadays imagine him to have been."*[38]

Photos and cinema vs. ideation—space vs. time

The preference by much of modern humanity for outer stimulation over inner effort is connected to the preference for space over time.

---

38 Ibid., chapter 6.

Photos and the cinema are both spatially oriented.[39] Ultimately, spiritual science strives to transcend the spatial.[40]

> Think of how difficult it is for people of the present day to follow an exposition purely of time. They are happy if space is brought in at least to the extent of drawing something on the blackboard. But if the feeling of space is conveyed by means of photographs, then modern people are verily in their element! "Illustration"—and by this they mean expression in terms of space—is what people of today strive to achieve in every exposition. Time, inasmuch as it is in perpetual flow, has become something that causes them discomfort. They still attach value to it in music; but even there the tendency toward the spatial is quite evident.
>
> We need only consider something that has become a definite feature of modern life and this mania of modern man to cleave to the spatial is at once apparent. In the cinema he is utterly indifferent to the element of time in the picture. He is content with the merest fraction of the time element and is entirely given up to the element of space.
>
> This orientation of the soul to the spatial is very characteristic of the present time, and whoever observes modern culture and civilization with open eyes will find it everywhere.
>
> On the other hand, in anthroposophical spiritual science we are striving, as you know, to get away from the spatial. To be sure, we meet the desire for it in that we too try to give tangible form to the spiritual, and that is justifiable in order to strengthen the faculty of ideation. Only we must always be conscious that this is purely a means of illustration and that what is essential is to strive, at least to strive, to transcend the spatial.
>
> Space "devotees" among us often cause difficulties by making diagrams of the consecutive epochs of time, writing "First Epoch

---

39 With movies, what appears as movement in time on a screen is a sequence of single images projected in rapid succession.

40 The transcendence of the spatial element through the experience of time arts such as eurythmy will be explored further in volume 2 in relation to sacred creation and the future development of technology.

with Sub-Epochs," and so on. Then follow a great many captions and what is sequential in time is dragged into a spatial picture.

    Our aim, however, is to transcend the spatial. We are striving to penetrate into the temporal and also into the super-temporal, into the element that leads beyond what is physically perceptible. The physically perceptible exists in its crudest form in the world of space and there thought is led in a certain direction.[41]

Even though Steiner viewed electricity as something associated with evil, he did not shy away from using it in the service of art. (See chapter three on electricity.) A primary example is his effort to develop a new stage lighting system for the performing arts—eurythmy and drama—in a building he designed and guided through construction.

At the Goetheanum in Dornach, Switzerland, he accomplished this, in part, by creating a separate building for the generation of power and heat so that the source of the heat was visible, not hidden within the building.

A key to neutralizing the demonic powers is to become conscious of their true nature, and when and where they exist.

As you know, we hope after some time to have a building at Dornach near Basel where we can nurture our spiritual stream in suitable surroundings. It is not a question of erecting this building to escape the pressures of our time in some way or other, but rather of building it entirely out of the pressures of our time. It was necessary, for instance, to design a lighting system out of the most ahrimanic forces of the present age, electric lighting, electric heating, and so on. It is a matter of using the architectural form as such to render such potentially harmful things harmless. It could have been the case that anyone entering the building in the future would have been surrounded with everything the ahrimanic culture of the present age leads to. The point, however, is not that it is present but that people do not notice it. We are not supposed to notice it. To achieve this, a number of friends

---

41   Rudolf Steiner, *Man and the World of Stars*, lect. 12/17/1922.

got together, and they are erecting a separate building for this, giving it a special form, so that the demonic ahrimanic forces are banished to this place. Anyone approaching the building, and also anyone entering it, will have it brought to their notice that the ahrimanic forces are at work there. For as soon as we know this, they are no longer harmful. The point is that the powers that have a bad effect on man cease to do so when we take a good look at the places where they are active, when we do not look at a machine thoughtlessly and say "a machine is simply a machine," but rather acknowledge that a machine is a place where a demonic ahrimanic entity may be found.[42]

Response to an idea of using of cinematography to enable the understanding of philosophical ideas

A philosopher of Steiner's day suggested that the use of slide images would help people understand the complex philosophical ideas of Spinoza and Kant. Steiner cautions against such an idea because such methods allow, if not encourage, the viewers to remain passive, without inwardly engaging in the ideas presented. Inner effort is essential for gaining insight into spiritual matters.

I am now going to consider another aspect of this quest of our age, which is as yet unable to understand itself inwardly. A philosopher who deserves our esteem has published a strange essay in a widely read journal. Among other things, he says that many people find Spinoza and Kant quite difficult to read. They get easier as you go on, but their concepts are always shifting and changing. Well, it cannot be denied that this holds true for many people. The author of the essay gives some advice, however, on how it may be done differently and in accord with the quest of our age. According to him, technology now provides us with the means of getting a good picture of the confusing, abstract ideas presented by Kant and Spinoza. He wants to use a kind of cinematography to show Spinoza sitting and grinding glass as the

---

42   Rudolf Steiner, *The Destinies of Individuals and of Nations*, lect. 1/19/1915.

idea of extension comes to him. This is to be shown in a sequence of changing images. The image of extension will then be transformed into the image of thinking, and so on. Cinematography could thus be used to create a visual image of Spinoza's whole ethics and philosophy, and this would satisfy those who follow the quest of our age. Oddly enough, the editor of the journal even commented that an invention which may seem no more than a toy to some people could therefore meet an ancient human need in a way which is entirely in accord with our age.

Now it may be possible, in some respects, to satisfy the questing minds of our time, though only with regard to outer things, by presenting Spinoza's Ethics *or Kant's* Critique of Pure Reason *cinematographically. Why not? It would be in line with the passive attitude so popular today. It is so popular that people find it hard to believe that the reality [of the things of the spirit] can only be found by going through everything yourself. Our age does not yet accept an approach where you bring the essential nature of these things to expression in your own inner life.*[43]

Promoting Waldorf education and social threefolding with photos and films

The following is a response by Steiner when informed that someone offered to make a film about Waldorf education and social threefolding.[44] While not overly enthusiastic, he didn't voice any strong opposition to someone who wanted to publicize the school and social threefolding ideas. His main concern was that the work of properly running the school continue without disruption. Although he didn't think it was useful to film classroom activity, he did not oppose outright the idea of himself being filmed giving a lecture.[45]

---

43 Rudolf Steiner, *The Inner Nature of Man*, lect. 4/6/1914.

44 For more on Waldorf education, see chapter 7, and for more on social threefolding, see chapter 6.

45 We have found no evidence that Steiner was ever filmed or recorded while giving a lecture, although he was photographed at least once while doing so.

I don't have any idea what to do here. If, for example, some-one wants to photograph the buildings, that will certainly hurt nothing. There is nothing wrong with that. If she wants to make a film publicizing the Waldorf school, we would have nothing against showing that publicly, since it is not our responsibility. Our responsibility is that the Waldorf school be properly run. We are not responsible for what she photographs any more than you are responsible for what occurs if you are walking along the street and someone offers you a ride. We can tell her we will do what we can do, but there is nothing we can do. She may want to photograph the eurythmy lessons. I did that in Dornach, but it was not very good. That is a technical question. I don't think much will come of it. She wants to film the threefolding? I was thinking, why shouldn't the film contrast something good with something bad? We certainly can have no influence if she creates a scene in the film where two people speak about the Waldorf school, but we do not need to let her into the classrooms. She can certainly not demand that we allow her to photograph anything more than a public eurythmy performance by the children. Since she wants to publicize eurythmy, that would be her contribution to the members' work. It is rather senseless if she wants to film the classes. She could film any school, there is nothing particular to see. She could, for example, record that terrible yelling in the fourth grade.

It would certainly not be proper to suppress offhandedly, due to false modesty, somebody who wants to publicize threefolding and the school. It would be better if we could hinder everything that is tasteless, but, due to false modesty, I would be hesitant to hinder anything. We have much interest in making the school as perfect as possible, but there is certainly nothing to be gained by preventing someone from photographing it. If she had set up and filmed my lecture, what could I have done against that?[46]

---

46   Rudolf Steiner, *Faculty Meetings with Rudolf Steiner*, faculty meeting, 6/14/1920.

Benefits of lantern slides of reproductions for a lecture

A technological device that Steiner thought could be put to good use is the lantern slide projector for displaying reproductions, particularly when speaking about the history of art.

> *It is a pity that a lecture like this [on Michelangelo] cannot be given with lantern slides or other visual aids, though fortunately you can easily get access to first-rate reproductions of the material necessary in any history of art and see for yourselves in actual detail what I am describing. When Herman Grimm set about writing his wonderful book on Michelangelo in the 1850s, he could not give any illustrations at all—though the second edition, published forty years later, was illustrated and thus reveals clearly the secrets of Michelangelo, which even Grimm's descriptions in his Life could not give. Modern reproductions make it even more possible to reach some insight into the basic ideas and forms which are to be found in the development of art through the ages.*[47]

Enigmatic indications on making photographic reproductions of the first Goetheanum cupola and windows

Steiner had quite a different and more complicated attitude regarding taking photos of the artistically painted cupolas and hand-carved stained glass windows in the first Goetheanum, which portrayed spiritual beings and activities.[48] He expressed little enthusi-

---

47   Rudolf Steiner, "Michaelangelo," lect. 1/8/1914 (Hudson, NY; unpublished ms., tr. E. Goddard, Rudolf Steiner Library), from CW 63.

48   The first Goethaneum was an artistically created lecture and performance hall made of wood designed by Rudolf Steiner. It consisted of two intersecting domes. All the interior structural features were handmade and/or artistically formed and enhanced, including windows, doors, ceiling, walls, and supporting columns. A wooden sculpture called the "Representative of Humanity," which depicts the central figure of the Christ maintaining a balance between the spiritual beings Lucifer and Ahriman, was to be placed centrally in the smaller of the two cupolas. The first Goetheanum was destroyed by fire in 1923 and was followed by the second Goetheanum, which is constructed of concrete. For more information and photographs of the first Goetheanum, see Rudolf Steiner, *Alchemy of the Everyday* and *The Goetheanum Cuploa Motifs of Rudolf Steiner*.

asm for the attempts to reproduce them with photographs, especially black-and-white photos. His comment that something could be achieved only if a photograph were the same size as the cupola suggests that what was artistically and spiritually important for Steiner was the multi-dimensional experience of the viewer standing in the cupola. Such an effect could not be created by photographs smaller than the cupola, regardless of whether they were black-and-white or color photographs. Nevertheless, there were photos taken of both the interior and exterior of the first Goetheanum.

> *What was painted in color in the cupola [in the first Goetheanum, which portrayed spiritual beings and themes] needs to be understood from the colors. If you reproduced it photographically, you could achieve something only if you enlarged it to the same size as in the cupola. It is just not something we can reproduce simply. The less the pictures correspond to those in the cupola, the better it is. Black and white only hints at something. It cries for color. I would never agree with these inartistic reproductions. They are only surrogates. I do not want to have any color photographs of the cupola paintings. The reproductions should not stand by themselves. I want to handle that so that what is not important is what is given.*
>
> *It is the same with the glass windows. If you attempted to achieve something through reproductions, I would be against it. You should not attempt to reproduce such things exactly. It is not desirable that you reproduce a piece of music through some deceptively imitative phonograph record. I do not want that. I do not want to have a modern, technical human being. The way these paintings appear in the reproductions never reproduces them. The reproductions contain only what is novel, not what is important. You then have a feeling that this or that color must be there.*[49]

---

49 Rudolf Steiner, *Faculty Meetings with Rudolf Steiner*, vol. 1, talk 6/14/1920.

Part 6: GRAMOPHONES AND CALCULATORS

The gramophone and the mechanization of art

Steiner viewed the gramophone, the precursor of various modern forms of recording music, as presenting a unique challenge to the human being. Whereas we can find ways to cope with technologies that provide us with some type of external service, such as cars and typewriters, we cannot do so if we develop an enthusiasm for listening to the likes of the gramophone, which mechanizes art. In this case, we need the help of the gods.

> *Where the kind of things are concerned that do us good service mechanically, human beings will find the means to stand up to them. And we can be assured that human beings will find a way to cope with everything that appears in the nature of cars, typewriters, and so on.*
>
> *With gramophones, however, it is different—and please forgive me for concluding on such an apparently trivial note. With their gramophones human beings are forcing art down to the level of mechanics. If people were to develop a passion for such things, which is really a mechanizing of what comes down to us as a reflection of the spiritual, if they were to become enthusiastic over the kind of thing represented by gramophones, then they would not be able to find the strength to stand up to it by themselves. In that case, the gods would have to help them.*
>
> *Now the gods are merciful, and today we certainly have the hope with regard to the way human civilization is heading that the merciful gods themselves will continue to come to our rescue where errors of taste such as the gramophone are concerned.*[50]

Calculators and laws: Eliminating the inner necessity of thinking and outwardly prohibiting it

Just as machine writing will replace handwriting, calculators will be developed to the point where we will no longer need to do arithmetic

---

50   Rudolf Steiner, *The Evolution of Consciousness*, lect. 8/29/1923.

or even think on our own. All that will be necessary, for example, to order things is the ability to push or press buttons.

Furthermore, to ensure that technology-based industry can function efficiently without individual resistance, laws will be enacted to limit any type of thinking that might disrupt the reigning social structures.

> Today we already have machines for adding and subtracting, don't we? All very useful and easy—we no longer need to calculate for ourselves. And this will become the norm for everything. It will take only a couple of centuries to arrive; and then people will no longer need to think or reflect, but only push things around. For instance, today if we send 330 balls of wool to Liverpool, we have to think how to do it, don't we? But soon you will need only to push or press and the thing will be done. And to ensure that the firm coherence of social structures is not disrupted in the future, laws will be issued that do not directly prohibit individual thinking but whose effect will be to exclude it, render it void. That is the other pole toward which we are tending. By comparison, life today is really not so bad. Today, we are allowed to think, aren't we, as long as we don't overstep a certain boundary. But what I have described is implicit in the development in the West and will emerge as the West develops.
>
> Spiritual-scientific development must also place itself into this overall course of development. It will have to perceive it clearly and objectively. We must be clear that what seems paradoxical today will come about. In the year 2200, roughly, and a little more, thinking will start to be suppressed in the world to the greatest possible extent. And spiritual science must engage with this tendency, must—and will—find enough to offer as a counterbalance in cosmic evolution to these tendencies.[51]

---

51   Rudolf Steiner, *The Human Spirit*, lect. 4/4/1916.

Keely, Strader, and the Development of Etheric Technology

The mechanical and the moral must interpenetrate each other because the mechanical is nothing without the moral. Today we stand hard on this frontier. In the future machines will be driven not only by water and steam, but by spiritual force, by spiritual morality. *(note 18)*

Purely mechanical mechanisms will be transformed into moral mechanisms. The spiritual-scientific worldview prepares for this ascent. *(note 15)*

FIVE

Keely, Strader, and the Development of Etheric Technology

Introduction

Rudolf Steiner not only critiqued the technology of his day, including those that were electricity-based. He also spoke about new forms of energy that will be created in the future. These will be created by harnessing, transmitting, and amplifying rhythms originating in the human soul, nature, and/or certain combinations of starry constellations and connecting them to mechanical devices. These new technologies will take on a beneficent or destructive character depending on the moral/ethical qualities of the inventors and operators, and the cosmic rhythms employed. An ideal combination of forces that will power technology in the future, insofar as what Steiner conveyed through his books, lectures, and conversations with close colleagues, are the moral force of selfless love on the part of the creators and the incorruptible morning and evening forces associated with the constellations of Pisces and Virgo. These indications should not be considered as the full spectrum of soul states and activities required, but as guiding thoughts for the initial research and development of new forms of etheric technology.

Chapter overview

From the perspective of the early twentieth century, Rudolf Steiner predicted that modern technology would, in a certain way, "cancel itself out" in the "comparatively near future." He also stated that if the economic arena in which technology is embedded continued to be based on egoism and competition, human civilization would descend into complete decadence.

On a more positive note, Steiner pointed to social forms that transcend private capitalism without succumbing to what is known as socialism[1] and to new forms of energy that would be developed that are not based on typical energy sources such as steam, waterpower, electricity, magnetism, or fossil fuels, but on harmonious resonance and amplification of etheric forces in the human being and the cosmos. With the development of these new forms of technology, ethically oriented social structures will become essential to safeguard against their misuse.

In describing preliminary efforts to develop this new technology, Steiner referred to the American inventor John Worrell Keely and the character Dr. Strader from the Mystery Dramas that he wrote. Both were working on the development of new energy sources based on the harmonious oscillation of human and cosmic forces. Neither succeeded, however, in real life, as in the case of Keely, or in the dramatic production, as in the case of Strader.

In addition to direct statements by Rudolf Steiner, this chapter will draw upon memories and reflections of people who worked directly with him in the effort to develop new forms of technology, most notably Ehrenfried Pfeiffer. In Pfeiffer's writings and transcribed lectures, we learn of the importance of Waldorf education, the threefold social organism, and the overcoming of materialistic thinking in the development of a morally based resonance technology.

The further elaboration of resonance technology will be the focus of volume two of this compendium of Rudolf Steiner's perspectives on technology.

---

1   See chapter 6, "Transcending Private Capitalism and Socialism: An Imperative in the Modern Age of Technology."

Part 1: ASPECTS IN THE EVOLUTION OF TECHNOLOGY

The limitations and decline of modern technology

Rudolf Steiner maintained that modern technology based on materialist natural science will reach a culmination or a peak in a relatively short period of time and implode on itself.

> *Humanity is now faced with having to solve certain quite specific problems... with today's much-admired technology—a consequence of natural science—which is also much admired by spiritual science. In the comparatively near future, this much-admired modern technology will reach a final stage where it will, in a certain way, cancel itself out.*[2]

> *Wireless telegraphy works across a distance from the transmitting station to the receiving station. The apparatus can be set to work at will, it is effective over great distances, and one can make oneself understood by it. A similar force to that by which wireless telegraphy works will be at humanity's disposal in a future age, without even any apparatus; this will make it possible to cause great devastation over long distances, without anyone being able to discover where the disturbance originated. Then, however, when the high point of this development has been reached, it will eventually come to the point where it falls back on itself.*[3]

Soul moods and technology

One of the great challenges and opportunities of our age is the development of a new form of technology that links human etheric forces and/or soul moods to machines. The ever-increasing connection between human beings and technology is inevitable and not something we should oppose outright. What is all important is how such connections are established. The worldview and motivation of the researchers, designers, inventors, and entrepreneurs are of primary concern. The

---

2   Rudolf Steiner, *The Karma of Untruthfulness*, vol. 1. lect. 12/18/1916.

3   Rudolf Steiner, *The Temple Legend*, lect. 1/2/1906.

essential issue is whether the development of future technology is done out of altruism or egotism.

> *Endeavors are to be undertaken to place the spiritually etheric element in the service of external, practical life. I have already pointed out that the fifth post-Atlantean period will have to solve the problem of how the temper of the human soul, the flow of human moods, can be transmitted to machines in wavelike movements. The human being must be linked with something that has to grow more and more mechanical....*
>
> *It would be quite wrong to think that we should try to prevent these things, for they will happen, they will come about. The only question is whether they will be brought about as a part of human evolution by people who are selflessly familiar with the great goals of earthly evolution and will do them in ways that are beneficial to humanity or whether they will be brought about by those groups of people who only want to make use of them egoistically or solely for the sake of their own group. It is not "what" is done that matters in this instance, for the "what" will happen anyway; the important thing here is the "how," how these things are tackled. The "what" will happen anyway because it is intrinsic in earthly evolution. Welding together human nature with mechanical nature will be a great and significant ongoing problem for the remainder of earthly evolution.*[4]

Transition from craft to industrial production and the understanding of spiritual forces at play

The transition from craft-based production to an industrial-based factory changed the nature of work. In the former, workers could derive a certain enthusiasm and joy from their work, which flowed as warmth into the products they produced; whereas little joy and enthusiasm can be experienced in the repetitive work in a factory based on using machinery and the division of labor. Consequently, the soul warmth that was engendered under the previous conditions of craft work was

---

4   Rudolf Steiner, *Secret Brotherhoods*, lect. 11/25/1917.

mostly lost. But something else became possible. The things produced will become "purer" and consequently susceptible to what flows from the human being as a motor force.[5]

> To the extent that the products of vocational labor can no longer be produced with special and absolutely necessary enthusiasm, what thus flows away from men and streams forth from them can become a motor force. The truth is that through the fact that individuals can no longer unite their emotions with the world of machinery, they, in a way, restore to this world the purity that arises from or serves their labor. In the future it will no longer be possible for people to bestow the warmth gained from the enthusiasm and joy derived from their work on the things produced. But these things themselves will be purer as they are put into the world by workers. They will also become more susceptible to what will emanate from, and be predetermined by, the human being as a motor force, as I have described.[6]

The beneficial development of this motor force can emerge only through an understanding of spiritual forces at play that can be discovered through spiritual-scientific research and the uniting of human beings above and beyond human labor and all professions.

> Such a direction to human evolution can only be given by concrete knowledge of the spiritual forces that can be discovered by spiritual science. In order that this development may occur, it is necessary for an ever-greater number of individuals in the world to gradually find the opposite pole. This consists in uniting one human being with another in what rises far above all vocational labor, while at the same time illumining and permeating it. Life in the spiritual-scientific movement furnishes the foundation for a united life that can bind all professions together.[7]

---

5   Here we are mainly focusing on inanimate or soon-to-be inanimate objects. Such detachment from what is being created does not necessarily apply to processes that are meant to enhance or retain life forces, as is the case in farming or preparing natural remedies.

6   Rudolf Steiner, *Karma of Vocation*, lect. 11/12/1916.

7   Ibid.

The connection of the soul disposition of human beings with machines and factories

The driving force in human beings that will set machines in motion will be transmitted through self-stimulated vibrations of one's ether body. Harmonious vibrations will become a practical application of modern science.

> In contrast [to the previously described decline of modern technology], something will come into being—I mentioned it in passing here—which will enable people to make use of delicate vibrations in their etheric bodies as a driving force with which to run machines. Machines will exist which are dependent on people and people will transfer their own vibrations to the machines. People alone will be capable of setting these machines in motion by means of certain vibrations stimulated by themselves. People who today see themselves as practitioners of science will, in the not-too-distant future, find themselves faced with the complete transformation of what they today call the practical application of science; for human beings are to be tuned in with their will to the objective sphere of feeling in the universe.[8]

Machines and the future preparation of medicines

In the future, the construction of machines themselves will evolve in such a way that they will become less objective and more humanized. In addition, the connection between what human beings are and what they produce will become more intimate. This will take place first in the treatment of the chemical constituents used in medicines. These substances that are intended to be used in medicines will be affected by subtle soul pulsations of the producer and will flow into products being made.

> Today, machines are constructed. Of course, they are at present objective, containing little of the human element. But it will not always be so. The course of the world tends to bring about

---

8   Rudolf Steiner, *The Karma of Untruthfulness*, vol. 1, lect. 12/18/1916.

a connection between what human beings are and what they produce and bring into existence. This connection will become ever more intimate. It will appear first in those areas that furnish the foundation for closer relations between one person and another—for example, in the treatment of chemical substances that are used in medicines. People still believe that when sulfur, oxygen, and some other substance—hydrogen or something else—have been combined, the product of this combination possesses only those effects that are derived from the individual substances. Today this is still true to a large extent, but the course of world evolution is tending toward something different. The subtle pulsations lying in the human being's life of will and disposition will weave and incorporate themselves gradually into what he produces. Thus, it will not be a matter of indifference from whom a certain preparation is received.[9]

Hand preparing biodynamic preparations and herbal remedies

Although Rudolf Steiner foretold new possibilities for creating medicines in the future with humanized machines, he also spoke about the benefits of making biodynamic preparations by hand stirring instead of using conventional machines, and about the difference between making certain herbal remedies by hand and making them with typical machines.

There is no question that stirring by hand has a quite different significance than mechanical stirring, although of course someone with a mechanistic worldview would never admit it. Just consider what a huge difference there really is: when you stir by hand, all the fine movements of your hand go into the stirring, and quite possibly all kinds of other things do too, including the feelings you have as you stir. People nowadays don't think that makes any difference, but in the field of medicine, for instance, the difference is quite noticeable. Believe me, it is really not a matter of indifference

9   Rudolf Steiner, *Karma of Vocation*, lect. 11/12/1916. In volume 2, we will describe how the development of anthroposophic pharmaceutical processes and the resulting remedies are a step in this direction

152

whether a certain medication is prepared by hand or by machine. Something is imparted to the things that are produced by hand— you mustn't laugh at this. I have often been asked what I thought of the Ritter remedies, about which some of you may have heard.[10] As you may know, some people sing the praises of these remedies while others go around saying they have no particular effect. Of course, they do have an effect, but I am firmly convinced that they would lose a great deal of their effectiveness if they became available commercially. With these medicines in particular, it makes a great difference when the doctor prepares the remedy and gives it directly to the patient. A certain enthusiasm is administered along with the remedy when this all occurs only in smaller circles. You may say that enthusiasm cannot be weighed or measured, but an enthusiastic doctor is an inspired doctor, and the doctor's enthusiasm supports the dynamic effect of the medicine. After all, light has a strong influence on remedies, so why shouldn't enthusiasm? As a mediator, enthusiasm can have a very great effect, and so can an enthusiastic doctor. That is why the Ritter remedies can be so effective. Great things can be accomplished with enthusiasm. However, if something like this were prepared by machine, the effects would probably disappear. That is what is involved here, whether something is done with everything that proceeds from the human hand—and this is a lot—or whether it is done by machine.[11]

Factories that reflect the disposition of their directors

Not only machines and technological devices will be influenced but whole factories will reflect the disposition of the directors. Machine operators will be able to step up to a device and set it in motion through certain hand gestures.

Even the most external and cold technical development tends toward a quite definite goal. Anyone who can form a vague conception of the future of technical development knows that an

---

10   Marie Ritter, a German pharmacist who developed "photo-dynamic" herbal remedies (not related to biodynamic agriculture).

11   Rudolf Steiner, *Spiritual Foundations for the Renewal of Agriculture*, First Discussion, 6/12/1924.

entire factory will operate in a completely individual way that will be in keeping with the one who directs it. The human attitude of mind will enter into the factory and will pass over into the way in which the machines work. Human beings will blend with this objectivity. Everything that they touch will gradually come to bear a human impression. No matter how stupid it may seem today to the clever people—in spite of St. Paul having said that what men consider to be clever is often foolishness in the eyes of God—people will realize that the time will come when an individual will be able to step up to a mechanism standing at rest and will know that to set it in motion, he must move his hand this way, that way, and another way. Through the vibrations of the air caused by this signal, the motor, adjusted beforehand to respond to it, will be set in motion.[12]

Morality as a creative driving force

Moral and immoral persons generate different types of soul vibrations. In the future, someone who is motivated by egoism or self-interest will not be able to operate machines that are constructed by people who are motivated by the force of selfless love, or the "Tau."

Just imagine what a truly good person who has reached an especially high level of morality will in future be able to do. They will construct machines with signals that can be governed only by individuals like themselves. Evil-minded people will produce quite different vibrations when they make these signals, and the machine will not respond.[13]

What is expressed by the Tau is a driving force which can only be set in motion by the power of selfless love. It will be possible to use this power to drive machines, which will, however,

---

12 Rudolf Steiner, *Karma of Vocation*, lect. 11/12/1916. There are electrical devices today that are motion activated by employing a motion sensor that transforms the detection of motion caused by animate or inanimate objects into an electrical signal. What Steiner is describing are machines that are activated by human soul vibrations generated by thoughts and feelings. In some cases, moral forces are the deciding factor.

13 Rudolf Steiner, *Karma of Vocation*, lect. 11/12/1916.

cease to function if egoistical people make use of them.... A driving force which can only be moral, that is the idea of the future; a most important force, with which culture must be inoculated, if it is not to fall back on itself. The mechanical and the moral must interpenetrate each other because the mechanical is nothing without the moral.[14]

Part 2: THE WORK OF JOHN WORRELL KEELY

John Worrell Keely and the development of etheric technology

The further development of morality will enable human beings to create forces beyond what nature provides directly. John Worrell Keely, a controversial American inventor, is cited by Steiner as someone who could set machines in motion through his own internal vibrations. He intimates that Keely had achieved a level of moral development that enabled him to do so.

By developing morality, we are able to create forces entirely different from those now present in the physical world. Keely set his motor in motion through vibrations he had created in his own organism. Such vibrations are connected to the moral nature of the human being and represent the first rays of light for what will become technology in the future. In the future we will have machines that can be set in motion only if the forces come from human beings who are moral. Immoral people will not be able to set such machines in motion. Purely mechanical mechanisms will be transformed into moral mechanisms. The spiritual-scientific worldview prepares for this ascent.[15]

---

14   Rudolf Steiner, *The Temple Legend*, lect. 1/2/1906.

15   "John's Gospel as a Record of Initiation: The First Twelve Chapters" (CW 97), lect. 2/12/1906, in Rudolf Steiner, *The Christian Mystery*. Keely was referred to as a fraud and a huckster by the media of his day. Despite this, and his apparent inability ultimately to create a motor based on a new form of energy, Steiner gives him credit for being a forerunner in harmonious oscillation technology.

Morality is a spiritual force that can set machines in motion that won't work for people driven by egoism. This force, as described above, has been depicted by the *Tau* sign and the poetical image of the Holy Grail.[16]

Human beings will be able to create life forms in the future, just as they have been able to shape and form the inanimate or mineral world. Hence, it is all the more important that this be done out of the highest sense of moral goodness. In the future, the mechanical and the moral will interpenetrate each other. Machines will not only be driven by water, wind, or electricity but also by spiritual forces of a moral nature.[17]

It is perhaps known to you that Keely invented a motor that would only go if he himself were present. He was not deceiving people about this, for he had in him that driving force originating in the soul that can set machines in motion. A driving force which can only be moral, that is the idea of the future—a most important force, with which culture must be inoculated if it is not to fall back on itself. The mechanical and the moral must interpenetrate each other, because the mechanical is nothing without the moral. Today we stand hard on this frontier. In the future machines will be driven not only by water and steam, but by spiritual force, by spiritual morality. This power is symbolized by the Tau sign and was indeed poetically symbolized by the image of the Holy Grail. The human beings are no longer merely dependent on what nature will freely give them to use; They can shape and transform nature. They have become the master craft workers of the inanimate. In the same way they will become the master craft workers of what is living.[18]

---

16 The *Tau* sign is a T-shaped cross. The Holy Grail is often identified with the cup that Jesus Christ drank from at the Last Supper and that Joseph of Arimathea used to collect Jesus's blood when he was crucified.

17 The moral realm, both good and evil, will be explored further in relation to technology in volume 2.

18 Rudolf Steiner, *The Temple Legend*, lect. 1/2/1906.

While acknowledging Keely's gifts and accomplishments, Rudolf Steiner suggests that Keely failed in his attempts to create a new energy source because, although he was of a certain moral character, he worked instinctively rather than through conscious knowledge of the forces he was working with. Nevertheless, the ahrimanic or materialistic[19] ideal of linking mechanics with spiritual elements will eventually take place.

It has to be clearly understood that Western culture is in its initial stages. We can see that this is most immediately apparent at the point where economic processes sprout from technological processes, if I may put it like this. A very typical example is the ideal once conceived by an American, an ideal that is bound to come to realization in the West one day. It is a purely ahrimanic [materialistic] ideal but one of high ideality. It consists of using the vibrations generated in the human organism, studying them in great detail and applying them to machines to the effect that if someone stood by a machine even his smallest vibrations would be intensified in that machine. The vibrations of human nerves would be transferred to the machine. Think of the Keely engine. It did not succeed at the first attempt because it had been largely developed from instinct, but it is something that will certainly be realized one day. Here something arises from the crude mechanistic material world that points to what is to come—material mechanics linking up with immaterial, spiritual elements.[20]

Notwithstanding Steiner's appreciation of Keely's attempts to develop a motor that could be set in motion through waves engendered when speaking or through our inner life in general, he suggested that the devastation of World War I would have been far worse if such a source of energy had been developed and employed in the conflict.

Keely harbored the ideal of building a motor that would not run on steam or electricity, but on the waves we create when we make sounds, when we speak. Just imagine that! A motor that runs on

---

19   For more on ahrimanic tendencies and trends, see chapter 8, "Ahriman and the Challenge of Evil."

20   Rudolf Steiner, *Polarities in the Evolution of Mankind*, lect. 11/8/1920.

the waves we set in motion when we speak, or indeed with our inner life in general! Of course, this was only an ideal, and we can thank God it was just an ideal at that time, for what would this war [World War I] be like if Keely's ideal had been realized? If it is ever realized, then we will see what the harmony of vibrations in external motor power really means.[21]

Part 3: POTENTIAL DANGERS OF TECHNOLOGY DEVELOPMENT DRIVEN BY INSTINCT OR EGOTISM

The development of these new forms of resonance technology requires that they be developed consciously out of spiritual-scientific knowledge rather than simply out of instinct and egotism. We have already read in the last passage of the danger that Keely could have unleashed if he had succeeded in developing his energy-producing device based on the amplification of sound waves produced by human speech.

We come to know certain forces that can easily be manipulated to unleash vast mechanical power over the whole world. Simply harmonizing certain vibrations can release tremendous powers. As a result, we will be able to instinctively exert some control over the realm of mechanics and machines, and then technology as a whole will be on dangerous ground. Our egotism will be pleased with this development and find it useful. To properly appreciate these concrete details concerning our development, we must develop a spiritual view of life. For without it, if we rely on an unspiritual view, these things will remain unclear to us.... Indeed, without spiritual understanding we would be much like the sleeping individuals who do not notice the thief coming at night to rob them and only see the damage later, when waking up, and by then it is too late.[22]

One way to consciously, rather than instinctively, develop new forms of technology based on reciprocal oscillations is to study the

---

21   Rudolf Steiner, *Toward Imagination*, lect. 6/20/1916.

22   Rudolf Steiner, *Death as Metamorphosis of Life*, lect. 10/9/1918.

rhythms of nature. The essence of a true natural science of the future will be understanding the rhythms of nature. Equally important is to recognize that great harm can befall humanity through attempts to develop reciprocal oscillation technology if we do not not strive simultaneously to develop a selfless social order.

> *If human beings will only give up looking for anything coarsely material as the basis of nature—and this they will do before the fourth millennium—they will come to something quite different; they will discover rhythms, rhythmical orderings, everywhere in nature. These rhythmical orderings are there, but as a rule modern materialistic science makes fun of them. We have given artistic expression to them in our seven pillars, and so on, in the whole configuration of our building. [The first Goetheanum, subsequently destroyed by fire.] This rhythmical order is there in the whole of nature. In the plants one leaf follows another in rhythmical growth; the petals of the blossoms are ordered rhythmically; everything is rhythmically ordered. Fever takes a rhythmical course in sickness; the whole of life is rhythmical. The discerning of nature's rhythms—that will be true natural science.*
>
> *By learning to understand the rhythms in nature we shall even come to a certain application of the rhythmical in technology. This would be the goal for future technics: harmoniously related vibrations would be set going; they would be small at first but would act upon each other so that they became larger and larger, and by this means, simply through their resonance, a tremendous amount of work could be done....*
>
> *No rhythmical technics can be introduced without causing harm to humankind, unless at the same time a selfless social order is striven after; to an egotistic society they would bring only harm.*[23]

One can gain insights for the development of technology not only from the rhythms of earthly nature but also from the related rhythmical movements of the sun and the planets. But in this case, Steiner

---

23   Rudolf Steiner, *Three Streams in Human Evolution*, lect. 10/12/1918.

expresses great concern when considering the steam engine developed by James Watt.

Watt was inspired by cosmic movements at a key point in the development of the steam engine. Just as the heavenly bodies radiate profound influences onto the earth, so it will be possible to radiate profound influences out into the universe. Steiner reflects that it is fortunate that no one has yet discovered how to reproduce such cosmic movements and radiate them back out into the heavens. But Watt's inventiveness indicates that a beginning has been made.

> It is astonishing that in a biography of James Watt you will find mention of the following fact; I shall refer to it in a way that will seem utterly insane to every modern and intelligent person. But of course, you yourselves must first understand the interpretation of this fact. Watt could not at first accomplish what he intended through his invention, his steam engine. You see, its development stretched from 1712 to 1769. When once a person has invented something, others, of course, imitate it again and again. Thus, much was constructed between these two dates. When Watt had finally made his machine really workable by means of other improvements, he had used a contrivance in it for which someone else held a patent; because of this, he could not proceed until he had thought out something different to replace it. He then discovered what he needed in a strange way. He was living, of course, in an age in which the Copernican view of the world had long been held.... It actually occurred to him to construct his mobile apparatus in such a way that he could call it the "movement of the sun and the planets." He spoke of it thus because he was really guided by what is conceived in the Copernican system as the revolution of the planets around the sun. He had actually brought down and concealed within the steam engine what had been learned in the modern age as the movement of the heavenly bodies.
>
> Now, bear in mind what I recently explained as something that will happen, but which is at present only in its beginnings; that is, that delicate vibrations will accumulate, and tremendous

effects will thus be produced. Thank God, it has not yet been achieved! But the beginning lies in the fact that the movement of the sun and the planets is copied. Since the movements of the sun and the planets possess a profound significance for our earth when they radiate inward, do you believe that they possess no significance when we copy them here in miniature and cause them to radiate outward again into cosmic space? What then happens has profound significance for the cosmos.[24]

Secret societies and the development of harmonious oscillation devices

There are secret circles in the West, particularly in the English-speaking world, that are working to develop motors and other devices based on reciprocal or harmonious oscillations in which certain vibrations or oscillations in the human soul are amplified and transformed into mechanical oscillation and ultimately into mechanical power.[25] This is kept secret by them in order to gain power over other regions of the earth.

The really important fact is that in groups in the West who keep their knowledge secret the greatest pains are taken to see that things shall develop in such a way as to insure under all circumstances the mastery of the West over the East.... The essence of the matter is to make the English-speaking peoples into a population of masters of the world....

Beginning with this fifth post-Atlantean epoch, definite forces will become prominent in the evolution of humanity.... Only through spiritual science, likewise, is it possible to indicate the forces that will develop in future in a wholly elemental manner out of the nature of the human being. The fact that such forces, which will transform life on earth, will develop out

---

24 Rudolf Steiner, *Karma of Vocation*, lect. 11/26/1916.

25 The activities of secret societies are often dismissed simply as unsubstantiated conspiracy theories without any credibility. However, their existence and activities can be known and understood through an examination of verifiable external facts together with spiritual-scientific perspectives. The topic of secret societies and their relation to technology from a spiritual-scientific perspective will be addressed more extensively in volume 2.

of the human being is known in those secret centers. It is this that is concealed from the East by people in the West who intend to retain it themselves....

First, there are the capacities having to do with so-called material occultism. By means of this capacity—and this is precisely the ideal of British secret societies—certain social forms at present basic within the industrial system shall be set up on an entirely different foundation. Every knowing member of these secret circles is aware that, solely by means of certain capacities that are still latent but evolving in humanity, and with the help of the law of harmonious oscillations, machines and mechanical constructions and other things can be set in motion. A small indication is to be found in what I connected with the person of Strader in my Mystery Dramas. [See the next section in this chapter on the Strader device.]

These things are at present in process of development. They are guarded as secrets within those secret circles in the field of material occultism. Motors can be set in motion, into activity, by an insignificant human influence through a knowledge of the corresponding curve of oscillation. By means of this principle it will be possible to substitute merely mechanical forces for human forces in many things.... The possibility will thus come about of rendering unnecessary nine-tenths of the work of individuals within the regions of the English-speaking peoples. Mechanistic occultism will not only render it possible to do without nine-tenths of the labor still performed at present by human hands but will give the possibility also of paralyzing every uprising attempted by the then dissatisfied masses of humanity.

The capacity to set motors in motion according to the laws of reciprocal oscillations will develop on a great scale among the English-speaking peoples. This is known in their secret circles and is counted upon as the means whereby the mastery over the rest of the population of the earth shall be achieved even in the course of the fifth post-Atlantean epoch.[26]

---

26 Rudolf Steiner, *Challenge of the Times*, lect. 12/1/1918.

Part 4: THE CHARACTER OF DR. STRADER IN RUDOLF STEINER'S MYSTERY DRAMAS

The Strader device: Based on a harmony of forces

Rudolf Steiner wrote four Mystery Dramas that were performed from 1910–1913. They relate the spiritual journeys of various characters through a series of incarnations. In the first scene of the third drama, *The Guardian of the Threshold*, we learn of the research efforts of Dr. Strader who is developing a new source of energy production. This new form of energy or power is meant to harness a "harmony of forces" that can be produced and made available to everyone, even in their own homes, rather than relying on a centralized energy system. Steiner uses the drama and the art form of dialogue to convey and expand upon ideas in his lectures and books.

We will begin first with some words by Ehrenfried Pfeiffer, a contemporary and student of Rudolf Steiner, who studied his Mystery Dramas intensively and attended performances over a ten-year period. It gives some further background to the Strader device.

> *Strader, in his studies, has discovered a nature force previously not known. Strader constructs an apparatus to collect hitherto unknown cosmic rays or cosmic energy. Then he makes an apparatus to transform vibrations of high amplitude and low force into low amplitude and high force. Dr. Steiner said the idea was of a motor by means of which everyone, in their home, could produce warmth, heat, and light. Such a device would revolutionize our present social concepts; it would free us from material cares and bring about a new social structure. It would mean a complete decentralization of industry.*[27]

Scenes from the Mystery Dramas

We begin with words from *The Guardian of the Threshold* spoken by Maria Treufels, a pupil of the spiritual leader Benedictus. In speaking

---

27   Ehrenfied Pfeiffer, *On Rudolf Steiner's Mystery Dramas*, lect. 11/14/1948.

to members of the public, she refers to Strader as a person who has the spiritual and practical abilities to be a leader in the development of new forms of technology that would not thwart individual spiritual development. She reveals that he has developed a model device that would be a first step in such technology.

MARIA TREUFELS

Many sure signs there are that clearly show
how many changes must take place in souls
accepting leadership in their life's course;
but fewer show us that the mystic path
can lead us surely to those blessed goals
that stimulate the forces of our souls.
I sadly fear that leaders now are lacking
who, in their harnessing of nature's forces,
combine both genius and agility,
and thus while working at their earthly tasks
show practical ability in action.
If such people plant the roots of spiritual work
in the good soil of plain reality,
they will be able, soberly,
to work in this world for the good of all.
Being convinced entirely of this view,
I see in Strader, rather than the mystics,
the forces needed for the leadership of humanity.
How long we have experienced with pain
that all our technical accomplishments
have only added to the heavy fetters
that hindered our free striving toward the spirit.
But now we can begin to have a hope,
a hope of which, till lately, none could dream.
In Strader's workshop, one can find already
amazing things still in the model stage,

> *which, if they work, may change technology*
> *in such a way that it will nevermore*
> *oppress our souls with dreary hopeless weight.*

DR. STRADER

> *Your words are optimistic, but my work*
> *seems headed in the right direction.*
> *It still must cross the gap that separates*
> *experiment from application,*
> *but up to now the expert eye inclines*
> *to find it technically feasible.*
> *I hope that the inventor of the thing*
> *may be allowed to give his own opinion*
> *of what he has accomplished at this stage.*
> *And since my words to some may seem immodest,*
> *I ask indulgence for them in advance.*
> *My aim is only to describe the feelings*
> *from which the forces for my work have sprung.*
> *It happens often in the course of life*
> *that all our labor soon becomes detached*
> *from feeling and from soul, becoming soulless*
> *the more our spirit learns to dominate*
> *the forces found here in the realm of sense.*
> *Our labor in producing needed goods*
> *grows more mechanical from day to day,*
> *and with the labor also life itself.*
> *For years much careful thought has been devoted*
> *to finding measures, finding ways and means,*
> *to rescue labor from technology,*
> *so that the soul would not be lamed by work*
> *but workers feel connected with the spirit.*
> *Yet little was achieved by all these efforts*
> *because one question only was considered—*

the right relationship of human being to human being.
I too devoted many weary hours
to groping for the answer to this riddle.
I always found that my deep cogitations
produced in actual life no real value.
I very nearly reached the harsh conclusion
that in this world our destiny ordains
that our great triumphs in material realms
can only prejudice the spirit's growth.
Then there occurred a seeming accident,
producing a solution from the muddle.
I had to institute experiments
which seemed at first remote from all these problems
but suddenly the thoughts sprang forth
that showed me the right way.
Through one experiment upon another
I finally discovered at my desk
a way by which to harmonize the forces
so that, when all the details are worked out,
through pure technique there will result that freedom
in which the soul can properly unfold.
No longer must our laborers be forced
to spend their days in soul-degrading sweatshops,
dreaming their lives away like vegetables.
The products of technology will now
be so distributed that everyone
will have what they may need for their own work
within a house arranged to suit themselves.[28]

In the fourth Mystery Drama, *The Souls' Awakening*, it is revealed through a conversation between a factory owner, Hilary, who is

---

28 Rudolf Steiner, *Four Mystery Dramas*, "The Guardian of the Threshold," scene 1.

supportive of Strader's efforts, and his skeptical business manager, that Strader is having trouble demonstrating the efficacy of his device when moving from an experimental to a production model.

HILARY

> *My friend, you know I do not follow dreams.*
> *How could I aim at such high goals if not*
> *good fortune had already brought the one*
> *who will accomplish all I'm striving for?*
> *I am astonished that you do not see*
> *that Strader is, in fact, this very man.*
> *The one who knows the essence of his spirit*
> *and senses highest human obligations*
> *should not be called a dreamer when he has*
> *conceived it as his duty to create*
> *a field of action here for such a man.*

MANAGER (showing his surprise)

> *What! Strader is the one you have in mind?*
> *Is it not clearly evident in him*
> *how human thinking's apt to go astray*
> *when it has lost a sense for what is real?*
> *He owes the mechanism he invented,*
> *without a doubt, to intuition's light.*
> *And if some day it can materialize,*
> *then from it countless blessings will flow forth,*
> *which Strader has believed were coming soon.*
> *But it will long remain experimental*
> *because the forces still are out of reach*
> *through which it could become reality.*
> *It saddens me that you can think that good*
> *will come about if you entrust your work*
> *to someone who's already suffered shipwreck*
> *with his so daringly conceived creation.*

In truth, this led his spirit to those heights
which always will entice the human soul
but will be scaled and conquered only then
when rightful forces shall have been acquired.

HILARY

Now see! You praise the spirit of the man
while seeking for the reasons to reject him,
and this significantly proves his worth.
You have implied that it was not his fault
that his invention did not meet success.
Then surely here within our circle is
his place, for here no outer hindrances
can set themselves against his spirit's aims.[29]

In scene four of *The Souls' Awakening*, Benedictus, who is a spiritual advisor and teacher to the main characters in the play, reveals he perceives spiritual beings connected to Strader that would work evil if they could take hold of certain spheres of human activities. Even though these beings are barred from doing so, they live as seed forces within Strader's soul that will ripen sometime in the future. These words of Benedictus are a portending of problems Strader will meet in the development of his device.

BENEDICTUS

All that has lately happened in our circle
has taught me, from your course of destiny,
to read in spirit light a certain word
which hitherto concealed itself from me.
I saw you joined with special kinds of beings
who would work evil if already now
they could take hold of human spheres of action.
Yet now they live as seeds in certain souls

---

29 Ibid., "The Souls' Awakening," scene 1.

to ripen for the earth in future times.
I saw such seeds alive within your soul.
That they're unknown to you is for your good.
They will first recognize themselves through you.
But as of now for them the road is barred
which leads them into realms of earthly matter.[30]

In the further course of the play, it becomes apparent that there is a flaw in Strader's device, which reveals itself when Strader works on a production model. The question arises whether Strader's machine does not work because of external circumstances or an internal flaw. Toward the end of the fourth play in scene twelve, a conversation takes place between the soul of Ferdinand Fox and the devilish spiritual being Ahriman, an adversary of the spiritual leader Benedictus. Ahriman enjoins Fox to convince Strader that his device is inherently flawed in order to undermine his confidence before he dies, thus disrupting Benedictus's beneficent efforts on behalf of humankind.

AHRIMAN

> *Do you know Doctor Strader, who's my servant?*

THE SOUL OF FERDINAND FOX

> *He roves about upon the earthly star,*
> *and tries to bring to life his learned drivel.*
> *Each windy puff of life will knock it down.*
> *He listens greedily to mystic snobs,*
> *and by their fumes already is half choked.*
> *And now he tries befogging Hilary*
> *whose friend, however, keeps him well in check*
> *because that bunch of charlatans would soon*
> *destroy the firm with spirit-blubberings.*

AHRIMAN

> *With such a line of chatter I'm not served.*

---

30 Ibid., scene 4.

It's Strader that I need—as long as he
can have unshaken faith still in himself,
will Benedictus easily succeed
in forcing humankind to hear his teaching.
The friend of Hilary might serve Lucifer;
however, I must try another course.
Through Strader I must damage Benedictus.
Should he lose Strader, he'll accomplish nothing
with all his other pupils, now or ever.
It's true, my enemies are still most potent,
and Strader, after death, will then be theirs.
If I can cause his soul to doubt itself
on earth, my gain would be that Benedictus
makes use of him no longer as forerunner.
Already, in the book of fate, I've read
that Strader's course of life will soon be run.
This Benedictus certainly can't see.
My faithful knave, you're almost super-cunning;
you take me for a stupid fool's invention.
Your reasoning's so good that people listen.
So go at once to Strader and explain
that his machine is faulty. It won't work—
not just because the time's unfavorable,
but through an error in the thought itself.

THE SOUL OF FERDINAND FOX

For that, I think, I'm well prepared. Quite long
I've racked my brain to prove to Strader
beyond the shadow of a doubt that he
is in the dark, astray, misled by error.
When someone ponders night for night such stuff
he will indeed believe that failure comes
not from the thoughts themselves but from outside.

In Strader's case it's truly pitiful.
If he'd stayed out of all that mystic fog
and used his intellect and common sense,
humanity would certainly have gained
immensely from his quite superior gifts.

AHRIMAN

See to it now that you are armed with shrewdness.
Your task shall be to undermine the trust
that Strader up to now has in himself;
he will no longer then desire to hold
to Benedictus, who must soon rely
upon himself alone and his own plans.
But these are far from pleasant for the people.
His aims will all the more on earth be hated,
the more their inmost truth reveals itself.

THE SOUL OF FERDINAND FOX

He roves about upon the earthly star,
I see already how to demonstrate
to Strader where his thinking's error lies.
His new machine embodies a mistake,
but he is unaware of it, because
the mystic darkness keeps him from this fact.
I, with my down-to-earth mentality,
can be of so much better help to him.
I've wanted this already for some time
but did not know how to accomplish it.
Now finally I feel myself inspired.
I'll concentrate on all the arguments
which must for sure convince him of the truth.[31]

---

31 Ibid., scene 12.

Fox is successful in convincing Strader his invention is fundamentally flawed, and, unsurprising, Strader is devastated. Hilary, the factory owner who supported Strader, and whose vision sustained him and gave purpose and direction to his work, is equally overcome.

HILARY

> *With grief I have to say to you, dear friend,*
> *the knot of destiny that forms itself*
> *among us in our circle here, for me*
> *is crushing. How are we to build upon*
> *this shaky ground? The friends of Benedictus*
> *are kept aloof, through you, from all our aims.*
> *And Strader suffers agonies of doubt.*
> *A man, who often shrewdly and with hatred*
> *has been opposed to all our occult strivings,*
> *was able to point out to him that he*
> *has made a bad mistake in his machine,*
> *so that it's going to be unworkable,*
> *and not because of outer hindrances.*
> *Life has not favored me with any fruits.*
> *I longed for actions. And yet I always lacked*
> *the thoughts that could promote them.*
> *Soul emptiness has tortured me most sharply.*
> *Alone my spirit vision has upheld me,*
> *and yet, in Strader's case, I was deceived.*[32]

Prior to his death, Strader writes to Benedictus, his spiritual teacher, acknowledging the design flaw in his device. He describes how a spiritual image or being appeared to him that embodied his own flawed thinking. Strengthened by meditative words given to him previously by Benedictus, Strader can dispel the being.

---

32   Ibid., scene 13.

BENEDICTUS *(reading Strader's last words)*
   "My friend, when I felt close to being crushed,
   and knew that opposition to my work
   did not arise alone from outward sources,
   but that the inner flaws of my own thought
   were obstacles to check my plan's success,
   I saw again that picture I described
   to you not long ago. Its outcome, though,
   was not the same. Not Ahriman arose
   as my opponent. A spirit messenger
   appeared where he had been, whose form I felt
   distinctly as my own erroneous thinking.
   Then I recalled those words that you had spoken
   about the strengthening of my own soul powers.
   And thereupon the spirit disappeared."[33]

Comments by participants and attendees of the early performances of the Mystery Dramas

While there is some disagreement about the apparent flaw in Strader's invention by reviewers of Steiner's Mystery Dramas, the following words of Alice Fels, a eurythmist who was a participant in the early production of the Mystery Dramas, supports the idea that there really was a flaw in the device as portrayed by Rudolf Steiner, and that Ahriman used that knowledge to undermine the confidence of Strader and Hilary, the factory owner.

> At that time Rudolf Steiner spoke in rehearsal of Ahriman's significance; we could perhaps think the fault in Strader's invention is just Ahriman's subterfuge. But that is not the case. Ahriman is a greater, more significant spirit remote from any petty intrigue. There really is a fault in Strader's plan and Ahriman has spotted

---

33   Ibid., scene 15.

it through his superior intelligence. The destructiveness in Ahri-man's scheming is in wanting to undermine confidence.[34]

In the following passage from a series of lectures on the Mystery Dramas, Ehrenfried Pfeiffer also confirms that there was a flaw in Strader's machine.

We have the drawings of Strader's machine, but it cannot work, because there is an error in it. People are not able to correct the error, because [they] are not spiritually advanced enough.[35]

Part 5: COMMENTS BY RUDOLF STEINER'S CONTEMPORARIES ABOUT KEELY AND ETHERIC TECHNOLOGY

Potential use of the Keely device in warfare

Rudolf Steiner told Pfeiffer that only people who bear within them an altruistic morality should serve the development of etheric oscillation machines. He further intimates that Keely was not allowed to fully develop his motor devices because they would have been used in warfare.[36]

Apparently, only certain people could activate the Keely motor; sometimes it only happened when Keely touched them on the shoulder.

---

34 Alice Fels, *Studien zur Einfuhrung in die Mysteriendramen Rudolf Steiners.*. Translation quoted is by Linus Feiten "Rudolf Steiner on Technology, A Review" (Dornach, Jupiter: *Astronomy, Mathematics, and Anthroposophy*, Verlag am Goetheanum, vol. 7, 2012).

35 Ehrenfried Pfeiffer, *On Rudolf Steiner's Mystery Dramas*, lect. 11/14/1948.

36 Presumably, he was prevented by spiritual beings concerned with the appropriate development of etheric oscillation machines. In an earlier passage quoted in this chapter, Steiner seemed to suggest that Keely was a person who manifested altruistic morality. However, other writings about the life of Keely reveal that he accepted much of his funding for his research from financiers who were mainly concerned about making a sizable return on their investments. An exception was Clara Bloomfield Moore, a poet, novelist, philanthropist, and an enthusiastic financial supporter of Keely. She is the author of *Keely and His Discoveries*.

The Keely Motor was mentioned. Mr. Keely could not realize his assertions because his invention would have been exploited for egoistical purposes (war). Only certain people could set the Keely Motor in motion, also many only when Mr. Keely touched them on the shoulder. With these experiments, the moral side of humankind definitely comes into question. Only persons with an altruistic morality could and should serve such etheric oscillatory machines, otherwise destructive mischief occurs.[37]

Early scientific research by Pfeiffer under the guidance of Rudolf Steiner: 1. Ether forces, social threefolding, altruistic technology

There now follow extracts from three different but overlapping descriptions by Pfeiffer about experiments he conducted under Steiner's guidance, and conversations he had with him about the development of new forms of technology. It is important to note that in response to certain experimental results obtained by Pfeiffer, Steiner told Pfeiffer they indicated that astral forces were operative rather than the desired etheric ones. This, Steiner said, was a message from the spiritual worlds that the time was not ripe for the development of etheric technology and that Pfeiffer should discontinue such experiments. A disappointed Pfeiffer then asked when the world would be ready for such technology. Steiner responded: When the threefold social organism and Waldorf education have a stronger presence in the world. In other words, the world will be ready when outer social conditions help guard against the misuse of such new technologies for selfish purposes and important spiritual leaders develop their unique capacities for the benefit of humanity.

Apparently, Steiner did allow Pfeiffer to conduct further energy research in private. In addition, Pfeiffer continued more openly his research and development of ways to substantiate the presence of etheric or life forces. It is worth noting that later in life, Pfeiffer did have some success in this regard, for instance, with the development of paper chromatography and sensitive crystallization methods.

---

37   Paul Eugen Schiller, *The Schiller File*, folio 4 a-c.

*The method of science, in a materialistic sense, is based on **analysis**, splitting apart (today atom-splitting and fusion, etc), disintegration, separation, dissecting, and all the procedures which have to destroy and take apart, to work on the corpse rather than to grow, to develop, to synthesize. That the human mind was captured by these methods of breaking apart: in that I saw the source of our present situation. My question, therefore, was: Is it possible to find another force or energy in nature which does not have in itself the ductus of atomizing and analysis, but builds up, synthesizes? Would we discover those constructive forces which make things alive and grow, develop adequate building-up methods of investigation, and eventually be able to use this force for another type of technology applied to drive machines? Then, because of the inner nature of this force or energy, we might be able to create another type of technology, another social structure, and constructive instead of destructive thinking. This force must have the impulse of life, an organization within itself, just as the so-called physical energies have the splitting, separating trend within themselves. My question to Rudolf Steiner during October 1920 and spring 1921, therefore, was: "Does such a force or source of energy exist? Can it be demonstrated? Could an altruistic technology be built upon it?"*

When these questions formed themselves in my mind, I met with Guenther Wachsmuth, a lifelong friend who pondered exactly the same problems.

Some discussions with Rudolf Steiner were carried out individually; others we both together had with Rudolf Steiner.

My questions were answered as follows: "Yes, such a force exists but is not yet discovered. It is what is generally known as the ether, not the physical ether, but the force which makes things grow, lives, for instance, in seed forces. Before you can work with this force, you must demonstrate its presence. As we have reagents in chemistry, so you must find a reagent upon the etheric force. It is also called formative etheric force, because it is the force which creates the form, shape, pattern of a living thing, growth. You might try crystallization processes to which organic substances are added.... It is possible, then, to develop machines which react upon and are driven by this force...." Rudolf Steiner then outlined the principles of the application of this force as the source of a new energy.... To me the task fell to start experiments. In this, the cooperation between us, the seed for the Forschungsinstitut am Goetheanum [research institute at the Goetheanum] was laid. I had to perform certain experiments which I do not feel at liberty to describe. The result of these experiments were reported to Rudolf Steiner, whereupon he said with utmost earnestness: "The outcome of the experiment points to another force, not the etheric one, but an astral one (i.e., forces which live in sentient matter, nerve, brain)." That the experiment did turn out this way was the answer of the spiritual world to him, and it meant that the time was not yet ready to make use of the etheric force. I asked when the time would be ready. He answered: "When the social conditions are such that no misuse of this force can be done for selfish purposes." That would only be the case if threefolding of the social organism would be practiced at least over a few territories on earth. Until this time, experiments in the direction of using the etheric forces would not be successful, or should not be done.[38]

Early scientific research by Pfeiffer under the guidance of Rudolf Steiner: 2. Laboratory as an altar, study of resonance, social threefolding, and Waldorf education

Rudolf Steiner was asked whether etheric formative forces [Bildekräfte] could be made available in the laboratory and also for technical purposes. This question arose from his lectures in which the Keely Motor and the future use of oscillations had been referred to (for example during a lecture on 11/25/1917). Rudolf Steiner had answered: "In the first place it is necessary to find a reagent for the etheric formative forces. One must be sure that the formative forces are active in any research arrangements. This could happen with phenomena of warmth and light, and even with cultures of bacteria too, that is, living substances." (Dr. Pfeiffer suggested that

---

38   Thomas Meyer (ed.), *Ehrenfried Pfeiffer: A Modern Quest for the Spirit*, "The Last Years with Rudolf Steiner," by Ehrenfried Pfeiffer.

Paramecium could also be used as a test medium.) Furthermore, for example, life ether could be obtained so that animals [bacteria, etc., Tr.] brought into the evacuated vessel would be killed. The life ether would then be extracted with ethyl alcohol.... Rudolf Steiner recommended the study of resonance and wave motion (oscillation); likewise, the influence of human rhythms on acoustic and magnetic phenomena. The transformation of delicate pulsations into larger waves. This means, above all, that substances must be found which react very sensitively. Here copper came into consideration.

Human vibrations could also be measured; for example, by using a fine copper strip in an evacuated tube (Geissler tube) and the influence of the light phenomena observed (or measured with an electroscope). A telephone receiver could also be used. There lies another possibility here, to set up a connection between the human tongue and a flame (via a wire or thread) and observe the changes.

In connection with the above, Dr. Pfeiffer had set up an experiment and observed that the approach (not touching) of a discharge tube to various parts of the human body produced color changes and shifts in the dark regions. When an evacuated glass globe was brought near the human body, he noticed light phenomena too. These light phenomena are quite different for different parts of the body. Dr. Pfeiffer told Rudolf Steiner about all this; Rudolf Steiner said that the observed changes in the discharge tube could be traced in the first place to the influence of the astral body, that is to say, not to etheric occurrences. However, he ruled out the course of the experiments up to that moment because the time was not yet ripe for the etheric forces to become operative. Dr. Pfeiffer asked: When would the time come? Dr. Steiner replied: When the threefold social order and Waldorf education were realized and humanity had another moral constitution. Until then, these studies should be carried out in the greatest privacy and secrecy.

Finally, Dr. Steiner mentioned that electromagnetic experiments would succeed better in America because greater concentrations of magnetic forces exist there. Such experiments should be conducted there.

In a further indication Rudolf Steiner suggested research into the reaction of the human being with a motionless burning flame.

[See folio 10 in the Schiller File.] One could also observe that when someone speaks the etheric body of the listener mimes the vibrations of the speech of the speaker. If one makes a eurythmic movement, the etheric body of the other mimes this movement in resonance. (In this connection see the lecture of 2/20/1917.) One must now investigate how far, for example, an 'I'-movement can be transmitted to a machine by means of resonance so that a lever arm, for example, of this machine follows the I-movement....

All these experiments will only succeed if the laboratory is made into an altar. Only when this requirement is met may one do experiments whereby the inner nature of the human being becomes outwardly effective; otherwise only greater mischief will be wrought.[39]

Early scientific research by Pfeiffer under the guidance of Rudolf Steiner: 3. Energy of life, social technology, social threefolding, incarnation of spiritual leaders

I came here to Dornach, [Switzerland], as a young man in 1919, 1920, 1921, when I was an apprentice. As I did all the various activities, I strove at the time to bring a very specific thought, a very specific question to Rudolf Steiner. The thought was this: Since present-day civilization leads to disintegration through the use of physical energies—i.e., electricity, magnetism, and other energies (atomic energy was not yet discovered)—since it is in the nature of these energies and their use in technology that they can lead only to destruction, would it not be necessary to introduce an energy of life into technology, a new energy containing the principle of constructiveness, of life, naturally eliciting in human beings such thoughts, feelings, will impulses that rather than continuing our technological destruction, disintegration, and bombardment, we could learn to equilibrate, that we could learn to build up, to synthesize, to grow, to develop?

This was a question that I put to Rudolf Steiner: whether there was such an energy that could then emanate from the Goetheanum out into the world as an answer, as constructiveness, as an

---

39   Paul Eugen Schiller, *The Schiller File*, folio 4 a-c.

antidote to the destruction. Rudolf Steiner pointed out that such an energy could be studied in certain substance transformations in the human body. He pointed out that this energy in general is what we designate as the etheric formative force, the etheric body, the warmth ether, light ether, etc. I am now not referring to courses and lectures, but to his direct answer to this problem. My thought was to ask whether it would not be possible through the discovery and application of such energies to bring about a social technology and a social order. In answer, Rudolf Steiner suggested a few quite simple experiments, which I then did for him. Concerning the results of these experiments, he said that he had received an answer from the spiritual world, and the answer was: It was not yet time for this etheric energy to be made known and introduced. I was then obligated, according to Rudolf Steiner's instructions, to remain absolutely silent concerning this whole topic. But then I asked: Under what conditions would the spiritual world agree that this new energy could be studied, known, and eventually applied? Rudolf Steiner replied—and this is the reason I wanted to present at least this part of his answer, with the thought that perhaps there may not be another chance: One necessary condition to keep this energy from being misused is that a social order in the spirit of the threefolding idea would have to happen, at least in a small region of the earth; a consequent social order along spiritual lines would need to come about. The spiritual world would not permit these ether energies even to be discovered unless this happened.

The second condition, said Rudolf Steiner, was that certain spiritual leaders must be able to incarnate on Earth in order to take over the guidance of humanity; but that these guides are unable to find bodies, because the present-day system of intellectual education does not make it possible to manifest through such a body; that there would be no possibility to manifest and that one must count with the possibility that these spiritual leaders may not be able to find bodies in this century unless Waldorf education becomes general. Only then, when such education enables certain spiritual leaders to incarnate who will then take over the guidance of humanity, and when a social order exists which guarantees against its misuse—then and only then could one continue working on this problem.[40]

Overcoming the erroneous concept that the heart is a pump in relation to creating proper machines and social life

A noteworthy additional perspective concerning the necessary prerequisites that need to be taken seriously to develop nondestructive machines can be found in a Pfeiffer lecture on the heart. In addition to the need for the threefold social organism and Waldorf education to be more prevalent, the erroneous concept that the heart is a pump must be overcome in order to safely create new forms of appropriate etheric technology and social problems.[41]

> *The heart is not a pressure pump but an organ in which etheric space is created so that the blood is sucked to the heart rather than pumped. [Steiner] also said that it was important to change the scientific concept from the idea of the heart as a pump to something else.*[42] *It is difficult to bring evidence on this point which can be presented. The matter needs more study; it is no help to quote Rudolf Steiner....*
>
> *Together with the wrong concept of the heart as a pump is connected the fact that we have a wrong social life today. A healthy social life can develop only if the old pump-concept is removed and is replaced by the proper one. So, this is a subject that should interest the student of social problems. Rudolf Steiner said that a true cognition in this regard would also make it possible to build machines that are in accord and in harmony with human beings and not destructive to them. He said that only when people know*

---

40 Thomas Meyer (ed.), *Ehrenfried Pfeiffer: A Modern Quest for the Spirit*, lect by Ehrenfried Pfeiffer, "The True Basis of Nutrition."

41 More insight into this issue can be found by the following authors in these publications: Branko Furst, *The Heart and Circulation: An Integrative Model* and Craig Holdrege (ed.), *The Dynamic Heart and Circulation.*

42 See lecture of 3/24/1920, CW 312.

that it is the invisible in people which moves the heart will it be pos-
sible to construct proper machines and to solve the social problem.[43]

Strader machine: A future power source that needs to be developed within twenty years

There are two references by Hans Kuhn, a contemporary of Rudolf Steiner who was active in efforts to implement Rudolf Steiner's ideas on a threefold social organism, that appear to contradict Steiner's reported statements to Pfeiffer that research and experimentation should not proceed until appropriate social conditions be in place to prevent the misuse of etheric energy sources. Unfortunately, it is not clear when Steiner was supposed to have said that a version of the Strader machine should be invented within twenty years, otherwise an ahrimanic counterpart would be developed in the meantime.

> *Summarizing our train of thought, we may describe the Strader*
> *machine as the power source of the future, of which Rudolf Steiner*
> *said that it should be invented... in the next twenty years, because*
> *otherwise the ahrimanic counterpart of it would be developed, that*
> *would serve only destructive ends.*[44]

---

43 Ehrenfried Pfeiffer, "The Heart as a Spiritual Organ of Perception," in Thomas Meyer, *Ehrenfried Pfeiffer: A Modern Quest for the Spirit*, lect. 12/17/1950.

44 Hans Kuhn, "Vom Strader-Apparat," in *Mitteilungen aus der anthroposophischen Arbeit in Deutschland*, 1971, 25 (98).

Transcending Private Capitalism and Socialism

The Necessity for a Threefold Social Organism

The three members of the social organism [economy, politics or rights, and culture] must stand in the right relation to one another, so that they may work on one another in the right way.... The point is ... to find how the three members can be brought together, so that they can really work in the social organism with inherent intelligence, just as the nerves and senses system, the heart and lungs system, and the metabolic system, for example, work together in our physical organism. (note 35)

Transcending Private Capitalism and Socialism

The Necessity for a Threefold Social Organism

Introduction

In this chapter we will explore why Rudolf Steiner told Ehrenfried Pfeiffer that the threefold social organism needed to be more widespread before the development of etheric technology should take place. In the next chapter we will also investigate why Steiner also said Waldorf education needs to be more prevalent.

Beneficial etheric technology needs to be developed through the activation of the soul-spiritual forces of selfless love in the human being in conjunction with certain types of cosmic forces.[1] We know from various statements by Steiner that he was in general concerned about these new and more powerful forms of technology being misused through warfare and the control of the masses.

It is not uncommon that society is portrayed as consisting of three main sectors, although they are called by differing names with varying characterizations.[2] It is not so much a question of whether society will still be recognized as having three main sectors. Rather, the crucial issue is, what kind of social threefolding will manifest in the future?

Steiner's vision of a threefold social organism consists of three unique and interdependent spheres: spiritual-cultural, rights, and

---

1 See chapter 5, "Keely, Strader, and the Development of Etheric Technology."
2 One example is "markets, state, and civil society."

economic.[3] All three need to be recognized as being equally important for a healthy social life, with each having its own distinct function,
jurisdiction, and basis.

In a threefold social organism, as characterized by Steiner, no sphere
dominates the others or obviates their function, as is often the case today
in industrialized countries when economic interests dominate politics
and culture. This imbalance harms the whole social organism, including
the realm from which the transgression originates, the economy.

The three realms can be briefly characterized in the following ways:
A spiritual-cultural life consists of human development and education
in the broadest sense, and encompasses science, art, and worldviews
ranging from materialism to those of deepest spirituality and religion.
The culture of a region can find expression in various traits, such as
family relations, cuisine, music, language, and philosophical or religious beliefs. The appropriate basis for a spiritual-cultural life is individual freedom regarding personal beliefs and choices (as long as they
do not cause harm to others). Such freedoms are sometimes referred to
as inalienable or birth rights, which are distinct from evolving rights
originating in laws.

The rights or political realm in modern life expresses itself most
appropriately in the principle of democracy based on equity and the
equality of *all* people. Its task is to recognize and uphold human rights,
including the rights of workers, and provide protection and safety to
all constituents. By extension, it would also include protection of the
environment that humans inhabit.

The economic realm's main function is to provide for material
human needs. It operates on the principle of efficiency,[4] and its range
of activities includes the production, distribution, and consumption of

---

3   In addition to "rights," Steiner also used the terms "politics" and/or "legal" for the
middle realm.

4   Efficiency in an associative economy in harmony with a threefold social organism
would be more of an ethical or social matter than one based merely on profit motive or
desire for power.

goods and services and the monetary functions that are required to support these activities. The basis for a healthy modern economic life needs to be a sense of togetherness, or unity, and caring for others.

The three sectors of the social organism—cultural, political/legal, and economic—need to work together with an innate intelligence like the intelligence that maintains harmony among the various systems within the human body: nerve-sense, the rhythmical ordering of the heart and lungs, and the metabolism.

Just as in the human organism illness arises if any one of the three systems is disrupted or intrudes inappropriately into one or both other realms, so too can the social organism become ill.[5]

A prime example of this in modern life is the intrusion of economic interests into the realm of politics. In turn, both the economic and political interests transgress the realm of culture, including education and scientific research.[6] Equally harmful are cultural wars, when vying cultural interests, religious or otherwise, try to impose their views and beliefs onto the whole of society through governmental means.[7]

The greatest security and prosperity are generated when each of the spheres can contribute the results of its activities on an ongoing basis to the overall social organism, unencumbered by the domination of one of the sectors over the others. Each sector has something vital to offer social life in addition to collectively providing a system of checks and balances within the whole social organism.

---

5 An example of transgression of one bodily system into another is when the metabolism becomes overactive in the head or nerve-sense region and sinusitis or migraines result.

6 An example of the economic and political interests in the United States teaming up in this way is the collaboration of big business with the state and federal governments to create and implement national educational goals, standards, and assessments that states are encouraged to adopt.

7 An example of this is when government (public) schools are subject to pressure by religious or secular groups who seek to impose their views and beliefs on all children and families.

However, there is more to social life than outer structures and arrangements. The social or antisocial behavior of institutions and organizations also reflect the ideals, moral character, motivation, thoughts, and feelings of their participants. While outer institutions and organizations can encourage or thwart socially responsible behavior, they are also dependent on what participants bring in their souls to situations. This is the all-important cultural aspect of life, which is dependent on one's upbringing, education, and social circumstances. For adults, this needs to include conscious inner development.

For the most part in this chapter, we will be focusing on outer social arrangements, while in the next chapter the focus will be on child development and education.

In our exploration as to why Rudolf Steiner thought that a threefold social organism and Waldorf education needed to be more prevalent for the research and development of moral technology to continue safely and productively, we need to consider four factors:

1. *Motivation of the people involved, including those active in financing, researching, developing, and distributing technology.*
2. *Quality of relations between the people working together and with the earth and the other beings that inhabit it.*
3. *Legal structures, organizational forms, and internal dynamics of initiatives.*
4. *Interrelations of the technology industry, and economic life in general, with government and cultural life.*

We will return to these factors in the summary at the end of the chapter.

Chapter overview

We need to recognize that the good or harm that technology can offer humanity and the earth is dependent on whether people become familiar with the spiritual goals of Earth evolution, and whether they can work selflessly in harmony with these goals to benefit humanity.

While it is important to understand that the technology industry or technical societies through the division of labor are in an *external* sense altruistic, such outer altruism can be thwarted at the outset because it was not fostered in one's upbringing and schooling. In addition, the demands of private capitalism thwart altruism by fostering, even requiring, self-interest as the primary motivation for entrepreneurs and investors. It also requires workers to, by and large, work for money to meet their needs by selling their labor. In an altruistic context, labor would be supported to freely work on behalf of society.

Notably, a threefold social organism as envisaged by Rudolf Steiner is inherently linked to a *fundamental social law* that is applicable to all economic endeavors: the more that people work out of interest in others rather than self-interest, the greater the wellbeing of a community or society will be. Conversely, human suffering caused by social conditions is ultimately linked in some way to egotism or self-interested behavior. The same could be said for the suffering we have inflicted on animals and the undue harm on the earth.

The rise of egotism, self-interest, individualism, and the associated antisocial forces in modern life necessitate that the social forces within the human being, and the cultivation of a greater interest in others, are continuously nurtured in various ways. One way this can be accomplished is through the development of the capacity to think in pictures or imaginations instead of abstract thinking. Thinking in pictures or imaginations allows us to envision the situation of other people, while abstract thinking causes people to be strongly attached to their own opinions and perspectives. The faculty of imagination or thinking in pictures can be fostered through the education of children and through various inner exercises that adults can do. In addition, social forces within the human being can be supported by outer social arrangements and structures in harmony with a threefold social organism as just described.

An economy within a threefold social organism can best serve society when it is guided by a collective or "group-born" intelligence arising from the respectful and equitable sharing of perspectives and insights among associations of producers, distributors, and consumers (or their representatives). This contrasts with a supposed intelligence arising from the interplay of the forces of supply and demand in an unregulated market, or from outside by commands of the state.

In a threefold social organism, which includes an associative economy, ownership of capital that can be utilized for personal gain under private capitalism will be replaced by the circulating rights of use of capital, including the means of production, that is made available at minimal or no cost to capable people who want to provide something that is needed and valued by the community.[8] When they can no longer do so, the rights to use the capital will be transferred to another capable person or persons through the associative processes. It would not be sold as private property to the next person but transferred as a gift to the new entrepreneur or group of entrepreneurs. Oversight of the transfer of capital, which in effect is a community asset, will be overseen by both the cultural and legal or rights sectors. Experienced and knowledgeable people working on behalf of the cultural sector will determine to whom the capital will be transferred, not through sale but through a granting process, and the political or legal realm will arrange and uphold the legal arrangements of such transfers.[9]

An important idea connected to a threefold social organism is that economic life needs to be subject to laws that uphold human rights. In addition, a healthy economy needs to be rejuvenated from outside by

---

8   *Capital,* in this instance, refers to any of the various means of production: land, buildings, machinery, inventory, monetary assets, and so on.

9   A modern-day example akin to this takes place to a degree in community land trusts, in which a not-for-profit board or trustee group acts as a cultural group overseeing the use of land and other common holdings within a given community.

constructive forces, which are generated in an independent spiritual-cultural life that continually flows into economic life. These constructive forces arise through the people participating in the economy. Ideally, they include ingenuity, creativity, practical skills, empathy, ethical ideals, and moral actions.

Part 1: EARTH EVOLUTION, TECHNOLOGY, ALTRUISM, AND EGOTISM IN RELATION TO PRIVATE CAPITALISM

Egotism and the application of technology

Until now, the motivation for the development and use of technological inventions has been primarily self-interest and egotism. On the producer side, the motivation is to obtain maximum efficiency and profits, and on the user side, the appeal is to gain greater convenience and comfort.

> Just try to imagine what is meant when one speaks about the technology [in our current age]. What is it there for? If you are able to form a comprehensive view of it you will see that, however great and impressive the result may be, when the forces of the intellect and manas [spiritual thinking] are applied to the inorganic mineral world it is nevertheless, in the main, only self-interest and egotism which is the motive behind the application of all these forces of discovery and invention.[10]

Technology and the great goals of Earth evolution

We will now revisit a passage quoted in the last chapter in relation to human motivation in economic life. The inevitable merger of human beings with machines and the harnessing of human soul vibrations and energy to power machinery must be accompanied by an understanding of the spiritual goals of human and Earth evolution and the will to work selflessly in harmony with them. This merger has already begun to a

---

10   Rudolf Steiner, *The Temple Legend*, lect. 10/7/1904.

significant degree with the use of medical devices and electronic communications, for instance, and will increase in the future.

> *Endeavors are to be undertaken to place the spiritually etheric element in the service of external, practical life. I have already pointed out that the fifth post-Atlantean period will have to solve the problem of how the temper of the human soul, the flow of human moods, can be transmitted to machines in wavelike movements. The human being must be linked with something that has to grow more and more mechanical....*
>
> *There is the will to harness human energy to mechanical energy. It would be quite wrong to think that we should try to prevent these things, for they will happen, they will come about. The only question is whether they will be brought about as a part of human evolution by people who are selflessly familiar with the great goals of earthly evolution and will [work toward] them in ways that are beneficial to humanity or whether they will be brought about by those groups of people who only want to make use of them egoistically or solely for the sake of their own group. It is not "what" is done that matters in this instance, for the "what" will happen anyway; the important thing here is "how" these things are tackled. The "what" will happen anyway because it is intrinsic in human evolution. Welding together human with mechanical nature will be a great and significant ongoing problem for the remainder of earthly evolution.*[11]

Modern technology and private capitalism: Altruism vs. egotism

Private capitalism is an outdated economic system that is predominately driven by self-interest, while at the same time, modern technology and the division of labor demand the opposite from economic life—that is, altruism (at least outwardly).[12] This means that in a technology-based society the pervasive use of technology can develop in a humane way only if the people who work in, or finance, the technology

---

11   Rudolf Steiner, *Secret Brotherhoods*, lect. 11/25/1917.

12   It is important to note that both private capitalism and socialism have tended for the most part toward oligarchic social orders as they evolve.

industry are motivated by interest in others and the greater welfare of humanity, rather than mere profit and personal gain.

> *Technical society [or civilization] has a very special character-istic—namely, it is at its core, a thoroughly altruistic society. In other words, technology can spread in a human way only when the people active in technology develop altruism, the opposite of ego-tism. Every new wave of technology in society shows, for those who can observe such things, that in a technological society it becomes increasingly necessary to work without egotism. At the same time, something else developed from capitalism that is not necessarily connected with technical society, or at least, need not remain con-nected. Capitalism, as private capitalism, must act egoistically since its nature is one of egotistical activity. In modern times, two diametrically opposed streams meet one another—namely, mod-ern technology, which requires human beings free of egotism, and private capitalism, which arose in an older period and can flourish only when people accept egoistical desires.*[13]

Technology and industrial manufacturing

To gain a sense of how modern technology is related to altruism, we need to consider the circumstances from which technology has emerged and developed through industrial manufacturing. A first step in this process is the evolution from craft production to manufacturing based on machines and the division of labor. The more that the divi-sion of labor advanced, the more workers, outwardly speaking, were required to produce things for others. From a purely economic per-spective, modern technology-based industry requires altruism, that is, working for others. However, to the degree that entrepreneurs work for profits and that workers must sell their labor, they both work out of egotism, in contradiction to this summons for altruism. As a result, societies based on technology demand something of an ethical, reli-gious nature from people that, for the most part, they cannot comply with under the pressures of private capitalism.

---

13   Rudolf Steiner, *Education as a Force for Social Change*, lect. 05/11/1919.

The more the division of labor advances, the more it will come about that one always works for others—for the community in general—and never for oneself. In other words, with the rise of the modern division of labor, the economic life as such depends on egotism being extirpated, root and branch. I beg you to take this remark not in an ethical but in a purely economic sense. Economically speaking, egotism is impossible. I can no longer do anything for myself; the more the division of labor advances, the more must I do everything for others.

The summons to altruism has, in fact, come far more quickly through purely outward circumstances in the economic sphere than it has been answered on the ethical and religious side.... Taking it, therefore, in its purely economic aspect, we see at once the further consequences of this demand for altruism. We must find our way into the process of modern economic life, wherein one does not have to provide for oneself but only for others; and so, each individual will, in fact, be provided for in the best possible way.

This point of view could easily be taken as idealism, but I ask you to observe once more that in this lecture I am speaking neither idealistically nor ethically, but from an economic point of view. What I have just said is intended in a purely economic sense. It is neither God, nor a moral law, nor an instinct that calls for altruism in modern economic life—altruism in work, altruism in the production of goods. It is the modern division of labor, a purely economic category, that requires it....

In recent times our economic life has begun to require more of us than we are ethically, religiously, capable of achieving. This is the underlying fact of many a conflict. Study the sociology of the present day [1922] and you will find that the social conflicts are largely because as economic systems expanded into a world economy it became more and more necessary to be altruistic, to organize the various social institutions altruistically; while, in their way of thinking, people had not yet been able to get beyond egotism and therefore kept on interfering in a clumsy, selfish way with the course of things.

We shall arrive at the full significance of this only if we observe not merely the plain and obvious fact, but the same fact in its more masked and hidden forms. Because of this discrepancy in the mentality of present-day humanity—the discrepancy between the demands of the economic life and of ethical and religious ability—the following state of affairs is largely predominant in practice. To a large extent, in present-day economic life, people are providing for themselves. That is to say, our economic life is actually in contradiction to what, by virtue of the division of labor, is its own fundamental demand....

To provide for oneself is to work for one's earnings, to work "for a living." To work for others is to work out of a sense of social needs. To the extent that the demand which the division of labor involves has been fulfilled in our time, altruism is actually present—namely, to work for others. But to the extent that the demand is unfulfilled, the old egotism persists. Egotism has its roots in the fact that people are still obliged to provide for themselves. That is economic egotism.[14] In the case of the ordinary wage earner, we generally fail to notice this fact because we do not think about what values are really being exchanged for in this case. The things that the ordinary wage earner manufactures have, after all, nothing to do with the payment for their work— absolutely nothing to do with it. The payment—the value that is assigned to their work—proceeds from altogether different factors. They, therefore, work for their earnings, work "for a living." They work to provide for themselves. It is hidden, it is masked, but it is so.

One of the first and most essential economic questions, therefore, comes before us. How are we to eliminate from the economic process this principle of working for a living? Those who to this day are still mere wage earners—earners of a living for themselves—how are they to be placed in the whole economic process,

---

14 There is also cultural egotism that includes biases, prejudices, antisocial feelings that people carry in their souls into social situations based on upbringing and education. See part 3 in this chapter.

no longer as such earners but as people who work to meet the needs of society.[15]

Part 2: EGOTISM, ALTRUISM, AND THE FUNDAMENTAL SOCIAL LAW

The fundamental social law and altruism

The fundamental social law can be characterized as follows: The more that people work out of interest and concern for others the greater the well-being of a society will be, and conversely, the more that people and institutions work out of self-interest or personal egotism the more will human exploitation in the form of poverty, want, and suffering take place somewhere, at some point in time.[16]

Another way of framing the fundamental social law is to say that the more that workers and institutions give over the proceeds of their work to the community, and the more that they are supported by the community at large to carry out work beneficial to the community, the greater the well-being of a society will be.

To be clear, this has nothing to do with government-based socialism in which the government directs the primary aspects of the economy and the distribution of wealth. Rather, it points directly to the individual motives and social structures required for an independent, prosperous, and socially attuned economy.

The fundamental social law stands in direct contrast to the idea that a society is served best if people are encouraged through their education and enabled, if not forced, through social structures to work out of personal self-interest or egotism. In fact, there is a consequential cause and effect relation between egotism and human suffering.

---

15   Rudolf Steiner, *Rethinking Economics*, lect. 7/26/1922.

16   The degradation of the environment, discrimination, and the exploitive use of artificial intelligence by companies are related consequences.

It is important not to take this social law simply as a moral platitude. It is meant to be applied practically in life in such a way that the proceeds or results of each person's work go wholly to the community, and that each individual is supported by the work of others. Thus, working for others must be separated from the income one receives.[17]

To recognize the validity of the fundamental social law requires that one understand that the effects of all social institutions are determined in the main by the thoughts and feelings of the people who are a part of such institutions.[18] Steiner described the fundamental social law as follows:

There is, then, a fundamental social law which anthroposophy teaches us, and which is as follows:

In a community of human beings working together, the well-being of the community will be the greater the less individuals claim for themselves the proceeds of the work they have done— i.e., the more of these proceeds they make over to their fellow workers, and the more their own requirements are satisfied not out of their own work done, but out of work done by the others.

---

17 This is not making a case for tax-the-rich, redistribute-the-wealth regulations or laws, rather that there is an inherent means within the economy for the overall proceeds to find their way to all members of society by means of "true prices" established by economic associations, as will be explained in a later section in this chapter. In other words, the emphasis is on distributing wealth, not redistributing it. The only role that the government would possibly have is to determine the minimum value of the resulting production that each person is entitled to. Rudolf Steiner suggested a social experiment in this direction through the creation of voluntary shared income communities, whereby each working person in the community would deposit their income into a common bank account and collectively they would determine how the overall proceeds would be distributed according to an agreed-upon scale of needs. See Rudolf Steiner, "Theosophy and the Social Question" (*The Threefold Review*, Philmont, NY: Margaret Fuller, 1996).

18 Regarding private capitalism, the "thoughts and feelings of the people who are a part of such institutions" refers firstly to those in power, those who own and control the capital. If they are motivated by egotism, there is little or no opportunity for management or workers to work out of altruism. Such economic power in the hands of people motivated by egotism imbues antisocial thoughts, feelings, and actions throughout such institutions. Thus, how capital is employed in a society is a crucial factor in any effort to implement the fundamental social law. For more on this topic, see *Steinerian Economics,* chapters 2 and 7.

Every institution in a community of human beings that is contrary to this law will inevitably engender in some part of it, after a while, suffering and want. It is a fundamental law which holds good for all social life with the same absoluteness and necessity as any law of nature within a particular field of natural causation. It must not be supposed, however, that it is sufficient to acknowledge this law as one for general moral conduct, or to try and interpret it into the sentiment that everyone should work for the good of others. No—this law only finds its living, fitting expression in actual reality, when a community of human beings succeeds in creating institutions of such a kind that no one can ever claim the results of one's own labor for oneself, but that they all, to the last fraction, go wholly to the benefit of the community. And everyone, again, must be supported in return by the labors of others. The important point is, therefore, that working for others and the object of obtaining so much income must be kept apart as two separate things.[19]

Human suffering [derived from social causes] is purely a consequence of egotism; and in every human community, at some point or another, suffering, poverty, and want must of necessity arise if this community is founded in any way upon egotism.[20]

Part 3: INDIVIDUALISM, HUMAN RELATIONS, AND NURTURING INTEREST IN OTHERS

The rise of individualism and antisocial forces

The rise of individualism and increased antisocial forces have accompanied the advancement of industrial societies. Inherently connected with the rise of individualism is an increase of antisocial forces and a diminishing of social forces within human beings. In trying to address these antisocial forces within ourselves, the goal should not be

---

19   Rudolf Steiner, *Anthroposophy and the Social Question*, part 3.
20   Ibid.

to eradicate them but to find the means to counterbalance increasing antisocial forces with ever stronger social forces.

We live in [an age]... in which human beings must become independent. But on what does this depend? It depends on people's ability... to become self-assertive.... It is the antisocial forces which require development in this time for consciousness to be present. It would not be possible for humanity in the present to accomplish its task if just these antisocial forces did not become ever more powerful; they are indeed the pillars on which personal independence rests. At present humanity has no idea how much more powerful antisocial impulses must become.[21]

The study of the reciprocal relation between the social and the antisocial is extremely significant for our time. Just this antisocial tendency is of the utmost importance to understand because it must make itself felt and must be developed in us. This antisocial spirit can only be held in balance by the social. But the social must be nursed, must be consciously cared for. And in our day, this becomes truly more and more difficult because the antisocial forces are really in accord with our natural development.[22]

We cannot rely solely on reforming outer institutions to instill social forces into people. The institutions themselves reflect the sentiments and thoughts of the people working within them.

[Those] alone can form a right judgment of the external institutions of life who see that they are nothing but the creations of human souls, who embody in these institutions their sentiments, their habits of mind, their thoughts.[23]

Interest in others: The foundation of social life

The most important social capacity that we need to develop in the current age is an ever-greater interest in others and the surrounding world. This is the foundation or "backbone" of all human interaction

---

21 Rudolf Steiner, *Social and Antisocial Forces in the Human Being*, lect. 12/12/1918.
22 Ibid.
23 Rudolf Steiner, *Anthroposophy and the Social Question*, part 2.

that can be called social. All social development, both individual and collective depends on this foundation.[24] As will be described in more detail later in this chapter, an inner requirement of any group of people working together, including the realm of moral technology development, is to continuously work on one's inner life and expand one's interest in others.

> *We shall see that in this ... [age] there is a tendency to take no notice of the social in merely acting naturally. [Social forces] must be acquired consciously in working with one's soul forces, while formerly it was felt instinctively. ... What is necessary and must be actively acquired is the interest of [one person in another]. This is indeed the backbone of all social life.[25]*
>
> *A favorable change in [a] social movement cannot come about in any other way than through an increase in the interest that a person feels in another human being.[26]*

Thinking in pictures and imagination

Pictorial or imaginative thinking will be an essential capacity that needs to be developed for people to take a greater interest in others and to live in a social manner. Abstract thinking, so prominent today, engenders a stubborn self-centered tendency that separates us from others and inhibits the ability to think and live in the spiritual world.

> *In our epoch it is of special importance to make the effort to form pictures, not really abstract, isolated judgments. It must be pictures, too, that will open a path to socialization.[27]*
>
> *Imaginations will be required by human beings, for only through them will the antisocial impulses, so rampant today, develop into social impulses. Thus, through imaginations, human beings will acquire the faculty to put themselves in the place of*

---

24 The connection between interest in others and moral goodness, and apathy and evil, will be taken up in volume 2.

25 Rudolf Steiner, *Social and Antisocial Forces in the Human Being*, lect. 12/12/1918.

26 Rudolf Steiner, *The Challenge of the Times*, lect. 11/30/1918.

27 Ibid., lect. 12/6/1918.

*other persons.... You cannot put yourself in the place of oth-
ers merely through abstract thinking. Abstract thinking makes
you stubborn; abstract thinking causes you to be attentive only to
your own opinion. Above all, abstract thinking generally leads us
to close ourselves off more or less from the mobility that is needed
for us to live with the spiritual world.*[28]

Imagination and the education of children

Because imaginative or picture thinking is so crucial for the development of social forces in the human being, it needs to be fostered in
the education of children. How this is done in Waldorf education will
be explained in the next chapter.

*Perhaps you will not feel that what I am saying now is extremely
important—but it is. For this ability to picture the other in oneself without love or hate, to allow the other individual to appear
again within our soul, this is a faculty which is decreasing week
by week in the evolution of humanity. It is something which people are, by degrees, completely losing. They pass one another by
without arousing any interest in each other. Yet this ability to
develop an imaginative faculty for the other is something that
must enter pedagogy and the education of children.*[29]

Imagination in relation to adult education and inner development

Adults can engage in two types of inner exercises to help advance
pictorial or imaginative thinking and interest in others. These exercises
will enable a person to picture and live into the situation of others.

One involves quietly yet vividly thinking of and picturing people
from the past who have helped us in some way. This is good preparation
for being able to imaginatively relate to people we meet in the present
in a social rather than antisocial way.

---

28 Rudolf Steiner, *The Time-Sequence and Spiritual Foundations for Threefolding,*
lect. 3/23/1919.
29 Rudolf Steiner, *Social and Antisocial Forces in the Human Being,* lect. 12/12/1918.

The precise need of the future is that the social shall be brought to meet the antisocial in a systematic way. For this there are various inner soul methods. One is that we frequently attempt to look back over our present incarnation to survey what has happened to us in this life through our relations with others. If we are honest in this, most of us will say: Nowadays we generally regard the entrance of many people into our life in such a way that we see ourselves, our own personalities, as the center of the review. What have we gained from this or that person who has come into our life? This is our natural way of feeling. It is exactly this which we must try to combat. We should try in our souls to think of others, such as teachers, friends, those who have helped us and also those who have injured us (to whom we often owe more than to those who, from a certain point of view, have been of use to us). We should try to allow these pictures to pass before our souls as vividly as possible in order to see what each has done....

For we can really develop this imaginative faculty in us if, instead of striving after the immediate sensations of life as is often done today, we are not afraid to look back quietly in our soul and see our relationships to other human beings. Then we shall be in a position to relate ourselves imaginatively to those whom we meet in the present. In this way we awaken the social instinct in us against the antisocial which quite unconsciously and of necessity continues to develop. This is one side of the picture.[30]

The other inner exercise that Rudolf Steiner recommends for adults to develop picture thinking is a self-review. This entails remembering oneself at an earlier age in certain situations as if one were someone else. This objectification process frees one from the past and enables a person to meet people in the present in an objective way.

The other [inner exercise for adults] is something that can be linked up with this review of our relations to others. It is when we try to become more and more objective about ourselves. Here we must also go back to our earlier years. Then we can directly,

---

30 Ibid.

so to speak, go to the facts themselves. Suppose you are thirty or forty years of age. You think, "How was it with me when I was ten years old? I will imagine myself entirely into the situation of that time. I will picture myself as another boy or girl of ten years old. I will try to forget that I was that; I will really take pains to objectify myself." This objectifying of oneself, this freeing of oneself in the present from one's own past, this shelling-out of the I from its experiences, must be specially striven for in our present time. For the present has the tendency toward linking up the I more and more with its experiences.[31]

Social forms

In addition to the education of children and conscious inner development by adults, our societal structures can be arranged in such a way that they foster social forces that counterbalance the rising antisocial forces.[32]

It is not a matter of finding prescriptions for resisting the antisocial forces but of so shaping, of so arranging the social order, the structure, the organization of that which lies outside of the individual, that a counterbalance is present to that which works as antisocial force within human beings. Therefore, it is vital for our time that the individual achieves independence, but that social forms provide a balance to this independence. Otherwise, neither the individual nor society can develop properly.[33]

Part 4: THE THREEFOLD SOCIAL ORGANISM

The threefold social organism as the basis for transcending private capitalism and socialism

As previously described in the chapter introduction, a threefold social organism consists of three independent spheres: spiritual-cultural;

31 Ibid.

32 One such arrangement is the creation of economic associations of producers, distributors, and consumers, which will be described in an upcoming section.

33 Rudolf Steiner, *Social and Antisocial Forces in the Human Being*, lect. 12/12/1918.

legal/political/rights; and economic. If we are to address a specific issue taking place in any of the spheres, we need also to take into consideration how the other spheres affect it. This requires an understanding of how the three realms of social life can be brought together in an intelligent way similar to how the three main systems in the human organism—nerves and senses, heart and lungs, and metabolic—work together.

> *A cultural problem, political problem, and economic problem are all contained in the social question, and we shall see that the smallest detail of that question cannot appear in its true light unless we look at it as a whole—fundamentally, in these three aspects: cultural, legal and political, and economic.*[34]

> *The three members of the social organism must stand in the right relation to one another, so that they may work on one another in the right way. This is the real meaning of the threefold nature of the social organism—not the splitting apart of the three members; the splitting apart is always there. The point is rather to find how the three members can be brought together, so that they can really work in the social organism with inherent intelligence, just as the nerves and senses system, the heart and lungs system, and the metabolic system, for example, work together in our physical organism.*[35]

Checks and balances through outside corrections

In the broad framework of a threefold social organism, each sector provides unique qualities to the overall society. Collectively they can create social unity and provide a system of checks and balances to ensure a healthy coordination of the whole social organism. Without such interaction and interdependence, a single sector on its own would eventually collapse.[36]

---

34 Rudolf Steiner, *The Social Future,* lect. 10/24/1919.

35 Rudolf Steiner, *Rethinking Economics,* lect. 8/2/1922.

36 These are important thoughts to consider in the twenty-first century when considering whether and what kinds of regulations would be appropriate for the technology industry.

It is essential that economic activity is corrected from outside by laws that have originated in an independent political/legal realm. Otherwise, laws and regulations would simply reflect economic interests and not the rights of citizens.[37]

> *Just as in a natural organism one single organic system would destroy itself through its specific activity if there were no other systems to keep it in balance, so does one function of the social organism need to be kept in balance by another. Work within the economic sphere would, over time, inevitably lead to comparable damage, unless it were counteracted by the political rights system that must rest on a democratic basis, just as the economic life* **cannot.** *In the sphere of democratic law-making, [governing by representatives] is appropriate. What is done there works within economic activity to counteract its innate tendency to cause damage. If one were to harness economic life to the administration of the state, one would deprive it of its efficiency and freedom of movement. Those engaged in economic work must* **receive** *the law from somewhere outside of economic life, and only* **apply** *it in economic life itself.*[38]

> *Only when laws are made in a field where business considerations cannot in any way come into question, and where business cannot gain any power over this legal system, will the two be able to work together in such a way that our sense of justice will not be violated, nor business acumen be turned into a curse instead of a blessing for the whole community.*[39]

> *To perceive clearly the idea of the threefold order, one must be willing to understand that the economic life needs to have its own forces continually corrected from outside, if it is not to call*

---

37 The technology industry consistently maintains that it can regulate itself to a large degree. Unfortunately, the technology industry is growing and developing new products at such a rapid rate that elected representatives are often ignorant of the harmful effects of these new technologies. And even if they are aware, the current laws and regulations are simply outdated and inadequate to uphold appropriate health and safety standards and the basic functions of democracy.

38 Rudolf Steiner, *The Renewal of the Social Organism*, "What the 'New Spirit' Demands."

39 Ibid., "Culture, Law, and Economics."

*forth out of itself obstacles to its own growth. This necessary corrective will be supplied when there is an independent cultural life and corresponding independent legal sphere to make provision for it. The **unity** of social life is not thereby destroyed; in reality, it arises thereby for the first time in its true sense.*[40]

The threefold social organism is not socialistic, communal control of industry under a different name. Such attempts only undermine the economy. An independent cultural life and political system are the means to counter the evils of private capitalism as they arise.[41]

*In the modern economic process, evils have risen through control of the means of production by private capital. If one tries to exterminate these evils by an **economic** measure, such as communal control of the means of production, one undermines modern industry. One can, however, work against these evils, by creating alongside the economy an independent legal system and a free life of the spirit. In this way, the evils that result—and result continually—from the economic life will be removed as they arise. It will not be the case of evils arising first and people having to suffer under them before they disappear, rather, the other organic systems that exist alongside the economic institutions will, in each instance, turn aside the mischief.*[42]

Origin and evolution of capital

The beginning of the accumulation of capital in the form of machinery, buildings, inventory, and money began with the transition from land-based production, as in forestry, agriculture, and fishing, to industrial production associated with the division of labor and machinery. Instead of the circumstances of nature determining the work process, the human spirit or intelligence becomes the determining factor

---

40 Ibid., "Law and Economics."

41 The initiative to establish a "precautionary principle" is an example of efforts to hold businesses to ethical and legal standards for environmental and public health policies. A leading proponent in the United States of the precautionary principle is the Science and Environmental Health Network (SEHN), www.sehn.org.

42 Rudolf Steiner, *The Renewal of the Social Organism*, "The Roots of Social Life."

in organizing labor. In the process, the workers who found themselves in factory settings felt disconnected from the natural world in their work setting and activities.

> *The point of origin of capital always lies in the division, the quali-tative division, of labor… In one respect or another, human labor is permeated by spirit [or entrepreneurial human intelligence]. It is labor permeated by spirit that arises in the process of the division of labor. Where we see capital arise in the course of the division of labor, we have, in the first place, nothing other than labor penetrated by spirit. The first phase of capital always consists in this. Where human labor hitherto was determined only by nature, it is now organized, divided, and so forth by spirit.*
>
> *It is indeed necessary to see capital and its formation very clearly from this point of view. Only from this point of view can we understand the function of capital in the economic process. The forming of capital is always a concomitant of the division— that is to say, the qualitative, organic division—of labor.*
>
> *In this process, however, something of the direct, immediate connection that the human being has with nature when working upon the earth is always loosened. You see, so long as economic life consists merely in the elaboration of nature, all that we deal with are the products of nature, which, on being transformed by human labor, acquire an economic value. The moment the human spirit organizes labor, however—organizes, that is to say, labor as such…an emancipation from nature begins to take place.*[43]

Division of labor, motivation, and the threefold social organism

Along with the diminution of their connection to nature, work-ers and even business owners began to experience a separation from the products they produced and the people they provided for. The pre-dominating incentive for owners became the accumulation of profits,

---

43 Rudolf Steiner, *Rethinking Economics*, lect. 7/27/1922.

while the workers were left to work for wages. Consequently, both lost an inner connection to and satisfaction from work itself.

The owners have goods produced because they bring them prof-its; workers produce them because they are obliged to earn a liv-ing. A personal satisfaction in the finished product itself is felt by neither. In fact, one touches a very essential part of the social question when pointing to the lack of any personal relationship between the producers and the goods produced in the modern industrial system. However, one must also be clear that this lack of a personal relationship is a necessary consequence of modern technology and the attendant mechanization of labor. It can-not be removed from the economic life itself. Goods produced by extensive division of labor in large industries cannot possibly be as closely associated with the producer as were the products of the medieval craftsman. One will have to accept the fact that, regarding a large part of human labor, the kind of interest that previously existed is past and gone. However, one should also be clear that without interest, individuals cannot work; if life com-pels them to do so, they feel their whole existence to be dreary and unsatisfying.

Whoever is honestly disposed toward the social movement must think of finding some other interest to replace the one that is gone. They will not be in a position to do so, however, if they insist on making the economic process the single main substance of the social organism, and on making the legal system and the cultural life a sort of appendage of the economy.[44]

The division of labor and of social function that has become necessary in modern times separates the laborer from the recip-ient of the product of his work. There is no changing this fact without undermining the conditions of modern civilization; nor is there any way of escaping its consequence—the weakening of one's immediate interest in one's work. The loss of this inter-est must be accepted as a result of modern life. Yet we must not allow this interest to disappear without finding other kinds to

---

44 Rudolf Steiner, *The Renewal of the Social Organism*, "Social Spirit and Socialist Superstition."

take its place, for human beings cannot live and work indifferently in the community.[45]

The need for new motivations to work that retain human dignity

Because of the disconnection from nature, from the products one makes, and from the people who use them, a social demand arose in workers seeking a more dignified relation to work than mere economic compulsion. However, the industrial economy based on private capitalism alone cannot create new incentives to work.

> *An economic management that does not include this profit motive among the forces at work within the economy cannot of itself exert any effect whatever upon the human will to work. And precisely because it **cannot** do so, it meets a social demand that a large part of humanity has begun to raise in the present stage of development. This part of humanity no longer wants to be led to work by economic compulsion. They want to work from motives more befitting human dignity....*
>
> *If the economic system is to be organized in a way that can have no effect on our will to work, then our will to work must be stimulated in some other way.*[46]

New incentives to work arising from independent cultural and political realms

The development of new incentives for work can only arise out of the perspectives of the independent cultural and political sectors. Within a threefold social organism, the cultural realm enables new types of human relations to arise, so that people understand the purpose and meaning of life beyond the purely economic. In an independent legal sector where equality and democracy prevail, a new sense of community can arise. Together, these two independent realms can enable people to experience new incentives to work for a community they feel a part of and love.

---

45 Ibid., "The Threefold Social Order and Social Trust: Capital and Credit."
46 Ibid., "Ability to Work, Will to Work, and the Threefold Social Order."

[The threefold social organism] aims at establishing within an independent, self-sustaining cultural life a realm where one learns in a living way to understand this human society for which one is called upon to work; a realm where one learns to see what each single piece of work means for the combined fabric of the social order, to see it in such a light that one will learn to love it because of its value for the whole. It aims at creating in this free life of spirit the profounder principles that can replace the motive of personal gain. Only in a free spiritual life can a love for the human social order spring up that is comparable to the love an artist has for the creation of his works. If one is not prepared to consider fostering this kind of love within a free spiritual-cultural life, then one may as well renounce all striving for a new social order. Anyone who doubts that men and women are capable of being brought to this kind of love must also renounce all hope of eliminating personal profit from economic life. Anyone who fails to believe that a free spiritual life generates this kind of love is unaware that it is the dependence of spiritual and cultural life upon the state and the economy that creates desire for personal profit—this desire for profit is not a fundamental aspect of human nature. It is this mistake that makes people say constantly, "to realize the threefold order, human beings must be different than they are now." No! Through the threefold order, people will be educated in such a way that they will grow up to be different than they were previously under the economic state.

And just as the free spiritual life will create the impulses for developing individual ability, the democratically ordered life of the legal sphere will provide the impulses for the will to work. Real relationships will grow up between people united in a social organism where each adult has a voice in government and is co-equal with every other adult: it is relationships such as these that are able to enkindle the will to work "for the community." One must reflect that a truly communal feeling can grow only from such relationships, and that from this feeling, the will to work can grow. For in actual practice the consequence of such a state founded on democratic rights will be that each human being will take his place with vitality and full consciousness in the common field of work. Each will know what he or she is working for; and each will want to work within the working community of which he knows himself a member through *his will.*[47]

Economic associations:
Fostering enhanced interest in others and collective economic wisdom

The economy needs to be based on the principle of association. Instead of relying on the chances of the market and the vicissitudes of supply and demand, economic decisions, such as pricing and determining the quantity and type of goods and services to be provided, need to be connected to specific circumstances. Associations of producers, distributors, and consumers can provide direct insight into what is taking place in the various sectors of the economy and facilitate imaginative or pictorial ideas based on concrete facts and situations.[48]

> *The judgments that have to be formed in the economic life must be formed out of immediate, concrete situations. And that is possible only in this way. For definite domains or regions (whose magnitude, as we have seen, will be determined by the economic process itself), associations must be formed, in which all three types of representatives will be present alike. From the most varied branches of economic life, there must be representatives of the three things that occur in it—production, consumption, and distribution.*[49]

Associations, picture thinking, and sound judgments

Economic associations foster picture thinking based on specific situations and shared perspectives and insights rather than relying on abstract ideas and theories. Only out of such insights can the values of products be determined.

---

47 Ibid.

48 The associative approach not only rejects the exclusive "wisdom" of the interplay of supply and demand in a so-called free market economy, it also rejects socialistic, state-run command economies.

49 Rudolf Steiner, *Rethinking Economics*, lect. 7/31/1922.

Specialized knowledge and down-to-earth objectivity can lead to a general harmony of interests within such an association. Not rules and regulations but people themselves determine production, circulation, and consumption of goods, through their direct insight and interests. By active participation in this associative way of working, people can develop the insights and skills they need for it; and goods can circulate at their proper value by means of contracts which balance one interest against another.[50]

No abstract concept can enable you to grasp the economic process; you must grasp it in pictures. Nonetheless, it is just this that makes the intellectual world so uneasy today—this demand, no matter in what sphere of thought, that we should pass from the mere abstract concepts to ideation of an imaginative kind. Yet we can never found a real science of economics without developing pictorial ideas; we must be able to conceive all the details of our economic science in imaginative pictures. And these pictures must contain a dynamic quality; we must become aware of how such a picture works under each new form that it assumes....

This means... that to act rightly in the economic sense, we must make up our minds to enter into the events of production, trade, and consumption with picture thinking. We must be ready to enter into the real process; then we shall get approximate conceptions—only approximate ones, it is true—but conceptions that will be of real use to us when we wish to take an actual part in the economic life. Above all, such conceptions will be of use to us when what we do not know by our own sensibility (supposing we ourselves have not arrived through sensibility at the corresponding pictures) is supplemented or corrected by others who are connected with us in associations. There is no other possibility. Economic judgements cannot be built on theory; they must be built on living association, where the sensitive judgements of people are real and effective; for it will then be possible to determine out of the association—out of the immediate experiences of those concerned—what the value of any given thing can be.[51]

---

50   Rudolf Steiner, *Towards Social Renewal*, preface to the fourth edition (1920).
51   Rudolf Steiner, *Rethinking Economics*, lect. 8/2/1922.

Economic associations are not only a means for all participants in the economic process to share their perspectives. These associations also provide the opportunity to be confronted by and understand the effects of their actions and the products they make directly on those who use them as well as the environment.[52]

> *Theoretically, no one will want to deny that a larger sense of responsibility is necessary in the present-day world of business and economic affairs. To this end, associations must be created that will work to confront individuals with the wider social effects of all their actions.*[53]

Rather than relying on the outcomes of the market by way of the intervention of the so-called "invisible hand," as described by Adam Smith in the *Wealth of Nations*, or state regulation imposed by a benevolent state, associations will rely on the collective wisdom derived from sharing detailed perspectives of the whole economic process by the participants involved or their representatives.

> *The "market" relationship must be superseded by associations that regulate the exchange and production of goods through an intelligent consideration of human needs.*[54]
>
> *The economic process can be sound only when such a wise self-active intelligence is working within it.*[55] *This can happen only if human beings are united together—human beings who have the economic process within them as pictures, piece by piece; and, being united in the associations, they complement*

---

52 Examples of this kind of dialogue between producers (farmers) and consumers can be found in the Community Supported Agriculture (CSA) movement. For more information on CSAs, visit the website of the Biodynamic Association: https://www.biodynamics.com/content/community-supported-agriculture.

53 Rudolf Steiner, *The Renewal of the Social Organism*, "The Threefold Social Order and Social Trust: Capital and Credit."

54 Ibid.

55 Which is like the inherent wisdom in the interaction of various systems with the human organism.

and correct one another, so that the right circulation can take place in the whole economic process.[56]

Associations and the determination of "true" prices

An associative-based economy within a threefold social organism will provide the necessary conditions for setting "true" prices, which would ensure that workers receive adequate income, including what is needed for the care of their dependents. In the process, true price formulation anticipates future conditions along with using information about the past.

> *You know, perhaps, that in my book* Towards Social Renewal *I tried to express in a formula how we may arrive at a conception of "true price" (as we will call it to begin with) in the whole economic process. Needless to say, such a formula is only an abstraction. It is the object of these lectures—which, I believe, in spite of the short amount of time, will really form a whole—it is our very object in these lectures to work the whole science of economics, at any rate in outline, into this abstraction.*
>
> *The formula that I gave in my* Towards Social Renewal *was as follows. "A 'true price' results when individuals receive, as counter-value for the product they have made, sufficient recompense to enable them to satisfy all of their needs, including of course the needs of their dependents, until they will again have completed a like product." Abstract as it is, this formula is nonetheless exhaustive. In setting up a formula, it is always necessary that it should contain all the concrete details. I do believe, for the domain of economics, that this formula is no less exhaustive than, say, the Theorem of Pythagoras is for all right-angled triangles....*
>
> *Today I intend to start from one essential feature of the formula. It is this: The formula does not point to what is past but to what is going to happen in the future. For I say in it, deliberately, that "the counter-value must satisfy the individual's needs in the future, that is, until he or she will have made a like product*

---

56 Rudolf Steiner, *Rethinking Economics*, lect. 8/2/1922.

again." This is an absolutely essential feature of the formula.... Economic or business life essentially consists in setting future processes in motion with the help of what went before.[57]

The collective insights and decisions of economic associations will replace the arbitrary results of the forces of supply and demand in a so-called free market. When determining true prices, associations will also take into consideration what the legal realm determines that workers require to meet their needs, provisions for those who are not able to work, health care, and the support of education.

How will price-setting be accomplished? It will certainly not be left to chance in the free market, as it has been so far in the national and international economies. In the context of associations between individual branches of industry and consumer cooperatives, individuals with the necessary expertise will set prices in a holistic and rational manner, avoiding the crises provoked by the haphazard effects of supply and demand. In the new [associative] economy, where determining the type and character of labor falls to the sphere of rights, what workers receive in exchange for producing goods will allow them to meet all their needs until the next production cycle is complete.... Of course, society will have to establish organizations to ensure that the needs of widows, orphans, and the sick and disabled are met, and to provide for education and the like. The setting of equitable and realistic prices, however, which is exclusively the jurisdiction of the socially responsible economy, will depend on the formation of corporate bodies for that purpose, whether elected or appointed by joint producer-consumer associations.[58]

Economic associations, interest in others, and community spirit

Economic associations are a practical means to foster person-to-person interactions, a greater interest in others, and an overview of the whole economic process. This interest in others and overall insight

---

57 Ibid., lect. 7/29/1922.
58 Rudolf Steiner, *Freedom of Thought and Societal Forces*, lect. 9/15/1919.

will be integrated into the decisions that are made. Moreover, these exchanges will transcend mere economic processes and thereby engender mutuality and an objective community spirit.

> *The moment the life of associations enters the economic process, it is no longer a question of immediate personal interest. The wide outlook over the economic process will be active; the interest of the other person will actually be there in the economic judgment that is formed. In no other way can a true economic judgment come about. Thus, we are impelled to rise from the economic processes to mutuality, the give-and-take between one person and another, and furthermore to what will arise from this, the objective community spirit working in the associations. This will be a community spirit, not proceeding from any [self-righteousness], but from a realization of the necessities inherent in the economic process itself.*[59]

Part 5: FROM PRIVATE CAPITAL TO COMMUNITY ASSETS

Beyond private capitalism: Capital and economic associations

Steiner associated private capitalism with egotism as a driving force, and with the transgression by the economy into political and cultural life. However, he also recognized that the accumulation and deployment of capital was essential to the modern economy and way of life. Capital itself is not the problem. It is the private ownership of capital that has become a social evil. However, the solution is not to do away with entrepreneurial access to capital by communalizing it within a state. The goal is to retain the use of capital in such a way that obviates the social harm that it causes under private capitalism.

> *It is easy to jump to the conclusion that... capitalism must be abandoned. The question is whether in so doing we would not also be abandoning the very foundations of modern civilization. Anyone who thinks the capitalist orientation a mere intruder*

---

59   Rudolf Steiner, *Rethinking Economics*, CW 341, lect. 8/2/1922.

into modern economic life will demand its removal. However, he who sees that division of labor and social function are the essence of modern life will only consider how best to exclude from social life the disadvantages that arise as a byproduct of this capitalist tendency. He will clearly perceive that the capitalist method of production is a consequence of modern life, and that its disadvantages can make themselves felt only as long as increase of capital is made the sole criterion of economic value.[60]

It is not capital itself that is harmful, but rather capital in private hands, especially if this private ownership is able to control the social structure of the economic body. But if society can be structured in the manner previously described [as in a threefold social organism], then capital can no longer have any antisocial influence. The beneficial social structure will always prevent the capital assets from being isolated from the management of the means of production. It will also put a stop to the attempts of those who strive only for capital assets but shirk participation in the economic process.[61]

Private capitalism and transgression of economic interests into political and cultural life

Modern industrialism and technology require a certain amount of economic power in the form of accumulated capital to operate efficiently. This power should be limited to what is required for the production and distribution of goods and services and not dominate and control the political state and cultural life. The transgression of economic interests under private capitalism into the other sectors of politics and cultural life is one of the most pernicious forms of social evil.

The modern industrial system has brought the means of production under the power of individual persons or groups. The achievements of technology were such that the best use could be made of them by a concentration of industrial and economic

---

60 Rudolf Steiner, *The Renewal of the Social Organism*, "The Threefold Order and Social Trust: Capital and Credit."

61 Ibid., "The Threefold Social Organism: Democracy and Socialism."

power. So long as this power is employed in the one field—the production of goods alone—its social effect is essentially different from what it is when this power oversteps its bounds and trespasses into the fields of law or culture. It is this trespassing into the other fields that, in the course of the last few centuries, has led to the social evils that the modern social movement is striving to abolish. Those who possess the means of production acquire economic power over others. This economic power has resulted in capitalists allying themselves with the powers of government, whereby they are able to procure other advantages in society, oppressing those who are economically dependent on them—advantages which, even in a democratically constituted state, are actually of a legal nature. This economic domination has led to a similar monopolization of the cultural life by those who hold economic power.[62]

Limiting capital to economic power, not including political and cultural advantages

Society benefits most when intelligent and skillful entrepreneurs can use capital to produce goods and services in an efficient manner for the common good. In the process, entrepreneurs gain a certain amount of economic power. But the arrangements of a threefold social organism will prevent capitalists from using economic power to gain political and legal advantages. This will help enable the political realm to create laws that uphold human rights and prevent exploitation of the environment that the economic sector must abide by.

Presently, the best services can be rendered to the community as a whole only by qualified persons through the control of large sums of capital. However, the nature of economics dictates that such services can only consist of the most efficient production of the goods that the community needs. A certain amount of economic power flows into the hands of the people who produce such goods. It cannot be otherwise, and the threefold social order recognizes

---

62   Ibid., "Culture, Law, and Economics."

this. Accordingly, it aims to bring about a society in which this economic power will still arise, but out of which no social evils can grow. The threefold idea does not propose to hinder the accumulation of large sums of capital in individual hands; it recognizes that to do so would be to lose the possibility of employing socially the abilities of these private individuals in the service of the general public.[63]

Out of the economic sphere one can develop only economic interests. If one is called out of this sphere to produce legal judgments as well, then these will merely be economic interests in disguise. Genuine political interests can only grow upon the field of political life, where the only consideration will be what are the rights of a matter. And if people proceed from such considerations to frame legal regulations, then the law thus made will have an effect upon economic life. It will then be unnecessary to place restrictions on the individual in respect to acquiring economic power; for such economic power will only result in his rendering economic services proportionate to his abilities—not in his using it to obtain special rights and privileges in social life.[64]

Access, administration, and transfer of capital in an associative economy

Capital in the form of the means of production should be limited in value to creation costs. Once the initial costs of the means of production are paid for, they should be made available free of charge to capable people who want to produce something of recognized value for society. Private ownership will be replaced by rights of access and use, as long as entrepreneurs are employing the capital in a productive manner. When the entrepreneurs are no longer able to use the capital to produce goods on behalf of the community, it will be transferred to another capable person as a free gift. No person or group could obtain productive capital simply through purchase, nor could they resell it for personal gain.

---

63 Ibid.

64 Ibid.

In a healthy social organism, capital goods and other means of production will have a one-time cost at the time of delivery. The producer will then be able to manage them, but only for as long as he can contribute to production by his management. The business will then have to be transferred to another not by sale nor by inheritance, but rather as a free gift to the one best able to manage it. It will have no sale value, and thus no value in the hands of an heir who does not work. Capital with independent economic power will work in the establishment of the means of production; it will dissolve itself instantly when the creation of the means of production is finished. Now, however, capital consists mostly of such "already established means of production."[65]

Free access to capital by capable people who want to produce something of recognized value for society is the most fruitful way to take advantage of those capacities.

At our present stage of development, the creative activity of individual capacities cannot usefully enter the economic process without free access to capital. This free access must be available if production is to be fruitful—not because it is advantageous to an individual or a group of people, but because it can best serve the whole community when based on proper social understanding.[66]

The transfer of capital is based on who is the most capable person, not on economic power or state directives. Such transfers will take place when an existing entrepreneur is no longer willing or able to continue as the overseer of the capital. The decision regarding the person to whom the enterprise should be transferred is a cultural question—that is, who has the knowledge and experience to determine what is required in a given situation, humanly and practically.

[The threefold idea] proposes... that the moment an individual can no longer attend to the management of the means of production within one's sphere of power, these means of production

---

65   Ibid., "The Threefold Order: Democracy and Socialism."

66   Rudolf Steiner, *Towards Social Renewal*, chapter 3.

> *should be transferred to another capable person. The latter will not be able to obtain these means of production through any economic power one possesses but solely because he or she is the most capable person.*[67]
>
> *It is essential that private individuals should have means, by the use of capital, of placing their abilities, unopposed, at the service of the community. When this individual is no longer willing or able to direct their abilities to the use of capital, this use must be transferred to other persons of similar abilities. It will not be transferred by state prerogative or by economic power, but by finding out, on strength of the training acquired under the free spiritual life, which person will make the most suitable successor from the social point of view.*[68]

In addition to the cultural sector, the legal realm will be involved in the transfer of capital. Cultural organizations or corporations would have the responsibility of ensuring that capital is transferred at the appropriate time and at no cost to capable people to produce goods and services for those who need them. The legal realm would ensure that the terms and rights of use would be clarified and upheld by law.

> *In* The Renewal of the Social Organism, *the administration of capital was made, on the whole, to depend on the spiritual organization in cooperation with the independent political-legal organization.*
>
> *We say today that capital makes business; it should always be possible to accumulate capital, but the impulse for the threefold social order requires that the provision of capital be administered by someone with the necessary capacity for business and a developed spiritual life, and that the accumulation of capital be administered by those to whom it belongs only as long as they are able to administer it themselves.*
>
> *When capitalists can no longer put their own capacities into the administration of the capital, they must see (or if they feel*

67 Rudolf Steiner, *Renewal of the Social Organism,* "Law and Economics."
68 Ibid., "Cultivation of the Spirit and Economic Life."

unable to fulfill such a task, a corporation of the spiritual organization must assume the responsibility for seeing) that the management of the business passes to a very capable successor, able to carry it on for the benefit of the community. In other words, the transfer of a business concern to any person or group of people does not depend on purchase or any other displacement of capital, but is determined by the capacity of individuals themselves. It is a matter of transferring from the capable to the capable, from those who can work in the service of the community to those who can also work in the best way for the common good.

The safety of the future society depends on this kind of transference. It will not be an economic transference, as is now the case; such a transference will result from human impulses, received from the independent spiritual-intellectual life and from the independent legal-political life. There will even be corporations within the cultural organization, united with all other departments of the culture, on which the administration of capital will devolve.[69]

Land should be treated as a community asset like the means of production. Therefore, it would not be treated as a private commodity to be bought and sold. Access and use of it would be gained through a free gift.

The transfer of land from one person or group to another must not be accomplished through purchase or inheritance, but by transfer through legal means based on the principles of the spiritual organization.[70]

Part 6: ECONOMY AND CULTURE

The necessary rejuvenation of the economy by cultural life

Human nature is more than mere economics. It rises above and beyond it. Left to its own devices, the economy is destructive and can

---

69   Rudolf Steiner, *The Social Future*, CW 332, 10/29/1919.
70   Ibid.

engage in unmitigated human and environmental exploitation. The economy needs to be continually renewed from the outside, not only by an independent rights or political life but also by an independent spiritual-cultural life. If it tries to rejuvenate itself through its own economic perspectives and thinking, it will not only accelerate its own destructiveness, but it will also wreak havoc on the whole social organism.

> *This is the inner meaning of the threefolding of the social organism; namely that, in a properly thought out threefold social organism... the economic thinking of the present is a destructive element which must, therefore, be continually counterbalanced by the* constructive *element of the spiritual realm of the social organism.*[71]
>
> *If economic life tries of itself to evolve a new form, it will only propagate and intensify its old evils. As long as economic life is expected to make of us what we may become, new evils will be added to the old. Not until humanity comes to understand that human beings—out of their own spirits—must give to the economic life what it needs will they be able to pursue as a conscious aim what they are demanding unconsciously.*[72]

> *An economy standing alone without constant fertilization by a cultural life founded on free human individuality cannot continue to develop and becomes rigid.... That quality of human individuality which must creatively influence and direct the social life has to be wrought from the very essence of human nature through impulses that economic life cannot produce. Economics are the foundation of human existence; but human spirit rises above it. Economic forces are confined within much narrower boundaries than human nature as a whole....*
>
> *Thus, self-administration of the cultural life is the only way to promote individual abilities. Only through self-administration will conditions exist that give rise not to a universal will that*

---

71 Rudolf Steiner, *The New Spirituality and the Christ Experience of the Twentieth Century*, lect. 10/24/1920.

72 Rudolf Steiner, *The Renewal of the Social Organism*, "Fundamental Fallacy in Social Thought."

*suppresses the fruitfulness of the individual for social life, but
rather a condition in which individual human accomplishments
can be taken up into the life of the whole for its benefit.*

*If the structuring of the social organism is done in such a way
that a self-governing cultural life can unfold within it, this will
not destroy the vital unity of the organism; on the contrary, it will
support and enhance it.*[73]

Education and the revitalization of economic and political life

The most urgent present and future need for a healthy social life
is for the schooling of children to be a key part of an independent
spiritual-cultural life. Every child in each rising generation must be
able to develop their latent capacities to the fullest out of their own
nature. This will enable regenerative forces to continually flow into economic and political life. Rather than the older generations determining
what is most worth doing in life, the children of each rising generation must have the opportunity to envision and forge their own future
unencumbered by the status quo. Only then can a spiritual-culturual
life provide the appropriate guidance and renewal for the future development of the economic and political realms. Without such revitaliza-
tion, economic life would ruin itself and the rest of society.

*The real need of the present is that the schools be totally
grounded in a free spiritual and cultural life. What should be
taught and cultivated in these schools must be drawn solely
from a knowledge of the growing human being and of individual
capacities. A genuine anthropology must form the basis of education and instruction. The question should not be: What does
a human being need to know and be able to do for the social
order that now exists? But rather: What capacities are latent in
this human being, and what lies within that can be developed?
Then it will be possible to bring ever new forces into the social
order from the rising generations. The life of the social order will
be what is made of it by a succession of fully developed human*

---

73   Ibid., "The Threefold Social Organism, Democracy and Socialism."

beings who take their places in the social order. The rising gen-
eration should not be molded into what the existing social order
chooses to make of it.[74]

In every generation, in the children whom we teach at school,
something is given to us; something is sent down from the spiri-
tual world. We take hold of this in education—this is something
spiritual—and incorporate it into economic life and thereby ward
off its destruction. For economic life, if it runs its own course,
destroys itself.[75]

Society has everything to gain by each person having the opportunity to fully develop their capacities. This full development maximizes
the possibility of a spiritual-cultural life to be able to imbue economic
life with constructive, rejuvenating forces.[76] This necessitates that the
education of children have its own administration. Otherwise, if it is
administered by economic and political interests, those interests will
give priority to and implant their perspectives and needs into the rising
generations, thus curtailing new and unique impulses.[77]

A healthy relation exists between school and society only when
society is kept constantly supplied with the new and individual
potentials of persons whose educations have allowed them to
develop unhampered. This can be realized only if the schools
and the whole educational system are placed on a footing of self-
administration within the social organism. The government and
the economy must receive people educated by the independent
spiritual-cultural life; they must not, however, have the power to
prescribe according to their own wants how these human beings

---

74 Ibid., "The Threefold Social Order and Educational Freedom."

75 Rudolf Steiner, *The New Spirituality and the Christ Experience of the Twentieth
Century,* lect. 10/24/1920.

76 These rejuvenating forces include mental capacities and knowledge, practical and
social skills, artistic creativity, motivation, ethical ideals, moral values, and the ability
to love.

77 The national education goals and standards developed since the 1980s in the
United States give priority to incessant economic growth, a requirement of modern
private capitalism. For more on how this took place, see Gary Lamb, *The Social Mission of Waldorf Education,* chapters 7–15.

*are to be educated. What a person ought to know and be able to do at any particular stage of life must be decided by human nature itself. Both the state and economic life will have to conform to the demands of human nature. It is neither for the state nor the economic life to say: We need someone of this sort for a particular post; therefore, **test** the people that we need and pay heed above all that they know and can do what we want. Rather, the spiritual-cultural organ of the social organism should, following the dictates of its own independent administration, bring those who are suitably gifted to a certain level of cultivation, and the state and economic life should organize themselves in accordance with the results of work in the spiritual-cultural sphere.*[78]

Part 7: SUMMATION: THE RELATION OF THE FOREGOING IDEAS TO SACRED CREATION AND THE DEVELOPMENT OF MORAL TECHNOLOGIES

We will now consider the four aspects of the development of new forms of morally based technology as presented in the chapter introduction in relation to the current state of technology and the ideals of a threefold social organism.

1) Motivation of the people involved, including those active in financing, researching, developing, and distributing technology

What is critically important is *how* future technology will be developed. This "how" includes two essential factors: a) the understanding of the goals of human and Earth evolution from a spiritual-scientific perspective, and b) the need for selfless devotion to a higher cause as the primary motivation of the people involved in its creation.

The first can be addressed only if people responsible for technology research and development make at least a minimal effort to gain a

---

78   Rudolf Steiner, *The Renewal of the Social Organism*, "The Threefold Social Order and Educational Freedom."

spiritual-scientific understanding of Earth and human evolution and what the overall goals are for both.[79]

Regarding the second, Steiner is clear that the primary motivation in economic life, which includes the development and use of technology, must become altruism, working for the good of others, which is the central principle of the fundamental social law. We need to rise above the motive of egotism that has driven private capitalism and technology up to now. A corollary to the fundamental social law is that human suffering endured by an individual in a social sense is a result of other people's personal egotism. To the degree this is true, the current increase in wealth inequity, social divisiveness, untruthfulness, and invasion of privacy has been to a large degree the result of the technology industry's manipulative, persuasive design for expanding consumer markets and maximizing personal profits, and its cavalier fail-fast, fail-often tactics regarding product development.

In contrast, when it comes to developing new forms of moral technology or any ethically oriented creation of new technologies, altruism is essential. But this does not mean that people need to give up their individuality. On the contrary, the power and focus of the I needs to expand through taking greater interest in others rather than remaining focused on itself. An inner requirement for any group of people working on moral technology together is to continuously work on one's inner life and expand one's interest in others, which Rudolf Steiner calls the foundation or backbone of social life.

2) The quality of human relations between the people working together and their customers

The development of morally-based technology should not be limited to a closed-off group of researchers and entrepreneurs. Rather, they need as far as possible to be in living association with all aspects of the supply chain, including manufacturers, suppliers of ingredients and

---

79   See Rudolf Steiner, *An Outline of Esoteric Science.*

parts, advertisers, and the distributors of the products, and ultimately, to the customers who use their products. Even with all of this, another group needs to be included in these associative conversations, the investors. It is essential for moral technology development that financiers are motivated by the good that will arise from their help rather than on maximizing returns as quickly as possible.

All of this is consistent with the principle laid out by Rudolf Steiner regarding economic associations, whereby people (or their representatives) from the whole supply chain can share their perspectives and fully consider those of others. In this way, a comprehensive picture can be created of how to produce new forms of technology in an ethical and socially responsible manner.

3) The legal structure, organizational forms, and business models of technology companies

Private capitalism runs on the fuel of egotism and self-interested behavior. This necessitates that ownership and organizational forms that succeed to the greatest degree are those that foster egotism and effectively harness it. The publicly traded stock company, an offspring of private capitalism, is a finely tuned corporate form that is powered by self-interest. In most of the United States, the legal duty of management under private capitalism is to maximize profits for shareholders. This type of corporation and financing will never do as a legal basis for supporting the development of moral technology. A corporate form is needed that encourages altruism in its various aspects and fosters dialogue and conversations within its organization, as well as being able to avail itself of the necessary financial resources. This means both gift money for research, and loan/investment money for production. We will consider some possibilities for this in volume two.

4) *The interrelations of the technology industry, and economic life in general, with government and cultural life*

The rapid expansion of the technology industry has outpaced the creation of necessary laws and ethical perspectives to keep it in check. This unbridled expansion also makes it nearly impossible for the government and ethical/religious organizations to keep pace with the potential harmful effects of technology products.

This situation is made worse by the fact that corporations and their CEOs play an inordinate role in determining the outcome of elections and the passage of legislation through lobbying and targeted donations. These corruptive influences also extend to the exploitation of cultural life, including education and scientific research.

One additional thing that must be taken into consideration, which Rudolf Steiner was surely aware of, is that existing energy companies would not take kindly to new forms of decentralized power sources that would compete with their products and jeopardize their wealth and supremacy. Thus, mighty diabolical forces of opposition will be unleashed.

Just because of these facts, it would be all important that moral technology initiatives strive to become agents of social change as exemplary research and economic enterprises that honor and support equity in the realm of rights, and freedom in the realm of education and research. New forms of ownership will need to be explored, such as purpose-driven trusts that create community-based ownership and governance forms that prevent the corruption of private capital.

Child Development, Waldorf Education, and Cultural Freedom in Relation to Technology

To use modern technology with no knowledge of how things work or how they were made is like being a prisoner in a cell without windows through which one could at least look out into nature and to freedom. Educators need to be fully aware of this.

(note 67)

It is the beginning of an antisocial life simply to accept inventions of the human mind without at least understanding them in a general way.

(note 65)

Child Development, Waldorf Education, and Cultural Freedom in Relation to Technology

Introduction

We will now provide an overall description of Waldorf education as described by Rudolf Steiner in the early 1920s. This is meant to help readers understand why he told Ehrenfried Pfeiffer that Waldorf education (in addition to the threefold social organism) needed to be more prevalent before any further research should take place concerning etheric-based technology as described in chapter five. This will include direct statements about technology in the curriculum and about the divine nature of the human being and its relation to the phases of child development. In addition, we will offer perspectives on how such an educational approach can best enable the current generation of children to meet the challenges of modern technology, which has advanced immensely since the 1920s.

Early twentieth-century educational methods such as those designed for Waldorf schools were developed long before the invention of computers and the internet. It might seem like a waste of time to refer to such outdated educational methods. Certainly, one can effectively do so only if such methods were proven to be prophetic in nature. Anthroposophical spiritual science as developed by Rudolf Steiner, the founder of Waldorf education, provides such a visionary perspective. The fact that there are technology industry workers in the Silicon Valley area that send their children to Waldorf schools to reduce exposure to computer technology and screen devices, thus allowing time for the development of essential human capacities and life skills necessary to navigate the digital age, is a testament that Waldorf education does offer something uniquely relevant in the technological age in the minds of people who design and develop those products.[1]

Before reviewing various aspects of Waldorf education that Steiner developed out of spiritual insight, it is important to consider some of the underlying factors behind the current efforts to expand the use of computers in education. For the technology industry, it is partly a matter of expanding its markets and developing brand loyalty at an early age. Its sales pitches often focus on enabling more efficient teaching to specific learning standards, offering personalized drills and skills instruction for students, and replacing direct experiences with supposedly cheaper and more convenient online experiences. This has a certain appeal to schools that are looking to reduce expenses and to certain human rights groups hoping to find more equitable results than the current public education system can provide for disadvantaged children.

But on the periphery, at a global level, there is also a much larger imagination of digital education that includes so-called lifelong learning from birth to death that relies on the predominance of online learning.[2] The current Covid-19 pandemic (2020–2021) has accelerated the process of transforming education from an in-person, teacher-based profession to one relying heavily on computers and virtual experiences and learning. The results are controversial.

---

1   Examples of such Waldorf schools are: the Waldorf School of the Peninsula, the San Francisco Waldorf School, and the Santa Cruz Waldorf School. Some resources on Waldorf education in the United States are the "Research Institute for Waldorf Education" (www.waldorfresearchinstitute.org); "Waldorf Publications" (www.waldorfpublications.org); "Association of Waldorf Schools of North America" (www.waldorfeducation.org); and "Alliance for Public Waldorf Education" (www.publicwaldorf.org).

2   One such international group, based in Russia with links to organizations worldwide, including the United States, is Global Education Futures. For more information, see Global Education Futures Agenda by Pavel Luksha (https://www.slideshare.net/edu2035/pavel-luksha-global-education-futures-agenda).

One factor that underlies these trends is a materialistic, mechanical view of the human being that underpins modern educational reform theory and planning. This includes the view mentioned in the previous chapter that economic considerations take precedence over cultural and democratic ones in a society based on private capitalism. It emphasizes the necessity of accelerated economic growth to maintain profits and prosperity, which in turn depends on the cultivation and promotion of self-interested behavior and competitive instincts to maximize production.

In support of the above, the development and widespread employment of a digital-based educational system implements three main components:

1. Universal—national and eventually international—educational goals, standards, and assessments linked heavily to supporting accelerated economic growth and needs of the economy;

2. An ever-expanding pool of data on child behavior and children's social, emotional, and academic progress;

3. Algorithms or formulas that use the collected data to enable children to reach the national or international educational goals, standards, and assessments.

Because algorithms can adjust an instructional sequence to be child specific, this approach is promoted as "personalized" instruction and learning. One might also call Waldorf education a form of personalized instruction but with significant differences from the normal use of the term in relation to computers. Waldorf education does not link its learning goals and standards to materialistic economic objectives that permeate and perpetuate the dominant social and power structures. Rather, it strives for a much broader and more balanced learning environment that helps prepare students in practical ways for college, work, and human and social development. This approach necessitates a teacher's ability to sense the latent capacities within each child. It is an approach meant to respect and support, not inhibit, the spirit of each child and the inherent intentions and innovations of the rising generation of children.

Waldorf education was, in part, designed to counterbalance the harmful effects of modern technology on the human being not only during Rudolf Steiner's time (early twentieth century) but far into the future. To be clear, it does not reject technology, but rather strives to be a preparation or training for the rising generations of children to engage in technology in a healthy way, at the right time in their development, and for the right reasons. The Waldorf methods and curricula, of course, will need to be adjusted as technology advances in degree and complexity.[3]

In order for teachers to work in harmony with such an approach to education, they need to be involved in modern life to such a degree that they know at least in general how technological devices are made and operate, when it is appropriate for children to use various technological devices, the potential harmful effects of technology use on children, and how to introduce appropriate pedagogical measures to counterbalance potential harmful effects.

The reader may notice a somewhat different approach to the annotations in this chapter compared to earlier chapters. The annotations will not only give a concise overview of the following passages, but the editor will add some reflections on how spiritual perspectives of child development and education relate to modern technology, and in particular the use of screen devices by children.

Chapter overview

The Waldorf curriculum is based on a spiritual-scientific understanding of the nature of the human being and the three phases of child

---

3   One experienced Waldorf high school teacher, upon reviewing this chapter, suggested that a more integrative, holistic approach could be taken by the editor by describing current educational ideas and teaching methods regarding technology that are employed in Waldorf schools in creative yet balanced ways. While this is an excellent idea and should be done, it goes beyond the scope of this work.

development up to the age of twenty-one. From birth to around the age of seven, children live strongly in their sense impressions and imitate what they see and feel in the environment in which they are immersed, including the moral nature of the thoughts, feelings, and actions of those around them. Thus, the best way to strengthen the body and soul of young children and prepare them for the development of thinking later in life, especially in the digital age, is for teachers and parents to create activities and a healthy environment worthy of imitating.

Also, in these early years, Waldorf education emphasizes the development of imagination. Games and toys that stimulate the imagination are particularly beneficial to the young child.

In the grade school years (grades 1–8), the experiences of beauty and artistic creativity are employed to balance practical activities and to support the understanding of how inventions work.

A future-bearing approach to learning reading and doing arithmetic is typically carried out in Waldorf schools. In both cases, students begin with a whole and then analyze the parts. For example, in learning to read, students start with writing whole sentences.[4] Then they move on to analyzing words in sentences and identifying letters in a word. Thus, analysis is introduced in the lower school as a habit of thought when there is an innate desire for it in the child. If this yearning for analysis is not met in grade school to some degree, then later in life there is an inclination to perceive the world in parts that build into a whole, which instills a tendency toward materialism.

---

4   One veteran Waldorf teacher who reviewed this chapter in advance of publication mentioned that some teachers in Waldorf schools use a combination of whole language (whole to the parts) and phonetics awareness (parts to a whole) reading approaches. Also, in the lecture cycle, *The Child's Changing Consciousness*, lect. 4/18/1923, Rudolf Steiner stated that three methods of learning to read can be drawn upon, depending on the circumstances. They are *whole word*, *phonetic*, and *spelling methods*. More information on these methods can be found in *Roadmap to Literacy: A Guide to Teaching Language Arts in Waldorf Schools Grades 1 through 3* (available at www.renewalofliteracy.com).

From a social perspective, our age requires a resolution of the polarity of capitalism versus socialism.[5] Educationally, this resolution begins to take place in the lower school when the children learn about a threefold social organism consisting of culture, law/politics, and economics in relation to the ideals of freedom, equality, and fellowship.[6]

From a practical perspective, the proper preparation for living and working in a technological society is learning to know how technology is made and operates. Steiner suggests that not doing so is a type of soul imprisonment, leaving individuals at the mercy of mechanisms they are not able to understand. A person is then cut off from comprehension of the world, from nature and from an experience of individual freedom. In addition to learning about various industries and how things are made, students should engage in practical, hands-on craftwork that can help strengthen mental discipline, manual dexterity, and comprehension of how things work. The building of practical understanding of how things work leads to a sense of "rightness," of an ethical sensibility that informs right actions, right thoughts, and wholesome feelings.

The issue of ethics is on the mind of many workers in the technology industry and will become more so in the future.[7] In Waldorf education, the development of moral capacities is cultivated in a variety of ways as children pass through the three phases of child development. Throughout all the phases, students should experience love and warmth from and for their teachers.

In the earliest years, when imitation is the prevalent way that a young child learns, the basis for morality is prepared through enriching a child's surroundings. The adults in children's lives need to surround them with moral thoughts and actions worthy of imitating as much as possible. The child should feel that the adults in their surroundings are good and that they have moral thoughts and actions worthy of

---

5   See chapter 6 for more on how to advance beyond private capitalism and socialism.

6   A description of a threefold social organism can be found in chapter 6.

7   For examples of this, see the film *Social Dilemma*.

imitating. The young child imitates these actions and in doing so builds up their own sense of what is right and good.

In the elementary school years, moral development can be best fostered by educating and refining students' feeling life through stories, images, and examples of good deeds that will help develop an esthetic sense for what is good and evil. Archetypes in legends, fairy tales, and ancient mythology provide pictures for the child's inner life that help make a bridge from their origin in the spiritual world through birth to life on earth. These pictures help the child comprehend the tools used for literacy and numeracy. Least effective are commands and preaching about moral qualities or virtues. Also, engaging in artistic activities and experiencing beauty are important factors in developing morality while the faculty of thinking is being developed. A sense for beauty helps the growing child to recognize what is moral.

In the high school years, students move on from myths and legends to biographies of people from various ages of humanity who made a difference in the world. Learning about inspirational people stimulates a moral sense of their own, enhances students' interest in other people in general and the world in which they live, and calls upon them to identify the deeds they are here on earth to accomplish. The high school teacher also helps with the development of moral judgment by leading students through objective analogy exercises of comparing and contrasting that build in complexity and subtlety.

Part 1: TEACHING IN THE MODERN AGE OF TECHNOLOGY

Counterbalancing the negative effects of technology

Teachers must be fully integrated in and have a deep understanding of life, including knowing how technology works (at least in a general sense), the appropriate age for children to begin using different devices, how these can affect the health of the human being and the environment, and how to counterbalance potential harm they may do to the children under their care.

> *There is no desire on our part to deride technical innovations, but we should be able to keep our eyes open to what they do to us, and we should find ways to compensate for any harmful effects. Such matters are especially important to teachers because they have to relate education to ordinary life. What we do at school and with children is not the only thing that matters. The most important thing is that school and everything related to education must relate to life in the fullest sense. This implies that those who choose to be educators must be familiar with events in the larger world; they must know and recognize life in its widest context.[8]*
>
> *When new inventions make their impact on modern life, we must take steps to balance any possible ill effects by finding appropriate countermeasures. We must try to compensate for any weakening of the human constitution due to outer influences by strengthening children from within. But, in this age of ever-increasing specialization, this is only possible through a new art of education based on a true knowledge of the human being.[9]*

The importance of understanding how technology works

One of the most important pedagogical and child development principles regarding the use of technology is to know how a particular piece of technology was made and how it works before using it.

> *It is the beginning of an antisocial life simply to accept inventions of the human mind without at least understanding them in a general way.[10]*
>
> *To use modern technology with no knowledge of how things work or how they were made is like being a prisoner in a cell*

---

8   Rudolf Steiner, *Soul Economy*, lect. 12/31/1921.

9   Ibid.

10   Rudolf Steiner, *A Modern Art of Education*, lect. 8/15/1923.

without windows through which one could at least look out into
nature and to freedom. Educators need to be fully aware of this.[11]

Teachers' deep understanding of and integration in life

The activity of teaching must be recognized as an activity essential to enabling new impulses to flow into modern civilization. Teachers need the moral support of society to accomplish this task. However, to accomplish such a mighty task, they need two things beyond knowing educational principles and methods, or knowledge and training in various subjects. They also need a deep understanding of life and to be fully integrated into life itself.[12]

> *[Teachers] need to be fully integrated into life. They need more than just the proper qualifications in educational principles and methods, more than just special training for their various subjects; most of all teachers need something that will renew itself again and again: a view of life that pulsates in a living way through their souls. What they need is a deep understanding of life itself; they need far more than what can pass from their lips as they stand in front of their classes. All of this has to flow into the making of a teacher.*[13]

Part 2: CHILDREN AS SPIRITUAL BEINGS, TEACHING AS A SACRED ACTIVITY

A new art of education and the principle of repeated earth lives

A new art of education needs to arise based on the profound spiritual insight that reincarnation is a human reality, and that the children before us have been through multiple earth lives. Teachers and parents

---

11 Rudolf Steiner, *Soul Economy*, lect. 1/5/1922.

12 Educators and the profession of teaching are often belittled and blamed for the apparent inadequacies of modern education, and consequently the viewpoints of educators are often ignored. This belittlement also leads to more testing and teaching to the test, which further stifle the freedom and creativity of teachers.

13 Rudolf Steiner, *The Child's Changing Consciousness*, lect. 4/20/1923.

can gain a sense of the intentions and tasks of the rising generations through observing their tendencies when they are young children. Thus, the art of education of the future based on spiritual insight will have a prophetic quality.[14]

> *The important thing [is] to establish a pedagogy, an art of teaching and education which would take into account the fact that in a child a soul is growing which has been through other earth lives. Hitherto, the teacher, however advanced in educational ideas, has felt no more than that he was dealing with the soul of a child whose capacities it was his duty to develop; but he could only, more or less, take note of what could be perceived through the bodily nature. That will not be enough for the teacher of the future. He will need a fine feeling for what is developing in the growing child as a result of earlier earth lives, and this comprehension will be the great achievement in the education of the future.... To hold the theory of repeated earth lives, based on intellectual philosophy, is not enough. The theory must become so practical that it forms the foundation of something like a real art of teaching and education. This is what first gives theory a living quality.... In the children of today, we have the tendencies which will grow in the next generation and the one after that—which means that education is prophetic.... What matters is*

---

14   This prophetic capacity, which includes sensing what wants to come about in the future through each child and collectively through each rising generation is a totally different phenomenon than computer-based predictions that are based primarily on data derived from past events, and projecting patterns exhibited by the data about the past onto the future. Such patterns do not allow for new and creative out-of-the-box thinking and inspired deeds. In addition, the recognition or lack of recognition of the spiritual nature of the human being and repeated earth lives will be a crucial factor in determining how and for what purpose technology will be used in the future. For instance, materialistic ideas such as transhumanism and singularity as espoused by Ray Kurzweil arise because he has no sense of the spiritual life and consciousness experienced by each human being prior to birth and after physical death. If such ideas about the eternal spirit and the continuity of consciousness of each person would become prominent, then macabre ideas such as freezing brains of dead people with the hopes of reviving their functioning with artificial intelligence at some future date would be acknowledged as serving no good purpose.

that we should educate prophetically, foreseeing the task of the next generation.[15]

Responsibility and love of the teachers

When adults view children as spiritual beings who have recently descended from spiritual realms into earthly bodies, it naturally can evoke a sacred feeling and responsibility in those who care for them. Love for the children needs to be the main driving force of teachers. The task of an educator is not to mold the child into some type of adult ideal (as is common in today's education reforms). It is to nurture what lies hidden within the child and to be spiritual helpers—midwives almost—to the birth and growing competence of spiritual capacities in each child who is here to accomplish some mission on Earth. This allows the will of the gods to manifest. Being aware that children are spiritual beings awakens a different kind of ethical responsibility than a materialistic view does.[16]

> *Being aware of life before birth arouses a totally different sense of responsibility, especially in teachers. It is no small matter to educate beings, who descend from eternal spiritual heights into human bodies, which they then shape to their own purposes more precisely with each passing year. Life before birth is the other half of the picture, the complement to the human soul's immortality after death.*[17]
>
> *When we deal with young children, we are faced with beings who have not yet begun physical existence; they have brought down spirit and soul from pre-earthly worlds and plunged into the physical bodies provided by parents and ancestors....*

---

15   Rudolf Steiner, *The Problems of Our Times*, lect. 9/12/1919; for current translation, see *Problems of Society*.

16   This is true not only for teachers, but also for many designers and investors in the technology industry who are currently gripped by the spell of materialism. All talk about ethics in the technology industry lacks potency unless it is based on a spiritual perspective on the human being.

17   Rudolf Steiner, *Freedom of Thought and Societal Forces*, lect. 12/30/1919.

What once lived among spiritual divine beings descended to live among human beings. We see the divine manifested in the child. We have a sense of standing before an altar. But there is one difference; in religious communities, it is normal for people to bring sacrificial offerings to their altars, so that those sacrifices can ascend into the spiritual world. Now, however, we have a sense of standing before an altar turned the other way; the gods allow their grace to flow down in the form of divine spiritual beings, so that those beings, acting as messengers of the gods, may reveal what is essentially human on the altar of physical life. We see in every child the revelation of divine spiritual, cosmic laws; we see the way God creates in the world. In its highest, most significant form this is revealed in the child. Hence, every single child becomes a sacred mystery to us, because every child embodies this great question. It is not a question of how to educate children to approach some ideal that has been dreamed up; it is a question of how to nurture what the gods have sent to us in the earthly world. We come to see ourselves as helpers of the divine spiritual world, and above all we learn to ask what will happen if we approach education with this attitude of mind.

True education proceeds from exactly this attitude. The important thing is to develop our teaching on the basis of this kind of thinking. Knowledge of the human being cannot be gained unless love for humankind—in this case, love for a child—becomes the mainspring of our efforts. If this happens, then a teacher's calling becomes a priestly calling, since an educator becomes a steward who accomplishes the will of the gods in a human being.[18]

The reunification of science, art, and religion through education

Waldorf education is meant to be a contributing factor in the greater evolution of humanity. As such, it brings into the activity of teaching the highest ideals of science, art, and religion in a practical form.[19]

---

18   Rudolf Steiner, *Human Values in Education*, lect. 7/17/1924.

19   This has significant importance for the potential development of future forms of etheric technology, which also needs to be a practical manifestation of the reunification

This [Waldorf] school is really intended to be integrated into what the evolution of humanity requires of us at present and in the near future. Actually, in the end, everything that flows into the educational system from such requirements constitutes a threefold sacred obligation.

Of what use would be all of the human community's feeling, understanding, and working if these could not condense into the sacred responsibility taken on by teachers in their specific social communities when they embark on the ultimate community service with children, with people who are growing up and in the becoming? In the end, everything we are capable of knowing about human beings and about the world only really becomes fruitful when we can convey it in a living way to those who will fashion society when we ourselves can no longer contribute our physical work.

Everything we can accomplish artistically only achieves its highest good when we let it flow into the greatest of all art forms, the art in which we are given, not a dead medium such as sound or color, but living human beings, incomplete and imperfect, whom we are to transform to some extent, through art and education, into accomplished human beings.

And is it not ultimately a very holy and religious obligation to cultivate and educate the divine spiritual element that manifests anew in every human being who is born? Is this educational service not a religious service in the highest sense of the word? Is it not so that all the holiest stirrings of humanity, which we dedicate to religious feeling, must come together in our service at the altar when we attempt to cultivate the divine spiritual aspect of the human being whose potentials are revealed in the growing child?

Science that comes alive!
Art that comes alive!
Religion that comes alive!

---

of science, art, and religion. This will be developed further in volume 2. It is important to note that Steiner held a spiritual-scientific view that transcends religious creeds, sects, and denominations to include ethical individualism and moral enthusiasm, goodness, and deeds. For more about this, see *Intuitive Thinking as a Spiritual Path: A Philosophy of Freedom.*

In the end, that is what education is.[20]

Part 3: FREEDOM TO TEACH, FREEDOM TO LEARN

The rising generation of children and the necessity for a free spiritual-cultural life

Modern government education reforms based on computer technology rely on several factors: data on past student performances, specific learning goals and standards for school-age children, and algorithms that connect the two. Thus, what is most worth knowing and doing in life is largely predetermined, all of which perpetuates and imposes the existing power structure and mindset of the adult generation on the rising generation.[21] In contrast, Waldorf education strives to liberate the latent capacities of each rising generation regardless of cultural or economic background, thereby allowing the maximum degree of renewing forces to continually flow into society from each new generation.

> *The real present need is for schools to be totally grounded in a free spiritual and cultural life. What should be taught and cultivated in schools must be drawn solely from a knowledge of the growing human being and of individual capacities. A genuine anthropology must form the basis of education and instruction. The question should not be: What does a human being need to know and be able to do for the social order that now exists? but rather: What capacities are latent in this human being, and what lies within that can be developed? Then it will be possible to bring*

---

20 Rudolf Steiner, *Rudolf Steiner in the Waldorf School*, address of 9/7/1919.

21 For more information on how U.S. federal and state reform measures were developed since the early 1980s and how the National Business Roundtable successfully promoted nine essential components in U.S. education reform (1995), which included using technology to raise teacher and student productivity and expand the learning process, see Gary Lamb, *The Social Mission of Waldorf Education*. These efforts have gone way beyond using computers simply as an information resource and for skills practices, especially since online learning has significantly expanded during the current global Covid-19 pandemic. In all cases, one of the most harmful aspects of computers in education is when they replace children's direct experience with the world and their teachers.

ever new forces into the social order from the rising generations. The life of the social order will be what is made of it by a succession of fully developed human beings who take their places in the social order. The rising generation should not be molded into what the existing social order chooses to make of it.[22]

Children are entrusted to us for their education. If our thinking in regard to education is based on spiritual science, we do not view a child as something to be developed toward some human ideal of society, or some such thing; a human ideal can be completely abstract. Such a human ideal has already assumed as many forms as there are political parties, societies, and other interests. Human ideals change according to one's adherence to liberalism, conservatism, or some other program, and thus children are gradually taken in some particular direction to become whatever is considered proper....

An abstract image of the human being, toward which children are to be led, is an idol; it has no reality.[23]

Selflessness of the teacher and a respect for individual freedom enable self-education to take place

The true task of education is to create the conditions that enable students to educate themselves in freedom. All true education is in essence self-education. Therefore, the goal of an educator is not to mold students to predetermined images. Nor is education meant to simply shape children according to the wants and needs of political, economic (including the technology industry), or cultural interest groups. All children bring capacities and intentions from the heavenly world from which they have descended.

Teachers must be able to educate not only pupils of their own capacity, but also those who, with their exceptional brightness, will far outshine them.

---

22 Rudolf Steiner, *The Renewal of the Social Organism*, "The Threefold Social Order and Educational Freedom."

23 Rudolf Steiner, *Human Values in Education*, lect. 7/17/1924.

However, teachers will be able to do this only if they get out of the habit of hoping to make their pupils into what they themselves are. If they can make a firm resolve to stand in the school as selflessly as possible, to obliterate not only their own sympathies and antipathies but also their personal ambitions, in order to dedicate themselves to whatever comes from the students, then they will properly educate potential geniuses as well as the less-bright pupils. Only such an attitude will lead to the realization that all education is, fundamentally, a matter of self-education.

Essentially, there is no education other than self-education, whatever the level may be. This is recognized in its full depth within anthroposophy, which has conscious knowledge through spiritual investigation of repeated Earth lives. Every education is self-education, and as teachers we can only provide the environment for children's self-education. We have to provide the most favorable conditions where, through our agency, children can educate themselves according to their own destinies.[24]

The removal of obstacles and the respect for freedom

Steiner outlined the most important task of the teachers in the first Waldorf School as creating the optimal circumstances for children to develop their full potential in freedom. One way for educators to do this is to identify and remove obstacles or hindrances within the being and surroundings of the child. Children have an innate capacity to learn and will do so if obstacles to learning are removed by their teachers.

In the Waldorf School, [the intention is that] everything is directed toward education in freedom. A person's inmost spiritual element remains essentially undisturbed by the Waldorf School.... A child's spiritual individuality is something completely sacred, and those with a genuine experience of human nature know that it will follow, of its own accord, the influences exerted on it by everything round about. The teacher thus has to set aside what can hinder this tenderly protected individuality in its development. The hindrances, which can result from

---

24   Rudolf Steiner, *The Child's Changing Consciousness*, lect. 4/20/1923.

the physical, the mental and even the spiritual sphere, can be discerned by a genuine knowledge of the human being, if it is developed on the pedagogic and psychological sides. And when we do evolve such a knowledge, we develop a fine sense for any impediment to the free development of individuality.... When we see that there is an impediment we must set aside, we set it aside. The individual will know how to develop through his own power, and his talents may then go far beyond what the teacher possesses.

Here is true respect for human freedom! This freedom is what enables human beings to find within themselves the impulses that lead and drive him in life.[25]

Each child in every age brings something new into the world from divine regions, and it is our task as educators to remove the bodily and soul obstacles, so that the child's spirit may enter with full freedom into life.[26]

Gratitude and the respect for freedom

It is not only important that educators love the children entrusted into their care and guidance, but they need to have a love for the profession of teaching.

There are three golden rules for the art of education: developing gratitude for the children, gratitude for what we do with the children, and respect for the freedom of each child.

*In a Waldorf school, **who** the teachers are is far more important than any technical ability they may have acquired intellectually.*[27] *It is important that teachers not only love the children, but also love the whole procedure they use. It is not enough for teachers to love the children; they must also love teaching, and love it with*

---

25 Rudolf Steiner, *The Tension between East and West*, lect. 6/7/1922.

26 Rudolf Steiner, *The Spiritual Ground of Education*, lect. 8/19/1922.

27 This does not imply that teachers do not need to work hard to master knowledge of the world. It does imply that all the intellectual knowledge in the world can't make up for a lack of love for the students and the profession of teaching.

objectivity. This constitutes the spiritual foundation of spiritual, moral, and physical education....

These must become the three golden rules in the art of education; they must imbue the whole attitude of teachers and the whole impulse of their work. The golden rules that must be embraced by a teacher's whole being, not as theory, are these: first, reverent gratitude toward the world for the child we contemplate every day, for every child presents a problem given us by divine worlds; second, gratitude to the universe and love for what we have to do with a child; and third, respect for the child's freedom, which we must not endanger, since it is this freedom to which we must direct our teaching efforts, so that the child may one day stand at our side in freedom in the world.[28]

Part 4: UNDERSTANDING THE NATURE OF THE HUMAN BEING, THE THREE STAGES OF CHILDHOOD, AND THEIR RELATION TO SOCIAL LIFE

The fourfold human being

In order to raise and educate children in a manner that enables them to develop the capacities they will especially need to meet the challenges of a technology-based society, teachers will need to understand the spiritual nature of the human being and the related phases of child development.

Spiritual science refers to three members of the human being beyond what is physically visible. In addition to the physical body, which is subject to the laws of the mineral world, there is also an etheric or life body, which we have in common with the plant and animal worlds; a sentient or astral body, which we have in common with animals; and an "I," the vehicle for our individuality, which is unique to each human being. As will be explained further, the ideal of Waldorf education is

---

28   Rudolf Steiner, *The Spiritual Ground of Education*, lect. 8/19/1922.

to understand and work with all these members in the appropriate way and at the appropriate time in the child's development.

> *If we want to perceive the nature of the evolving human being, we must begin by considering hidden human nature as such. What sense observation learns to know in human beings, and what the materialistic concept of life would consider as the only element in human beings, is for spiritual investigation only one part, one member of human nature: that is, the physical body. This human physical body is subject to the same laws of physical existence and is built up of the same substances and forces as the world as a whole, which is commonly referred to as lifeless. Spiritual science, therefore, designates that humankind has a physical body in common with all of the mineral kingdom. And it designates as the* physical body *only what, in human beings, are those substances that mix, combine, form, and dissolve through the same laws that also work in the substances within the mineral world.*
>
> *Now beyond the physical body spiritual science recognizes a second essential principle in the human being. It is the* life body, or etheric body....
>
> *For those who have developed the higher organs of perception, the etheric or life body is an object of perception and not merely an intellectual deduction.*
>
> *Human beings have this etheric or life body in common with plants and animals. The life body works in a formative way on the substances and forces of the physical body and thus brings about the phenomena of growth, reproduction, and inner movement of vital body fluids. It is therefore the builder and shaper of the physical body, its inhabitant and architect. The physical body may even be spoken of as an image or expression of the life body. In human beings the two are nearly—although by no means totally—equal in form and size. However, in animals, and even more so in the plants, the etheric body is very different in both form and extension from the physical.*
>
> *The third member of the human body is called the* sentient or astral *body. It is the vehicle of pain and pleasure, of impulse, craving, passion, and so on—all of which are absent in a creature*

that consists of only the physical and etheric bodies. These things may all be included in the term sentient feeling, *or* sensation. ...

Humankind, *therefore, has a sentient body in common with the animal kingdom only, and this sentient body is the vehicle of sensation or of sentient life.* ...

Human beings *also possess a fourth member of their being, and this fourth member is shared with no other earthly crea-ture.*[29] *It is the vehicle of the human "I." The little word I—as used, for example, in the English language—is a name essentially different from any other name. To anyone who ponders rightly on the nature of this name, an approach to the perception of true human nature is opened up immediately. All other names can be applied equally by everyone to what they designate. Everyone can call a table "table," and everyone can call a chair "chair," but this is not true of the name "I." No one can use this name to designate another. Every human being can only call themselves "I." The name "I" can never reach my ear as a description of myself.* ...

From what has been said, it is clear that we may speak of four members of human nature: the physical body, *the* etheric or life body, *the* astral *or* sentient body, *and the* "I" body. ...

The educator works on these four members of the human being. Therefore, if we want to work in the right way, we must investigate the nature of these parts of human beings. One must not imagine that they develop uniformly in human beings, so that at any given point in life—the moment of birth, for exam-ple—they are all equally developed; this is not the situation. Their development occurs differently in the different ages of a person's life. The correct foundation for education and for teach-ing involves a knowledge of these laws of development of human nature.[30]

Imitation, authority, and love in relation to the first three phases in human life and a healthy threefold social organism

29 Elsewhere Rudolf Steiner speaks of a group "I" for each species of animal.

30 Rudolf Steiner, *The Education of the Child*, essay from the journal *Lucifer–Gnosis*, 1907.

The way we educate children and the experiences they have during the three seven-year cycles up to the age of twenty-one will have profound implications not only for the individual child in the future but also for the whole of society.

A strong, healthy experience of imitation up to the time of the change of teeth transforms itself within the child into an experience of freedom in adulthood. The experience of being surrounded by positive role models who a child can look up to and trust leads to a clear sense of rights later in life, and if a loving interest in humanity and the world in general is developed after puberty, it develops into a sense of fellowship so necessary for the future development of economic life.

> *In the future, we must attend to the fact that the [young] child's behavior is imitative. In raising children, we need to continually keep in mind how we can best create the most favorable environment for their imitative behavior.... People will need to remind themselves that if children are to grow up to meet the needs of the social organism, they must be free. People become free only if they were intensively imitative as children....*
>
> *You also know that from the age of seven until puberty, that is, until the age of fourteen or fifteen, children have a strength we could call "acting upon authority." Children experience a great uplifting if they can do everything because a person they look up to [adult role models] says it is the right thing to do. There is nothing worse for children than attempting to develop their judgment too early, before puberty.... We must, with increasing consciousness, direct all upbringing and education during these years toward awakening in children a pure and beautiful feeling toward authority....[31] What we implant during these years will form the basis for what adults within the social organism experience as equal rights for their fellow human beings. A feeling for equal rights for other human beings cannot exist in adults if a feeling for authority is not implanted in them during childhood.*

31   Authority in the sense meant here is a natural response, not an outer compulsion, when children look up to and receive guidance from an adult or adults whom they respect and trust.

Otherwise, adults will never become mature enough to recognize the rights of others....

After puberty, from the age of fourteen to twenty-one, more than sexually oriented love develops in people. That form of love is only a special form of a general love of humanity. The strength that arises from a general love of humanity needs particular care at the time when children leave elementary school and go on either to higher education or into an apprenticeship....

The kind of fraternity we must strive for in future economic life can exist in human souls only if we form education after the age of fifteen so that we work completely consciously toward a general love of humanity ... or, more generally speaking, a love of the external world.

We must base what should bloom within future humanity upon these three aspects of education....

These things are completely interwoven, and thus I must say: imitation in the proper manner develops freedom; authority, justice; and fraternity or love, economic life.

However, the reverse is also true. If we do not develop love in the proper manner, freedom is missing, and if we do not develop imitation properly, then animalistic urges prevail.[32]

Part 5: FROM BIRTH TO THE CHANGE OF TEETH AROUND SEVEN YEARS OF AGE

Early childhood: Imitation and forming the physical body

From birth to the change of teeth (around seven years old) all the physical organs are developing to a greater degree than at any other time in life. The physical and emotional environment of the child is an important factor in this development. Children strongly imitate what they perceive and sense in their physical environment. This process works inwardly in the permanent shaping of the physical organs. The physical environment includes everything the child senses, including

---

32   Rudolf Steiner, *Education as a Force for Social Change*, lect. 8/9/1919.

both moral and immoral actions. Moral admonitions do not affect a child as strongly as what they see, hear, and feel, and consequently imitate. Love and warmth provide the ideal environment for a young child. Most importantly, educators and parents need to surround the young child with activities that are worthy of imitation and guard them from things that are not. These are important guiding thoughts when considering to what degree and under what conditions young children can be safely exposed to and use technology, especially screen devices.[33]

> Before the change of teeth in the seventh year, the human body has to accomplish a task on itself that is essentially different from the tasks of any other period of life. In this period the physical organs must form themselves into definite shapes; their whole structural nature must receive particular tendencies and directions. Growth takes place in later periods as well; but throughout the whole succeeding life growth is based on the forces developed in this first life-period.... Just as nature causes the proper environment for the physical human body before birth, so after birth the educator must provide for the proper physical environment. The right physical environment works on the child in such a way that the physical organs correctly shape themselves.
>
> Two "magic" words indicate how children enter into relationship with their environment. These words are imitation and example.... Children imitate what happens in their physical environment, and in this process of imitation their physical organs are cast into forms that become permanent. "Physical environment" must, however, be understood in the widest sense imaginable. It includes not just what happens around children in the material sense, but everything that occurs in their environment, everything that can be perceived by their senses, that can work on the inner powers of children from the surrounding physical space. This includes all moral or immoral actions, all wise or foolish actions that children see.

---

33 Helpful resources on the latest research on the effects of screen devices on young children are the Research Institute for Waldorf Education (waldorfresearchinstitute.org) and

It is not moralistic talk or wise admonitions that influence children in this sense, but it is, rather, what adults do visibly before their eyes....

[Young] children, however, do not learn by instruction or admonition, but through imitation. The physical organs shape themselves through the influence of the physical environment. Good sight will be developed in children if their environment has the proper conditions of light and color, while in the brain and blood circulation the physical foundations will be laid for a healthy moral sense if children see moral actions in their environment....

The joy of children in and with their environment must therefore be counted among the forces that build and shape the physical organs. They need teachers that look and act with happiness and, most of all, with honest, unaffected love....

The children who live in such an atmosphere of love and warmth, and who have around them truly good examples to imitate, are living in their proper element. One should thus strictly guard against anything being done in the children's presence that they should not imitate.[34]

The young child as a sense organ

A young child can be viewed as a complete sense organ, perceiving not only physical phenomena but also soul-spiritual phenomena, including our soul attitude. As educators and parents, we need to keep in mind that the most important factor in a child's education and upbringing is the environment in which the child is immersed. The child lives in and absorbs the surrounding environment. Thus, the impact of screen devices and social media in modern life is a crucial issue for teachers and parents.[35]

Fair Play (fairplayforkids.org).

34 Rudolf Steiner, *The Education of the Child*, lect. 1/10/1907.

35 This includes the way children observe how and why adults use such technology. Are they using self-control or yielding to external stimuli? Are the adults using technology as a substitute babysitter or child pacifier that replaces opportunities for the child to experience the real world and real people with videos and virtual people?

Because children have very subtle organs of sensory perception, they are receptive not only to surrounding physical influences, but also to moral influences, particularly those of thoughts. As odd as this may seem to materialistic thinking today, children perceive what we think when we are around them. As parents or teachers, when we are around young children it is important not only to avoid acting in ways that we should not in front of children, but we should also be inwardly true and moral in our thinking, which children can sense. Children form their being not just according to our words and actions, but also according to our attitudes, thoughts, and feelings. During this first period of childhood, before the age of seven, the most important thing for education is a child's environment.[36]

The child is like a sense organ. The surrounding impressions ripple, echo, and sound through the whole organism because the child is not so inwardly bound up with its body as is the case in later life but lives in the environment with its freer spiritual and soul nature. Hence the child is receptive to all the impressions coming from the environment.

We need to become more aware of how anything acting as a stimulus in the environment continues to vibrate in the child....

Whether in perception, feeling, or thought, whatever we do around children must be done in such a way that it may be allowed to continue vibrating in their souls.[37]

Processing sensations through play

When children play, they are imitating what they have taken in from their environment. Imitating what they have observed and taken in is a liberating experience for them, which gives them joy if they are imitating something worthwhile.

[We] know that children are playing when they copy. Fundamentally, the playful instinct is not completely original, but an imitation of the things the child sees in its environment. If we are

---

36 Rudolf Steiner, *A Modern Art of Education*, lect. 8/10/1923.
37 Rudolf Steiner, *The Essentials of Education*, lect. 4/9/1924.

sufficiently objective, we become aware of the fact that play is completely rooted in imitation.[38]

All children play. They do so naturally.... The child's play is connected with an inner force of liberation, endowing the playing child with a feeling of wellbeing and happiness. You need only observe children at play. It is inconceivable that they are not in full inner accord with what they are doing. Why not? Because playing is a liberating experience to children, making them eager to release this activity from the organism. Freeing, joyful, and eager to be released, this is the character of the child's play.[39]

Play and the higher being of the child

The higher self of a child can be observed when it is engaged in focused play. Play is true self-education on the part of the child. The child learns through doing things and observing how the outer world responds to its willed actions. It learns through direct involvement with the world by testing things out, which requires that adults give as much free rein as possible to the child.[40]

Where do we find [the] higher self, active as a higher entity belonging to the child but not entering his awareness? It may sound strange, but we find this active in the child in absorbed, focused play. In the child at play we can only create the context, the conditions for education to happen. What is achieved through play is basically achieved through the child's own activity, through all that we cannot harness within strict rules. That is the key thing about play, its educational value: that our rules cease here, our pedagogical and educational arts, and we leave the child to its own powers.... In play he uses outer objects to see if something

---

38 Rudolf Steiner, "Teaching and Practical Life Questions from the Point of View of Anthroposophical Spiritual Science," lect. 2/24/1921; in *Education, Teaching, and Practical Life*.

39 Rudolf Steiner, *Waldorf Education and Anthroposophy 2*, lect. 3/25/1923.

40 This direct experience of the natural world lays the broadest and most healthy foundation for both practical and theoretical thinking later in life, whereas computer games take place in a limited, virtual world with simplistic rules unlike actual life experiences.

works through his own activity. He activates his own will, brings it into movement. And through the way in which external things behave in response to his will, the child educates itself quite differently from an education undertaken by another person or in line with his pedagogical principles. He educates himself directly through life, albeit only playfully. This is why it is so important that we refrain as far as possible from bringing logic and intellect to bear upon the child's play.... The less predetermined and conceptually designed play is, the better it will be. And this is because a higher element cannot be forced into human awareness, but only enters as the child tries out and tests things in a living context, non-intellectually.[41]

Toys, imagination, and brain development

Young children live in an imaginative world. Playing and pretending with appropriate toys helps them to develop their own world of inner pictures. In so doing they engage and strengthen their will powers and ability to maintain equanimity in the face of diverse circumstances. Beautiful, perfectly formed dolls provide little to stimulate the imagination.[42]

Imitation should not curtail imagination. Children have to live in an imaginative world; they should be occupied by playing and pretending and thus develop their own forces in creating their own world of inner pictures. And a "beautiful" doll will not activate this inner force. Children's play is done in imitation of

---

41 Rudolf Steiner, *Good Health: Self-education and the Secret of Wellbeing*, lect. 3/14/1912.

42 This section requires an answer to the question: What effect does screen technology, in particular social media and entertainment, have on the young child's ability to self-produce living inner pictures or imaginations? Certainly, there is a threefold problem. One is that there is no stimulation for children to create their own pictures because vivid, technologically formed pictures are already presented on a screen. Another is that young children will naturally imitate the images that they see on screens, images that are often unworthy of imitation and difficult for parents to monitor, limit, or prohibit. And finally, it is common knowledge that much of social media and screen-based entertainment are purposely designed to monopolize attention or instill obsessions, if not addictions, in viewers, and especially in children.

what they hear and see; playing demands exercise of will. This awakens certain energies, and two things will be fostered: dexterity and the ability to maintain equanimity in the face of a great diversity of circumstances.[43]

The work of creating imaginations in a young child helps to form the brain. A simple doll made from a cloth napkin calls on the imagination of the child, which, in turn, stimulates brain development, whereas a life-like pretty doll does not stimulate the child's imagination, and hence does nothing positive for brain development but leads to atrophy instead.[44]

As the muscles of the hands grow firm and strong through doing the work for which they are suited, so the brain and other organs of the physical body of human beings are guided into the correct course of development if they receive the proper impressions from their environment. An example will best illustrate this point. You can make a doll for a child by folding up an old napkin, making two corners into legs, the other two corners into arms, a knot for the head, and painting eyes, nose and mouth with spots of ink. Or you can buy the child what is called a "pretty" doll, with real hair and painted cheeks.... If the children have the folded napkin before them, they have to fill in from their own imagination what is necessary to make it real and human. This work of the imagination shapes and builds the forms of the brain. The brain unfolds as the muscles of the hand unfold when they do the work they are suited for. By giving the child the so-called "pretty" doll, the brain has nothing more to do. Instead of unfolding, it becomes stunted and dried up.[45]

Between the ages of two-and-a-half and five, the desire to play is an outer expression of a child's power of fantasy. Providing children with

---

43 Rudolf Steiner, "Questions on Education" in *On the Play of the Child*, lect. 3/3/1906.

44 Research on screen time and brain development can be found at the website of the "Research Institute for Waldorf Education" (https://www.waldorfresearchinstitute .org/research-brain-development).

45 Rudolf Steiner, *The Education of the Child*, lect. 1/10/1907.

appropriate toys is most important at this time in life. Building blocks or bricks and erector sets at this age accentuate intellectual capacities, which lead to a materialistic mentality and encourage atomistic thinking, forcing the imaginative powers into rigid forms. The main criterion for determining the appropriateness for games or toys for children in early childhood is the degree to which they allow the imagination to be active.

> Whatever one's attitude may be, as educators we must respond to the imagination and fantasy of children, which tries to express itself outwardly when they play with toys or join in games with other children. The urge to play between the ages of two-and-a-half and five is really just the externalized activity of a child's power of fantasy.... The most important thing now is to meet their inborn urge to play with the right toys. People in the past responded to this need according to their own particular understanding.
>
> Perhaps this also happened in the West, but at one time a regular epidemic spread throughout Central Europe of giving children boxes of building bricks, especially at Christmas. From separate cubic and quadrilateral stones, children were expected to build miniature architectural monstrosities. This sort of thing has a far-reaching effect on the development of imagination in children, since it leads to an atomistic, materialistic attitude—a mentality that always wants to put bits and pieces together to form a whole. In dealing with practical life, it is far better to give full freedom to children's flexible and living powers of imagination than to nurture intellectual capacities that, in turn, encourage the atomistic nature of modern thinking. Imagination in children represents the very forces that have just liberated themselves from performing similar creative work within the physical formation of the brain. This is why we must avoid, as much as possible, forcing these powers of imagination into rigid, finished forms.[46]

---

46 Rudolf Steiner, *Soul Economy*, lect. 12/29/1921.

I would also like to point out that the main thing one has to assess in games is to what degree the imagination of the child is allowed to be active.[47]

Discipline and the imitation of adults

Imitation can be put to good use in certain instances of discipline. If, for example, adults want to deny the wish of a child to do something that should not be done, then they should deny themselves the same or similar activity in such a way that the child is aware of it. This is obviously an important example of how adults need to approach disciplining children in relation to the use of screen devices.

> *[If parents or teachers]... deny a wish of a child that the child could otherwise do, they are apt to awaken the child's antipathy.... What, then, is to be done? The answer is for the person guiding the child or pupil to deny himself or herself the wish in such a way that the child becomes aware of the denial. There is a strong imitative impulse at work here in the child, especially during the first seven years, and it will soon become evident that the child will follow the example of its elders and, consequently, deny itself such wishes. What is thereby achieved is of untold importance.*[48]

Play and its relation to health and illness and meeting one's destiny in later years

It is important for educators and parents to know that there is a connection between how children play during the early childhood years, the development of their physical organism, and their state of health in old age, particularly regarding digestion and blood circulation. This is an important consideration when determining when it is appropriate for children to play with and use complex forms of toys and technology.

---

47 Rudolf Steiner, *On the Play of the Child*, lect. 12/29/1920 (answer to a question).
48 Rudolf Steiner, "Overcoming Nervousness" (Spring Valley, NY, Anthroposophic Press, 1969), lect. 1/11/1912.

> *It is necessary ... that teachers see precisely all that takes place*
> *when a small child plays. Play involves a whole constellation of*
> *soul activities: joy, sometimes pain, sympathy, antipathy, and*
> *especially curiosity and a desire for knowledge. Children want*
> *to investigate the objects they play with and see what they are*
> *made of. When we observe this free and entirely spontaneous*
> *expression of soul—still unconstrained into any form of work—*
> *we must look at the shades of feeling and whether it is satisfying.*
> *When we guide children's play toward contentment, we improve*
> *their health by promoting an activity that is indirectly connected*
> *with the digestive system. And the way a person's play is guided*
> *during childhood can determine whether a person's blood circu-*
> *lation and digestive system become congested with old age. There*
> *is a delicate connection between the way a child plays and the*
> *growth and development of the physical organism.*[49]

How children play in early childhood also has an effect on how they
meet their destiny in their mid-to-late twenties.

> *And howsoever the child plays in the fourth, fifth, or sixth year,*
> *all this then sinks as a force into the deeper layers of the soul.*
> *The child becomes older, we do not notice at first how one or*
> *another typical way of playing reappears in the child's later*
> *character traits. The child develops other forces, other capacities;*
> *the unique quality of his play, as it were, slips into the hidden*
> *recesses of the soul. But it reappears later, and actually reappears*
> *in unique ways, between the ages of twenty-five to thirty, at the*
> *time of life when the person needs to find his/her way in the world*
> *of external experience, eternal destinies. One person approaches*
> *it nimbly, another awkwardly. One person tackles the world in*
> *such a way as to gain some satisfaction from dealings with the*
> *world; another person doesn't manage to find any point at which*
> *to engage his own activity and has a difficult destiny.*
>
> *We need to acquaint ourselves with the life of the whole per-*
> *son; we must see how, in hidden ways, the sense of play reappears*
> *in the twenties in the form of the sense of life. This way, we will*

---

49 Rudolf Steiner, *The Spiritual Ground of Education*, lect. 8/24/1922.

gain an artistically shaped idea of how to guide and channel the playful instinct so as to give the person the wherewithal for a later stage in life.[50]

Gratitude, love, truthfulness, and piety

Feelings of gratitude in young children are important for both their soul and physiological development. Gratitude will arise naturally in them through imitation if it already lives in the adults around them. The feeling of gratitude in the young child engenders the first delicate feelings of the love of God and becomes a foundation for the development of a religious attitude and piety later in life.

> *Gratitude is something that must already flow into the human being when the growth forces, working in the child in an inward direction, are liveliest, when they are at the peak of their shaping and molding activities.... Gratitude will develop very spontaneously during the first period of life, as long as the child is treated properly. All that flows with devotion and love from a child's inner being toward whatever comes from the periphery through the parents or other educators, and everything expressed outwardly in the child's imitation, will be permeated with a natural mood of gratitude. We only have to act in ways that are worthy of the child's gratitude and it will flow toward us, especially during the first period of life. This gratitude then develops further by flowing into the forces of growth that make the limbs grow, and that alter even the chemical composition of the blood and other bodily fluids. This gratitude lives in the physical body and must dwell in it since it would not otherwise be anchored deeply enough.*
>
> *It would be very incorrect to remind children constantly to be thankful for whatever comes from their surroundings. On the contrary, an atmosphere of gratitude should grow naturally in children through merely witnessing the gratitude that their elders feel as they receive what is freely given by their fellow human beings and in how they express their gratitude. In this*

---

50   Rudolf Steiner, *Education, Teaching, and Practical Life*, lect. 2/24/1921.

situation, one would also cultivate the habit of feeling grateful by allowing the child to imitate what is done in the surroundings. If a child says "thank you" very naturally—not in response to the urging of others, but simply by imitation—something has been done that will greatly benefit the child's whole life. Out of this an all-embracing gratitude will develop toward the whole world....

This universal mood of gratitude is the basis for a truly religious attitude; for it is not always recognized that this universal sense of gratitude, provided it takes hold of the whole human being during the first period of life, will engender something even further. In human life, love flows into everything if only the proper conditions present themselves for development. The possibility of a more intense experience of love, reaching the physical level, is given only during the second period of life between the change of teeth and puberty. But that first tender love, so deeply embodied in the inner being of the child, not as yet working outward, this tender blossom will become firmly rooted through the development of gratitude. Love, born out of the experience of gratitude during the first period of the child's life, is the love of God.... The love of God will develop out of universal gratitude, as the blossom develops from the root....

If, during the first period of life, we create an atmosphere of gratitude around children... then out of this gratitude toward the world, toward the entire universe, and also out of an inner thankfulness for being in this world at all (which is something that should ensoul all people), the most deep-seated and warmest piety will grow. Not the kind that lives on one's lips, or in thought only, but piety that will pervade the entire human being, that will be upright, honest, and true.[51]

---

51   Rudolf Steiner, *The Child's Changing Consciousness*, lect. 4/20/1923.

Part 6: LOWER SCHOOL, GRADES 1–8: ART, MORALITY, TECHNOLOGY, ANALYSIS AND SYNTHESIS, PRACTICALITY, COURAGE

Goodness and evil, morality and religion

The development of morality in children in the lower school years also takes place through the feeling life of the child. Taking pleasure in goodness and acts of goodness, and displeasure or antipathy regarding immorality and wickedness are important educational experiences. Imposing morality on the child through dogmatic commands or intellectualizing at this age are inappropriate. Developing a healthy relation to inner morality and a sense of good and evil will take on ever greater importance as modern life becomes increasingly pervaded by social media, gaming devices, and virtual reality technologies.

Children must never feel a separation between spirit and body. The moral and religious elements thus truly come to life in their feelings. The important thing to keep in mind is that, between the change of teeth and puberty, we must never indoctrinate morality and religion into children dogmatically, but by working on their feeling and perception according to this period of life. Children must learn to delight in goodness and to loathe evil, to love goodness and hate wickedness. In history lessons, the great historical figures and the impulses of various eras can be presented so that moral and religious sympathies and antipathies develop in the children. Thus we achieve something of supreme importance....

If we begin by telling children that they should do this or not do that, it stays with them throughout their life, and they will always think that such things are right or wrong. Convention will color everything. But those who have been educated properly will not stand within convention but use their own judgment, even regarding morality and religion, and this will develop naturally if it has not been engaged prematurely....

There is no better heritage in the moral and religious sense than to raise children to regard the elements of morality and religion as an integral part of their being, so that they feel fully human because they are permeated with morality and warmed by religious feelings.

This can be achieved only when we work, at the proper age, only on the life of feeling and perception, and do not prematurely give the children intellectual concepts of religion and morality. If we do this before twelve to fourteen, we bring them up to be skeptics—men and women who later develop skepticism instead of healthy insight into the dogmas instilled in them—and not just skepticism in their thinking (the least important), but in feeling, which injures their feeling life. And, finally, there will be skepticism of volition, which brings moral error with it. The point is that our children will become skeptics if we present moral and religious ideals to them dogmatically; such ideals should come to them only through the life of feeling. Then, at the right age, they will awaken their own free religious and moral sense, which becomes part of their very being. They feel that only this can make them fully human. The real aim at Waldorf schools is to raise free human beings who can direct their own lives.[52]

Physiology, art, and morality

After the change of teeth, the rhythmic system (breathing and blood circulation, for example) becomes dominant. Art is an activity that has a strong effect on it, and everything that is taught must be done in an artistic manner. It is also a time to encourage moral development, which is the most important aspect of education. The best way to do this during the lower school years is by presenting real-life examples of moral actions and people rather than making commands and abstract judgments of what is good and bad. This can be done through aiding the children in developing an aesthetic sense for what is right and wrong through feelings of sympathy and antipathy, like and dislike for good and evil.

In children after the change of teeth around the seventh year, we find that the nervous system no longer dominates; it has become

---

52   Rudolf Steiner, *A Modern Art of Education*, lect. 8/17/1923.

more separate and is turned more toward the outer world. In these children, until puberty, it is the rhythmic system that dominates and takes the upper hand. It is most important to keep this in mind during elementary school, when we have children between the change of teeth and puberty. Hence, we must see that it is essential to work with the rhythmic system, and that anything affecting the other systems is wrong. But what affects the rhythmic system? It is affected by art—anything conveyed in an artistic form....

Before our teaching can become truly educational, we must know that everything children are taught throughout this period must be conveyed artistically. According to Waldorf principles, the first consideration in the elementary school means composing all lessons in a way that appeals to the rhythmic system of children....

If we now turn to the moral aspect, we must find the best way to encourage children to develop moral impulses. Here we are concerned with the most important of all educational issues. We do not endow children with moral impulses by giving them commands, saying that they must do this or that, or such and such is good.... We must not force moral judgment on children; we merely lay the foundation so that, when children awaken at puberty, they can form their own moral judgments by observing life.

The least effective way to attain this is by giving children finite commands. Rather, we work through examples or by presenting images to their imagination—say, through biographies or descriptions of good or bad people; or by inventing circumstances that present a picture of goodness to their mind. Because the rhythmic system is especially active in children during this period, pleasure and displeasure can arise in them, but not judgment of good and evil. They can experience sympathy with what is good in an image, or a feeling of antipathy toward the evil seen in an image. It is not a matter of appealing to children's intellect by saying, "Thou shalt...." or "Thou shalt not...." It is rather a matter of nurturing aesthetic judgment, so that children begin to feel pleasure and sympathy when they see goodness and feel dislike and antipathy when they see evil.... Working through imagery, we must train them to take an esthetic pleasure in goodness and feel an esthetic dislike of evil. Otherwise, when children do awake after puberty, they will experience an inward bondage—perhaps not consciously, but throughout life they will lack the important experience of moral discernment awakening and developing within. Abstract moral instruction will not accomplish this awakening; it must be prepared by working correctly in this way in children.[53]

Experiencing beauty and understanding how technology works

Engaging in art and the appreciation of beauty are important preparations for understanding how technological devices work and for doing practical work in life.

We really have to ask ourselves whether there is any possibility of encouraging children between their second dentition and puberty [grades 1–8] to become more practical and skillful. And if we look at life as it really is—guided by life and not by abstract ideas or theorizing—we find that the answer is to bring children as close as possible to beauty. The more we lead them to appreciate beauty, the better prepared they will be at the time of puberty to tackle practical tasks without being harmed for the rest of their lives. Our students will not be able to safely understand the workings of conveyances or railroad engines unless an aesthetic appreciation of painting or sculpture was cultivated at the right age. This is a fact that teachers should keep in mind. Beauty, however, needs to be seen as part of life, not separate and complete in itself. In this sense, our civilization must still learn a great deal, especially in the field of education.[54]

Learning practical craftwork and chemical and mechanical processes used in technology

It is important for children in the lower school to experience and understand basic chemical and mechanical processes used in technology. They should do so by reproducing them on a small scale with their own hands. Also, it is important for students to engage in practical craft

---

53 Rudolf Steiner, *The Spiritual Ground of Education*, lect. 8/19/1922.
54 Rudolf Steiner, *Soul Economy*, lect. 1/5/1922.

work. The mental discipline and feelings involved in making crafts is key to becoming a full human being.

> Knowledge of the human being calls on us to make adequate provision in our curricula and schedules for preparing pupils for the practical side of life....
>
> They should be taught not only mechanics and chemistry, but also how to understand at least simple examples of mechanical and chemical processes used in technology. They should reproduce these on a small scale with their own hands so they will know how various articles are manufactured. This change of direction toward the more practical side of life must certainly be made possible....
>
> I would consider it a sin against human nature if we did not include bookbinding and box making in our Waldorf school craft lessons, if it were not introduced into the curriculum at a particular age determined by insight into the students' development. These things are all part of becoming a full human being. The important thing in this case is not that a pupil makes a particular cardboard box or binds a book, but that the students have gone through the necessary discipline to make such items, and that they have experienced the inherent feelings and thought processes that go with them.[55]

Augmenting material utility with the love of beauty

It is important in the modern age that children not only are guided in their actions by utility but also by the love of beauty and artistry. Children even from the poorest backgrounds should be surrounded by artistic beauty.[56]

> Our actions should not be guided only by utility but by our pure delight in what is beautiful. Everything created by human beings to satisfy their artistic needs, in pure love of beauty, will also assume life in the future and contribute to their higher evolution.

---

[55] Ibid., lect. 4/21/1923.

[56] In volume 2, we will learn more about the necessity that technology in the future not only be useful but artistically beautiful as well.

> *It is terrible to see today how many thousands of human beings are forced, from earliest childhood on, to engage only in activities founded upon material utility; they are cut off all their lives from everything that is beautiful and artistic. In the poorest primary school, there should hang the finest works of art; that would be an endless blessing for human evolution. The human being is today building his future.*[57]

Music and courage

Singing and playing music are important aspects of the education of children in the lower school. Among other things, they are preventive measures that help remove obstacles from the development of will forces that are imbued with courage, an essential attribute that certainly will be needed to persevere through the social disruption and personal challenges that are and will be part of future technology development.

> *Right from the beginning in the first grade, all lessons are permeated by a musical element according to various ages and stages.*
>
> *I have already indicated (with unavoidable briefness, unfortunately) how our pupils are being directed into artistic activities—into singing, music-making, modeling, and so on. It is absolutely necessary to nurture these activities. Simply through practicing them with the children, one will come to realize exactly what it means for their entire lives to be properly guided musically during these younger years, from the change of teeth through the ninth and twelfth years until puberty. Proper introduction to the musical element is fundamental for a human being to overcome any hindrance that impedes, later in life, a sound development of a will permeated with courage. . . .*
>
> *One learns to recognize that we have an extremely sensitive and refined musical instrument in the raying out of the nerves from the spinal marrow, from the entire system of the spinal cord. One also learns to see how this delicate instrument dries up and hardens, whereby, inwardly, the human being can no longer properly develop qualities of courage if musical instruction*

---

57   Rudolf Steiner, *Guidance in Esoteric Training*, lect. 1/16/1908.

and the general musical education do not work harmoniously with this wonderfully fine musical instrument. What constitutes a truly delicate and unique musical instrument is coming into being through the mutual interplay between the organs of the nerves and senses with their functions, on the one hand, and on the other hand, the human motor functions with their close affinities to the digestive rhythms and those of sleeping and waking.[58]

Using analytical activities to counter materialism

One of the reasons why materialism is so prevalent in our times is because the innate desire to analyze things by children has not been met between the change of teeth and puberty when it is most appropriate. In a Waldorf school, this need to analyze is met, for instance, through its method of learning to read and to do arithmetic by proceeding from the whole to the parts.[59]

Why have people in our age developed such an inclination for atomism? Because they have developed insufficient analytical activities in children. If we were to develop in children those analytical activities that begin with unified word pictures and then analyze them into letters, the child would be able to activate its capacity to analyze at the age when it first wants to do so; it would not have to do so later by inventing atomic structures and so forth.[60] *Materialism is encouraged by a failure to satisfy our desire for analysis. If we satisfied the impulse to analyze in a way that I have described here, we would certainly keep people from sympathizing with the materialistic worldview.*

For this reason, in the Waldorf school we always teach beginning not with letters, but with complete sentences. We analyze the sentence into words and the words into letters and then the letters into vowels. In this way we come to a proper inner understanding as the child grasps the meaning of what a sentence or

58 Rudolf Steiner, *The Child's Changing Consciousness*, lect. 4/22/1923.

59 It is important for educators to distinguish between objective analysis and biased criticism.

60 See note 4.

word is. We awaken the child's consciousness by analyzing sentences and words.

In our Waldorf school it is very pleasing to see the efforts the children make when they take a complete word and try to find out how it sounds, how we pronounce it, what is in the middle, and so forth, and in that way go on to the individual letters. When we atomize or analyze in this way, children will certainly not have any inclination toward materialism or atomism such as everyone does today, because modern people have been taught only synthetic thinking in school and thus their need to be analytical, their need to separate, can only develop in their worldviews.[61]

When children enter class one, they are certainly ready to learn how to calculate with simple numbers. And when we introduce arithmetic, here, too, we must carefully meet the inner needs of children. These needs spring from the same realm of rhythm and measure and from a sensitive apprehension of the harmony inherent in the world of number. However, if we begin with what I would call the "additive approach," teaching children to count, again we fail to understand the nature of children. Of course, they must learn to count, but additive counting as such is not in harmony with the inner needs of children.

It is only because of our civilization that we gradually began to approach numbers through synthesis, by combining them. Today we have the concept of a unit, or oneness. Then we have a second unit, a third, and so on, and when we count, we mentally place one unit next to the other and add them up. But, by nature, children do not experience numbers this way; human evolution did not develop according to this principle. True, all counting began with a unit, the number one. But, originally, the second unit, number two, was not an outer repetition of the first unit but was felt to be contained within the first unit. Number one was the origin of number two, the two units of which were concealed within the original number. The same number one, when divided into three parts, gave number three, three units that were felt to be part of the one. Translated into contemporary terms, when

---

61   Rudolf Steiner, *The Renewal of Education*, lect. 5/5/1920.

reaching the concept of two, one did not leave the limits of num-
ber one but experienced an inner progression within number one.
Twoness was inherent in oneness. Also three, four, and all other
numbers were felt to be part of the all-comprising first unit, and
all numbers were experienced as organic members arising from it.

Because of its musical, rhythmic nature, children experi-
ence the world of number in a similar way. Therefore, instead
of beginning with addition in a rather pedantic way, it would be
better to call on a child and offer some apples or any other suit-
able objects. Instead of offering, say, three apples, then four more,
and finally another two, and asking the child to add them all
together, we begin by offering a whole pile of apples, or whatever
is convenient. This would begin the whole operation. Then one
calls on two more children and says to the first, "Here you have a
pile of apples. Give some to the other two children and keep some
for yourself, but each of you must end up with the same number
of apples." In this way you help children comprehend the idea
of sharing by three. We begin with the total amount and lead
to the principle of division. Following this method, children will
respond and comprehend this process naturally. According to our
picture of the human being, and in order to attune ourselves to
the children's nature, we do not begin by adding but by dividing
and subtracting. Then, retracing our steps and reversing the first
two processes, we are led to multiplication and addition. Moving
from the whole to the part, we follow the original experience of
number, which was one of analyzing, or division, and not the
contemporary method of synthesizing, or putting things together
by adding.[62]

Whole-being learning

Modern education tends to focus on intellectual or head learning.
This will only increase as computer use becomes more prevalent in
instruction and learning. Waldorf education strives to enable children

---

62   Rudolf Steiner, *Soul Economy*, lect. 12/31/1921.

to learn with their whole being and to transform what they think into action in a balanced and healthy way.

It is interesting to observe children when they learn something about the human organism—for example, the sculptural formation of skeleton or muscle formation. If they are given an artistic concept of the structure and functions of the human body, they begin to express, in a sculptural way, their ideas of the shape of some limb, not in a strict sense of imitation, but freely and creatively. Our children are allowed great freedom, even in their practical work, and they are allowed to follow their own sense of discovery. Their souls create wonderful forms once they learn to observe certain things in people or in animals with a truly artistic feeling for nature.

*We teach this way, so that whatever children know, they know it with their whole being. Our culture is calculated to make us know everything with our heads. Facts rest in the head as though sitting on a couch; they rest in the head as though in bed; they are asleep, "meaning" only one thing or another. We carry them around, stored up in so many little compartments, which we otherwise prefer to leave alone. In the Waldorf school, the children do not merely "have an idea" in their heads; they feel the idea, since it flows into their whole life of feeling. Their souls live in the **sense** of the idea, which is not merely a concept but becomes a shaped form. The whole complex of ideas eventually becomes the human form, and finally passes into their volition. Children learn to transform what they think into action. When this happens, we do not find thoughts arising in any one part of the human being, with the will in another part nourished only by instinct.*[63]

Becoming fully human through harmonizing thinking, feeling, and willing

Learning with one's whole being as just mentioned can be achieved through developing and harmonizing thinking, feeling, and willing.

---

63 Rudolf Steiner, *A Modern Art of Education*, lect. 8/17/1923.

An example of this is how children are taught about plants and animals. Out of the proper cultivation of the feeling life for the whole world, the cultivation of thinking can be developed through plant studies, and the will can be strengthened through learning about animals. The primary purpose of education is to develop the whole human being through such strengthening and harmonizing of these three soul forces: thinking, feeling, and willing.

> *When we teach about plants, we work toward the proper cultivation of intelligence, and we cultivate volition by teaching about animals. In this way, we help children of nine to twelve relate to these other creatures of the earth, so that, through proper intelligence and self-confident will, they may find their way properly through the world.*
>
> *Above all, in education we must see that human beings develop in relation to both intelligence and volition. Out of feeling, which we have cultivated in children of seven to nine-and-a-half, we develop intelligence and a strong will. Thinking, feeling, and volition are thus harmonized instead of being developed in the usual unnatural way. Everything is rooted in feeling. We must begin with the feelings of children. From their feeling in relation to the world, we cultivate thinking through an understanding of plants, because the life of the plants never allows dead concepts. Out of feeling, we also develop the will by leading children to what connects them properly with the animal world, while raising children above them.*
>
> *Thus, we work to nurture the appropriate intelligence and a strong volition in human beings. This is in fact our primary purpose in education, because only this can make children fully human, and such development is the goal of all education.*[64]

---

64   Ibid., lect. 8/13/1923.

Part 7: HIGH SCHOOL YEARS: CONNECTING ALL KNOWLEDGE TO PRACTICAL LIFE, MAKING SENSE OF LIFE EVERMORE PERVADED BY TECHNOLOGY

Preparing for high school: Understanding how things work

Prior to puberty, it is appropriate and necessary to focus on the relation of the human being to nature. With the approach of puberty, however, it becomes important for teenagers to learn about inventions and how machines work, and not just use them with indifference. To take no interest in such things leads to an antisocial attitude. In contrast, if students do take an interest in technology, it will help them find their place in society.

> *Consider how many people there are today who get into a train without the faintest idea of how it operates or what makes it move.... It is the beginning of an antisocial life simply to accept inventions of the human mind without at least understanding them in a general way.... Human beings open up to the world at puberty. Previously, children lived more internally, but now they are ready to understand other people and the world's phenomena. So, we act according to the principles of human development when, before children reach puberty, we concentrate on all that relates the human to nature. But, at the age of fourteen or fifteen, we must focus our energy on connecting children with the inventions of the human mind. This helps them understand and find their place in society.*[65]

All learning needs to be connected to practical life

Everything a child learns in the high school years should be presented in such a way that it can be seen in its connection to the practical aspects of life. It is essential that children learn about the human-made world in which they live and the contrivances that they use. One way

---

65 Ibid., lect. 8/15/1923.

this can be done is by learning about various industries and the manu-facturing processes that take place in them.

> *Imagine even how many people see a steam engine rushing by without having any clue as to the workings of physics and mechanics that propel it. Consider what position such ignorance puts us in with regard to our relationship with our environment, that very environment we use for our convenience....*
>
> *The very worst thing is to experience and live in a world made by human beings without bothering ourselves about this world.*
>
> *We can work against these things only by starting during the last stage of the lower school. We must really not let the fifteen- and sixteen-year-olds leave school without at least elementary ideas about the more important processes taking place in life....*
>
> *It is entirely beneficial for children between the ages of thir-teen and sixteen to be given... condensed descriptions of differ-ent branches of industry. It would be very good if during these years they were to keep a notebook in which to record [various processes of manufacturing]....*
>
> *Every single thing children learn during the course of their schooling should in the end be presented so broadly that threads may everywhere be found linking it with practical human life. Very, very many things that are now antisocial in the world would be made social if we could at least touch upon an insight into matters that later need not have any direct bearing on our own work in life.*[66]

Necessity of knowing how technology works

The failure to learn how various technologies are made and operate is a form of soul imprisonment that cuts people off from nature and a sense of freedom.

> *To use modern technology with no knowledge of how things work or how they were made is like being a prisoner in a cell without windows through which one could at least look out into nature and to freedom.*

---

66   Rudolf Steiner, *Practical Advice to Teachers*, lect. 9/3/1919.

Educators need to be fully aware of this. When adolescents experience differentiation between the sexes, the time is ripe for understanding other differentiations in modern life as well.... We must try to familiarize our students with the ways of today's civilization so they can make sense of it. Even before the age of puberty, teachers must prepare the chemistry and physics lessons so that, after the onset of puberty, they can build on what has been given and then extend it as a basis for understanding the practical areas of life.[67]

---

67   Rudolf Steiner, *Soul Economy*, lect. 1/5/1922.

Ahriman's Pervasive Influence in the Age of Modern Technology

How to Meet Its Challenge

The true nature... of the human being is essentially the effort to hold the balance between the powers of Lucifer and Ahriman; the Christ impulse helps contemporary humanity to establish this equilibrium. (note 27)

We have to be clear that a realistic view of the structure of the cosmos requires us to recognize the role that the number three plays in it. We must acknowledge the opposing roles of luciferic and ahrimanic powers, while recognizing that the role of divine beings consists in holding a balance between the two. (note 57)

EIGHT

Ahriman's Pervasive Influence in the Age of Modern Technology

How to Meet Its Challenge

Introduction

This chapter refers to three spiritual beings whom Rudolf Steiner indicated are involved with Earth and human evolution: Lucifer, Christ, and Ahriman. The focus will be mainly on Ahriman, the being who is strongly associated with electricity, modern technology, and the materialistic worldview that underlies the development and application of both.

Rudolf Steiner makes an important contribution to the understanding of evil in this chapter. He reveals that there is not just one adversarial being and form of evil but two that human beings need to contend with: Ahriman and Lucifer. These are not beings who simply work together toward a common goal. Rather, they both have their own objectives and following in the spiritual world. Of the two beings, it is Ahriman who is dominant in our current age, with Lucifer playing a supporting role.

Christ is the spiritual being who is devoted to helping human beings meet the challenge of both forms of evil manifested by Ahriman and Lucifer that threaten human and Earth evolution.[1]

---

1 The mission of the Christ, the being who is committed to aiding humanity throughout Earth evolution, will be featured more extensively in volume 2. In addition, Ahriman's specific influence and strivings in relation to secret societies, those who have died, and technology development will be explored further in volume 2.

Chapter overview

Both Lucifer and Ahriman oppose the divine powers who care for Earth evolution, foremost of which is the Christ. However, these two oppositional beings do so for different reasons and in different ways.

Lucifer is interested in enticing human beings into forsaking the divine powers and abandoning life on the Earth altogether. In doing so, he inspires people to become visionaries whose thoughts are disconnected from reality.

In contrast, Ahriman encourages cold, intellectual thinking and seeks ways to bind people to the earth, in part by encouraging them to be endlessly busy with mundane matters. Ahriman's purpose is to make the Earth his own dominion. Ahriman can be characterized as the lying spirit, a promulgator of falsehoods and half-truths, while Lucifer is known as the great tempter who appeals to and inflames a person's passions, desires, and egotism.

It is important to understand that opposition between certain spiritual beings is a legitimate means for cosmic evolution to take place, but the accompanying strife and hostility should not extend into the physical world.

Luciferic and ahrimanic powers collaborate with one another even though they have different goals for human evolution. Even so, one of them is more dominant than the other during a given time period, with the other playing a supporting, albeit self-serving, role. Since the Renaissance in the 1400s, Ahriman has been the dominant adversarial spirit. He has been active in spreading materialism and fostering intellectual thinking for the advancement of modern industrial life.

Just as Lucifer incarnated in a physical body in China in the third millennium BC, and Christ was incarnated in the Middle East, Ahriman is preparing for his incarnation in the West in the early part of the third millennium AD. His goal is to further his efforts to wrest control of Earth evolution from the divine powers. It would be a great benefit to Ahriman if he could incarnate completely unnoticed.

It is imperative that human beings become ever more aware of the trends and influences in outer life that Ahriman is using to prepare for his incarnation. It is startling to consider how prevalent these trends and influences are now in the early part of the twenty-first century.

Some of these trends and influences in human relations and earthly events are:

Lying and deceitfulness.
Prejudices of all kinds, and using them to instigate conflicts among races, religions, and peoples.
Racism, nationalism, and corrupted patriotism.
Obsession with personal and group power and domination.
Perpetual strife and warfare.
Rulers who are dominated by economic thinking and moneyed interests.
Fear and anxiety.
Reliance on abstract thinking and statistics instead of lived experiences.
Giving priority to material over spiritual needs of the human being.
A restricted interpretation of the Gospels instead of an expansive interpretation based on an understanding of spiritual science.
A despiritualized, mechanical view of the cosmos.
Domination and polarization of political parties in government.
Opposition to individual and cultural freedom and to the threefold social organism.

For humanity to come to a right relationship to both Lucifer and Ahriman, human beings need to think in terms of a triad consisting of Lucifer, Christ, and Ahriman rather than dualities, such as God and the devil. One of Rudolf Steiner's most important artistic creations is the large wooden sculpture, "Representative of Humanity," on display at the Goetheanum in Dornach, Switzerland, which portrays the Christ maintaining a state of balance between the beings of Lucifer and Ahriman.

Another helpful image of the appropriate relations among all three of them is a balance beam with luciferic forces on one side and ahrimanic forces on the other. The beam represents human life, and the fulcrum, which retains a balance between the two opposing forces, represents the Christ force or a human being imbued with the Christ force. Indeed, one of the primary tasks in life is to understand how the luciferic and ahrimanic powers are at play and how they can be brought into balance with the aid of the Christ.

There are also ways people can prepare to fend off the influences of either Ahriman or Lucifer more directly than employing the counterbalancing measures just described. For instance, by developing moral attributes such as modesty and humility we can keep the temptations of Lucifer at bay. Similarly, developing self-directed, wholesome thinking in earthly life, especially with the help of spiritual science, helps to defend oneself against the cold, abstract views and cleverness of Ahriman. Through such measures we also have the possibility to redeem both Lucifer and Ahriman.

Part 1: CHARACTERISTICS AND INFLUENCES OF AHRIMAN AND LUCIFER

Characteristics of Lucifer and Ahriman

Both Lucifer and Ahriman want human beings to oppose the divine powers that are responsible for human and Earth evolution, but in quite different ways. Lucifer encourages human beings to emancipate themselves, to reject earthly life and flee to another realm. In contrast, Ahriman wants to influence and dominate people in such a way that they become bound to the Earth, forever under his control.

We may contemplate luciferic beings in terms of the kind of interest they take in cosmic existence. We find that their chief interest lies in making the world, particularly the human world, unfaithful to the spiritual beings whom we must regard as the true creators of humanity. Their one desire is to make the world

281

disloyal to these divine beings. They are not interested in claiming the world for themselves.... Their aim is rather to make human beings forsake their divine creator-beings—they wish to free the world from the beings felt by humankind to be the real divinities.

The ahrimanic beings have a different interest. Their firm intention is to get the human kingdom and thereby the earth along with it into their sphere of power, to make human beings dependent on them, to control humanity. Whereas luciferic beings strive, and have always striven, to alienate us from the beings whom we feel to be our gods, ahrimanic beings seek to draw humanity and everything connected with it into their power.

In other words, luciferic beings striving for universal freedom, and ahrimanic beings striving for lasting dominion.... The world we live in is permeated by luciferic and ahrimanic beings, and as we have described it there is a tremendous contrast between the emancipating tendency of the luciferic beings and the power-seeking tendency of the ahrimanic beings.[2]

Lucifer inspires human beings to be visionaries living in an inner world of fantasy with little inclination to be active in the world, while Ahriman instills human beings with a dry intellect, a materialistic view of life, and the desire to mechanize everything. Rather than inducing people to inaction like Lucifer, Ahriman prefers people to be as busy as possible, but in predictable and fixed ways.

The luciferic beings want to hold human beings back from any action at all, and make them into dreamers, mystics, who in course of time would have no more use for earth existence and could therefore be removed from it. The ahrimanic beings want to keep human beings bound forever to earth existence. This is why they want to mechanize everything, i.e., press things down into the mineral kingdom. By doing this they would transform the earth in their way and not allow it to continue into the Jupiter existence [a future stage of earth evolution]. They do not have

2   Rudolf Steiner, *The Incarnation of Ahriman*, lect. 11/21/1919.

the desire to rob human beings of action; perhaps they want to leave them to be as busily active as they possibly can, as long as it is all done in a routine and stereotyped way.[3]

Let us for the moment focus on the outermost aspects of these luciferic and ahrimanic beings, who also dwell in the spheres that human beings occupy. We may say that we picture the outward characteristics of **luciferic** *beings properly when we imagine that they possess such forces as we human beings manifest when we become visionaries, when we abandon ourselves one-sidedly to fantasy, let ourselves be carried away, and, speaking metaphorically, lose our heads. In other words, whenever we tend to go out beyond our heads, we are dealing with forces that, while they play a certain role in our organism, actually belong cosmically to the beings we term luciferic. If we imagine beings who are wholly formed of that tendency in us that strives to go out beyond our heads, we are picturing the luciferic beings who are related to our human world in certain ways.*

Now, in contrast, think of everything that presses us down upon the earth, that makes us dull and philistine, leading us to develop materialistic attitudes, penetrating us with a dry intellect, and so on: there you have a picture of ahrimanic powers.[4]

Soul influences of Lucifer and Ahriman on the human being

Ahriman's influence on human thinking and intelligence is one of coldness and rigidity, while being fixated on material existence. In contrast, Lucifer promotes a disdain for the material world and a mystical desire to rise above it.

We find the ahrimanic influence at work in everything that drives the soul toward purely intellectual rigid laws. Our natural science today is almost totally ahrimanic. As we develop toward ahrimanic soul elements, we discard anything that might fill our concepts and ideas with warmth. We submit only to whatever makes concepts and ideas ice-cold and dry as dust....

---

3   Rudolf Steiner, *Guardian Angels*, lect. 10/23/1921.
4   Rudolf Steiner, *The Incarnation of Ahriman*, lect. 11/21/1919.

The luciferic influence in the human soul is found in everything that makes us desire to fly upward out of ourselves. This can create nebulous, mystical attitudes which lead us to regions where any thought of the material world seems ignoble and inferior. Thus, we are led astray, misled into despising material existence entirely and into wanting instead to indulge in whatever lies above the material world, into wanting wings on which to soar above earthly existence, at least in our soul.[5]

Part 2: COMPREHENDING AND MEETING
THE CHALLENGES OF AHRIMAN AND LUCIFER

Appropriate attitude regarding Lucifer and Ahriman

Sometimes people are confused as to what attitude is best to take regarding Lucifer and Ahriman. It is important to know that even though Lucifer and Ahriman do not belong to the physical world, they have important spiritual tasks to perform from outside the physical world in relation to human evolution. Conflicts arise when they become active in the physical realm and misappropriate functions not assigned to them.

It is easy to understand the human feeling that leads a person to ask: "What is the right attitude to adopt toward Lucifer and Ahriman; am I to love them or to hate them? I really don't know what to do about them." How does all this come about? It should be quite clear from the way in which one speaks of Lucifer and Ahriman that they are beings who by their whole nature do not belong to the physical plane but have their mission and task in the cosmos outside the physical plane, in the spiritual worlds.... The progressive gods have assigned to Lucifer and Ahriman roles in the spiritual world; and that discrepancy and disharmony appear only when they bring down their activities

---

5   Rudolf Steiner, *Old and New Methods of Initiation*, lect. 1/1/1922.

into the physical plane and arrogate to themselves rights which are not allotted to them.[6]

Opposition and hostility in the spiritual realm

Human beings need to understand and appreciate the fact that opposition to the intentions of the divine gods and hostility in the spiritual worlds are legitimate means for the universe to evolve and progress. This is not true, however, for life in the physical world. It is wrong for spiritual beings such as Lucifer or Ahriman to work within human souls in such a way as to induce strife on earth.

> *If we say, "one power is hostile to another," then on the physical plane it is quite right to say, "enmity is improper, it ought not to exist." But the same thing does not hold good for the higher planes. There, judgment must be widened. Just as in the realm of electricity, positive and negative electricity are necessary, so is spiritual hostility necessary in order that the universe may exist in its entirety; it is necessary that the spirits should oppose one another. Here is the truth in the saying of Heraclitus, that strife as well as love constitute the universe. It is only when Lucifer works upon the human soul, and when through the human soul strife is brought into the physical world, that strife is wrong. But this does not hold good for the higher worlds; there, the hostility of the spirits is an element that belongs to the whole structure, the whole evolution, of the universe. This implies that as soon as we come into the higher worlds, we must adopt other standards, other colorings for our judgments. That is why there is often a feeling of shock when we speak of Lucifer and Ahriman on the one hand as the opponents of the gods, and on the other hand as being necessary for the whole course of the cosmic order. Hence, we must, above all things, hold firmly in our minds that a man comes into collision with the cosmic order if he allows a judgment which holds good for the physical plane to hold good for the higher worlds also.*[7]

------

6   Rudolf Steiner, *Christ and the Human Soul*, lect. 7/15/1914.
7   Ibid.

Forces that work above and below the life of the soul

In our current age, it is important for human beings to not only comprehend forces that work within human existence but also those that work below and above human soul life. As we become more aware of the challenges that Lucifer and Ahriman place before humanity, we should not simply avoid them. That would only ensure their success. Human beings can achieve individual freedom only if they have the potential to think incorrect thoughts and make errors. One example of this is succumbing to the belief that prosperity is equivalent to the good.

> We must endeavor to understand how real and concrete forces work in human existence, and what is at work beneath and above the conscious life of soul in the culture of the fifth post-Atlantean epoch. If you recognize this leitmotif you will be able to understand many things. Only you must not give way to the delusion that everything luciferic and everything ahrimanic must for these reasons be avoided. That would be the very way to succumb to these forces! Everyone who lives together with humanity must realize that Lucifer and Ahriman have been granted their places in the world. If errors could not take place, the human being would never reach inner freedom; freedom could never come to man if he were incapable of forming the erroneous conception that prosperity and the good are identical; he would then have no opportunity of rising above this error.[8]

Part 3: LIES AND TEMPTATIONS, EFFECTS VS. FACTS

Ahriman as the lying spirit and Lucifer as the tempting spirit

Ahriman can be described as the lying spirit, just as Lucifer can be call the "tempter." They both have a legitimate function in the spiritual world. From there, Ahriman was permitted to insert himself in the realm where the human being attempts to correctly harmonize ideas

---

8   Rudolf Steiner, *Inner Impulses of Evolution*, lect. 9/24/1916.

with facts. However, Ahriman corrupts this activity as much as possible, which results in falsehood and lies.

In modern life, we must be prepared to meet the challenge of ahrimanic influences at every moment. This is not an easy task because he is with us so closely in earthly life that we often fail to recognize him and his influence in our lives. More will be said about ahrimanic trends and influences later in this chapter.

> *Ahriman is the "Lying Spirit," in contrast to Lucifer who is the "Tempter." This, then, is how they may be described: Lucifer, the Tempter; Ahriman, the Lying Spirit.*
>
> *Much exists in the world for the express purpose of guarding mankind from temptation by Lucifer: rules of conduct, maxims, moral precepts, instituted customs, and so forth. But there is less to help man to protect himself in the right way from falling prey to the ahrimanic impulse—namely, untruthfulness.*
>
> *All that is luciferic in man has to do with the emotions, the passions. On the other hand, the ahrimanic influence which asserts itself in human evolution has to do with lying, with untruthfulness. And in our age man must be armed not only against the attacks of Lucifer. It is high time for him to forge his armor against the attacks of Ahriman....*
>
> *The facts and objects are around us and we make images of them in our conceptions and ideas. The agreement of the images in our thought with the facts or objects or events, we then call physical truth.*[9]

If Ahriman never accessed the realm between ideas and reality, the human being would automatically think and express ideas that were in total harmony with physical reality, which is the opposite of freedom of thought and choice.

> *When we speak of physical truth, this implies that our conceptions fit the facts of the physical plane. In order that this*

---

9   Rudolf Steiner, *Memory and Habit: The Sense for Truth, the Phenomena of Metamorphosis in Life* (London, Anthroposophic Publishing, 1948), CW 170, lect. 8/26/1916.

truth-relationship may arise, it is absolutely necessary to live in a physical body and perceive things in the outer world through the physical body.... It is only because we live in a physical body that this agreement between ideas and external facts can arise at all. But here Ahriman's field of action is opened up for him. In what sense is it thus opened up before him?

*From what has been said we can perceive the interplay between the spiritual and the physical world. Ahriman has his own good task in the spiritual world and must, furthermore, send forces from there into the physical world. But **he** must not enter the physical world! The fact that this realm is denied him makes it possible for ideas we acquire in the physical body to fit the facts in the outer world.... He should, if I may be allowed to use the expression, "keep his fingers off" the realm in which man makes his ideas harmonize with the outside facts. But this is precisely what Ahriman does not do. If he did, there would be no lying in the world!...*

But whenever there is lying, it is a proof that Ahriman is at work in the physical world in an unjustified way. This particular activity of Ahriman in the world is something which man has to overcome....

Why, then, has Ahriman been allowed access to the physical world!... If he were not there we should be like innocent lambs, for the impulse would continually be never to form concepts which did not tally with the facts. We should only express what we actually observed as fact—but we should do this of necessity. It would be impossible for us to do anything else and there would be no question of free spiritual activity. In order to be able to speak the truth as free beings.... We must acquire the power to conquer Ahriman within us at every moment. Ahriman must be there "enticing, working, creating, as the devil." Ahriman must be there, but the trouble is that men follow him so closely and do not recognize him as the devil who entices, works, and creates, and who must be overcome.[10]

---

10 Rudolf Steiner, *Memory and Habit*, lect. 8/26/1916.

Ahriman's focus on effects instead of facts and truth

Ahriman is totally indifferent to whether expressed thoughts and ideas are in accordance with facts and reality, or whether they are simply lies. He is only concerned with the effects of his communications on people.[11]

> *This unbiased relationship to truth, where we strive for truth as the accordance of idea with objective reality, is beyond Ahriman's ken. He neither knows nor is concerned with it. Ahriman's position in the universe makes it entirely a matter of indifference to him whether, in the forming of a concept, this concept agrees with reality. In everything which Ahriman conceives as truth (in the human sense, of course, one would not call it "truth") he is concerned only with* effects. *What is said is said not because it fits the facts, but in order to produce an effect. This or that is said in order that some particular effect may be produced....*
>
> *I am sure you realize that these things actually happen: that a man may think out some scheme, be utterly indifferent as to whether his ideas are in accordance with objective reality or not, and then make use of them in such a way that they will have a certain effect upon those who listen to him....*[12]
>
> *We find, therefore, that Ahriman is never concerned as to whether an idea fits the facts* but only with the *effects produced.*[13]

Luciferic influences:
Disconnection between thoughts and reality, and crippled will forces

Lucifer also does not concern himself with correct relations between thoughts and reality. However, he comes from a quite different perspective than Ahriman. While Ahriman is focused on the effects of what is communicated, Lucifer's focus is on a premature expansion

---

11   This is a common phenomenon found among U.S. national politicians that can be greatly amplified when using modern social media.

12   The trait of speaking for effect, stirring up instinctual or prejudicial feelings rather than imparting factual truth, is an all-too-common characteristic of U.S. politicians and media outlets.

13   Rudolf Steiner, *Memory and Habit*, lect. 8/28/1916.

of consciousness and the attainment of inner visions that are disconnected from reality.[14]

> [As with] Ahriman, Lucifer is never concerned with the agree-
> ment of an idea with actuality. Lucifer is out to cultivate such
> ideas as will generate in man the highest possible degree of con-
> sciousness. Understand me well: I mean by that, cultivation of
> the most enhanced consciousness, of the widest possible expan-
> sion of consciousness. This expanded consciousness in which
> Lucifer is interested is associated with a certain inner volup-
> tuousness in man.... Prematurely to induce consciousness in
> man, that is to say, to call forth consciousness whereas under
> proper conditions this particular degree of consciousness should
> unfold at another period of time—this is the aim of Lucifer. Luci-
> fer does not want the attention of men to be directed altogether to
> externalities. He would like everything that works into the con-
> sciousness to work from within. Hence all visionary life—which
> is, as it were, an exudation of forces in the inner organs—is of a
> luciferic nature....
>
> It is therefore correct to say that both Ahriman and Lucifer
> are equally unconcerned as to whether ideas agree with actuality.
> Ahriman is concerned with the effects of what is said, Lucifer's
> aim is to bring about an enhanced consciousness in man of what,
> in a particular situation, should really not become conscious.[15]

A premature and overly enhanced consciousness inspired by Lucifer not only creates a disconnection between thoughts and reality, but it
also cripples the human will to take decisive actions.

> The luciferic angel beings... have every interest in actually hold-
> ing human beings back from being active. They would like to keep
> [actions]... at the level of inner soul life. Human beings have
> become personalities. But these angel beings want to prevent

---

14 The yearning to enter prematurely into a state of expanded consciousness
that is disconnected from reality is often intensified by substance abuse, including
hallucinogens.
15 Rudolf Steiner, Memory and Habit, lect. 8/28/1916.

human beings from performing the kind of deeds in which their will impulses really come to manifestation as an experience. They would like to hold them in inner contemplation. They seduce them into mysticism and into false theosophy. They mislead them into leading a life merely of inner contemplation instead of being active. They make them into dreamers who would like nothing better than to sit all day long and think irrelevant thoughts about all manner of puzzling world mysteries, but who do not want to bring what is in their minds into outer reality.[16]

Part 4: AHRIMAN AND LUCIFER AS COLLABORATORS, OPPONENTS, AND ALTERNATING POWERS

Ahriman and the rise of post-Renaissance mechanics and technology

Up to the Renaissance in the fifteenth and sixteenth centuries, Lucifer was the dominant influence in European cultural life. Since the Renaissance, Ahriman has become the dominant force. He has been instrumental in turning human intellectual life from contemplations and activities of the soul to the creation of machinery, either in the form of industrial technology or machinery of the state.

Ahriman has his finger in the construction of things of a mechanical and technological nature, of everything that works in the direction of pulling the intellect away from the human level and pushing it into machines, either mechanical instruments or the machinery of the state. This is essentially the only reason why those things have arisen, particularly since the time of the Renaissance, and are now living among modern humanity. We are tempted to say: During the time of the Renaissance luciferic activity came to a kind of impasse; ahrimanic activity then started up on the other side of the blockage. And we see [what] has been taking place since the Renaissance; the pull toward

---

16   Rudolf Steiner, *Guardian Angels*, lect. 10/23/1921.

mechanization, toward science without spirit; all this bears the hallmark of Ahriman.[17]

Ahriman…has a hand in everything to do with the kind of science that deals only with the surface of things and does not penetrate through to the spirit, and in every aspect of human action that entails mere mechanization.[18]

Common mission, differing goals:
The anger of Lucifer and the pain of Ahriman

Luciferic beings are continually trying to prevent human beings from finding happiness on the earth by luring them to a realm of inner experiences that disengages them from the world. Luciferic beings experience profound anger when humans go about life connected to the earth. In contrast, ahrimanic beings experience great pain because they are not able to take on human form and stand on the earth. The only thing that can subdue this pain is if they can take control of a human being's intellect. Consequently, they try to merge with human beings and take hold of their intellect, while shunning anything to do with higher forms of spiritual cognition.

The human soul is a battleground between warring luciferic and ahrimanic powers.

We could say that the luciferic beings are beings of anger who ensoul human beings, but with the intention of preventing them from finding happiness on earth and are forever trying to pull them away from it so as to raise them constantly on to a super-human level. They would far rather have them as angels who do not get embroiled in the lower functions of the physical organism.

The luciferic beings feel a terrible fury toward humans who go about the world on two legs and are bound to the earth through their lower functions; they would like to strip them of everything of an animal nature, and now, for instance, in the present period of human existence, they are reluctant to let them descend again

17 Ibid.
18 Ibid.

into physical incarnation but would like to keep them back in the life between death and rebirth.

In contrast to these beings, we could call the other ones ahrimanic, beings of pain. For they are actually trying to acquire human form but cannot achieve it. Fundamentally speaking it is a terrible pain these ahrimanic beings suffer. It is as though an animal were dimly to feel that it ought to stand upright and ought to be human. They feel the pain completely tearing them to pieces. The ahrimanic beings actually feel this terrible pain. It can be alleviated only if they approach human beings and take hold of the intellect. The intellect cools this pain down. Therefore, they are obsessed by the human intellect and hold on to it with tooth and claw. Ahrimanic beings fill themselves as it were with human intellect until it hurts. They want to merge with human beings to become intellectual beings themselves.

So, the human being is the scene of conflict between the luciferic and the ahrimanic beings. The truth of it is that the luciferic beings have a hand in everything that is artistic or of an abstract theological nature, whereas with the ahrimanic beings it is as though they were rising up out of the material world and having passed through the animal kingdom were reaching out with painful longing to the human condition. They want to grasp hold of the intellect, but they are repelled by the supersensible part of the human being. They recoil from it every time, but they would like to take the intellect with them. These are beings who are trying ever and again to enter human beings and keep them at the level of the intellect, not letting them rise to imagination or inspiration [higher, more spiritual forms of cognition] because they want to keep hold of them to relieve their agony.

All that has taken shape in humanity since the beginning of this recent ahrimanic period, particularly in the way of materialistic science, of a science that stems from what is going on in human beings in the way of this cooling down of the pain of material existence, is of an ahrimanic nature. We actually see this materialistic science arising. Human beings are working on it, and in that they do so, Ahriman connects himself, within them, with this science.[19]

Collaboration:
Unconscious eating of food and preservation of knowledge

Even though Lucifer and Ahriman oppose each other in many ways, they find ways to collaborate. It is more a question of which one is the dominant force at any given time. Lucifer's influence is diminishing as we approach Ahriman's incarnation. Even so, Ahriman and Lucifer have made an agreement regarding the consumption of food and the preservation of abstract knowledge. Lucifer is given jurisdiction over people's stomachs, meaning that what they take in through the stomach in a dulled state of consciousness instilled by Ahriman, with no spiritual awareness, serves as nourishment for Lucifer's entourage. Ahriman, on the other hand, lays claim to knowledge in the form of theses or dissertations not based on real human experience and preserved in libraries, created with little or no interest or enthusiasm, and hardly ever read.

> *Ahriman and Lucifer will always work hand-in-glove with each other. It is only a question of which of them gains the upper hand in human consciousness at any time. A strongly luciferic culture held sway until sometime after the Mystery of Golgotha, from the incarnation of Lucifer in China in the third millennium BC onward. From this incarnation a particularly strong influence was exerted until the early Christian centuries and has still gone on working in our own era.*
>
> *But now the signs and traces of Lucifer are growing fainter since an incarnation of Ahriman is approaching in the third millennium, and the signs of Ahriman are becoming particularly discernible in things such as those I have described.*
>
> *You can say that Ahriman has signed a contract with Lucifer, the words of which can be put as follows: "I, Ahriman, consider it especially beneficial for me to claim use of the canned preserves,*

---

19   Rudolf Steiner, *Guardian Angels*, lect. 10/23/1921.

leaving people's stomachs to you. This latter on the condition that you will allow me to keep their stomachs—that is, human awareness of their stomachs—in a dulled and twilight state."

What I mean by this is that the people I referred to as soul and spirit devourers remain unaware of the stomach, and what they introduce into their stomachs they lead directly into the luciferic stream unless they bear spirituality in their human nature. What they have eaten and drunk without spirituality goes straight through the stomach to Lucifer!

And what do I mean by the canned preserves? I mean libraries and suchlike, which store academic knowledge undertaken without true interest; knowledge that does not live in people but in books in a library. Look at these academic pursuits, these disciplines that are undertaken without reference to human experience. There are huge numbers of books in libraries everywhere. Whenever a student must write a scholarly thesis or a doctorate, these are sent off to as many libraries as possible. But quite apart from this, people write, and write, and write nowadays, and only a very little of what is written is read. Only when people must prepare themselves in some way for something do they resort to the library shelves and in turn quote whatever they find there, what is preserved there. These "preserved cans of wisdom" are highly beneficial to Ahriman and further his preparations.[20]

Material substance devoured unspiritually means that the spirit slides off on an erroneous path. It is hard to say such things to people today. But try to really grasp for a moment how much of modern culture must be characterized once one knows this fact. And maintaining the human being in this kind of soul- and spirit-devouring state is one of Ahriman's impulses to support and prepare his coming incarnation.[21]

20   Rudolf Steiner, *Understanding Society*, 11/1/1919.
21   Ibid.

From envy to falsehood and egotism:
Further collaboration between Lucifer and Ahriman

Lucifer and Ahriman inhabit and work through different parts of the human soul. Ahriman lives in the etheric or life-force body, and Lucifer in the astral body or the realm of feelings.[22]

When Lucifer has an opportunity to instill envy into people's astral bodies, there is a natural soul reaction to dispel it. He then seeks help from Ahriman, who clouds a person's thinking and inspires false judgments of other people. If, in turn, these falsehoods are innately rejected or restrained, then Ahriman goes back to Lucifer for help, and Lucifer responds within the astral body by riling up profound egotism.

> Lucifer and Ahriman live in human nature. Ahriman lives in the etheric body and Lucifer in the astral body of human beings.
>
> Lucifer is a power that tempts the human soul by drawing it down morally and by leading it away from its origin. He casts us into the depths of earthly nature and we should beware of this. Lucifer is the power that draws us down into the depths of passion.
>
> Ahriman, on the other hand, is the spirit of falsehood and error and he falsifies our judgments.
>
> Both Lucifer and Ahriman are powers which are hostile to human progress. Yet they get on very well with each other. Envy is a quality in which the luciferic power comes to expression. It is a detestable quality and that is why people dislike it. They seek to get rid of it, to overcome it and drive it away. When a person first discovers that his soul is filled with envy, he begins to fight against Lucifer, the source of envy. What does Lucifer do in that case? He simply hands over the matter to Ahriman, and Ahriman darkens the human judgment.
>
> When we fight against Lucifer in the astral body, Ahriman can easily insinuate himself into the etheric body, darkening our

---

22   For more on the etheric and astral bodies, see chapter 7, "Child Development, Waldorf Education, and Technology."

judgments of other people. This is falsehood, and falsehood is an ahrimanic quality.

People also feel a strong dislike for falsehood, and they try to fight against it. When we try to overcome falsehood, we can see that Ahriman hands over the scepter to Lucifer, so that a quality creeps into the astral body which appears in the form of an extremely pronounced egotism. Egotism is restrained falsehood.

These two qualities, falsehood and envy, are a crass expression of the way in which Lucifer and Ahriman work within the human soul.[23]

Part 5: CONTRASTING INFLUENCES OF AHRIMAN AND LUCIFER IN ART

Lucifer, Ahriman, and art

From a spiritual perspective, Lucifer and Ahriman have domains where they can legitimately work in relation to human evolution. Negative consequences arise when they transgress their boundaries. However, there is no simple map that shows where Ahriman or Lucifer can legitimately operate. Art is a good example of how complex things are. Even though art is primarily related to and influenced by Lucifer, Ahriman has a strong influence on certain realms of art, in particular architecture and sculpture, where outer form is important.

With the art of painting, we find both ahrimanic and luciferic tendencies prevailing in different methods such as Impressionism and Expressionism, respectively. Matters can be much more complicated when considering things from a spiritual perspective, rather than with our earthly ordering and classification.

The luciferic element is present to the greatest extent in the development of art. But something more must be added. There are,

---

23 Rudolf Steiner, "Morality and Karma," lect. 11/12/1910, *Anthroposophical News Sheet,* Dornach, Switzerland, Oct. 15, 1944; available at the Rudolf Steiner Library, Hudson, NY.

in general, five principal arts to be found in the physical world: the art of building or architecture, sculpture, painting, music, and poetry. Other arts combine and mix together the elements of these five....

Of the five arts, architecture and sculpture are those most particularly open to the ahrimanic impulse. In these arts we are concerned with form. To accomplish anything in architecture and sculpture we must find our way into the form element, which is dominant on the physical plane....

It is important, we will see, especially in such cases, not simply to assert in a superficial way that we must protect ourselves from the ahrimanic element. We should always realize that such beings as the luciferic and ahrimanic ones have their particular domains, where normally they live and work, and that bad effects come about only when they overstep their boundaries. The ahrimanic impulses have their absolutely legitimate domain in architecture and sculpture.[24]

Lucifer and Ahriman: Stylistic influences in architecture

Even though Ahriman is more dominant in architecture, Lucifer tries to introduce old styles of architecture that are influenced by outdated spiritual impulses. They instill in human beings a loathing for new, spiritually inspired artistic styles. Ahriman, on the other hand, is not concerned with style at all. His interest is in utilitarian service to industry and what maximizes mechanical productivity.

[Luciferic beings] want nothing but Renaissance, i.e. [a revival of] what lived in olden times. They instill into human beings' hatred against any new stylistic form that can really spring from the modern human spirit. They want to perpetuate the old styles because these are still adopted from the extraterrestrial unearthly [spiritual] element.

The ahrimanic character is not to let things acquire spiritualization or style at all, but for people to have only totally prosaic utility buildings, for example, have everything mechanized,

---

24 Rudolf Steiner, *Secrets of the Threshold,* lect. 8/29/1913.

everything solely at the service of industrial existence, inspire human beings not to appreciate any form of handicraft as art, but to deal solely in models of which an endless quantity of mechanically made copies can be distributed, in the same way as Ahriman can make himself manifest in many people.[25]

In the realm of painting, two distinct movements arose in reaction to modern industrial life. Expressionism, based in Germany and Austria, which is influenced primarily by Lucifer, focused on showing subjective emotions related to the dehumanizing effect of early twentieth-century industrialization. And Paris-based Impressionism, under the influence of Ahriman, was a reaction to the effect of industrialization on urban environments. A main emphasis in this movement was a focus on changes in the quality of light.

The goal of artistic endeavors should be to consciously bring about a balance between the luciferic and ahrimanic influences.

Today people live out their ahrimanic inclinations in science and their luciferic ones in religion. And in the realm of art, they oscillate between the one and the other. In recent times some artists tended more toward the luciferic, others toward the ahrimanic. Those of a more luciferic bent became expressionists, while those of a more ahrimanic inclination became impressionists. And those who wish neither to follow the one nor the other school oscillate between them, with no proper judgement either of the luciferic or the ahrimanic, seeking to avoid both....

But that is not what it's about. Rather we should regard ahrimanic and luciferic impulses as two necessary scales. The scale beam, balancing both, is what we ourselves must be. That is the important thing.[26]

25 Rudolf Steiner, *Guardian Angels*, lect. 10/23/1921.
26 Rudolf Steiner, *Understanding Society*, lect. 11/2/1919.

Part 6: THE INCARNATION OF AHRIMAN: PREPARATIONS, INFLUENCES, AND TRENDS

Background

In the third millennium, the spiritual being Ahriman will incarnate in the West just as Lucifer did in the East and the being of Christ in the Middle East.

Ahriman has been preparing for his upcoming incarnation in Western humanity by instilling certain tendencies or trends in people and into so-called civilized society. The true nature and task of the human being in the current age is to establish a balance between the polar influences of Lucifer and Ahriman within our souls with the help of the Christ being.

> Just as Lucifer incarnated at the beginning of the third pre-Christian millennium, and Christ incarnated at the time of the Mystery of Golgotha, so there will be an incarnation of Ahriman in the West not long after our present times, in the third post-Christian millennium in fact. To gain a right conception of the historical evolution of mankind over approximately 6,000 years, one must grasp that at the one pole stands an incarnation of Lucifer, in the center the incarnation of Christ, and at the other pole the incarnation of Ahriman. Lucifer is the power that stirs up all fanatical, all falsely mystical forces in human beings.... Ahriman is the power that makes people dry, prosaic, philistine—that ossifies them and anchors them in the superstition of materialism. And the true nature and being of the human being is essentially the effort to hold the balance between the powers of Lucifer and Ahriman; the Christ impulse helps contemporary humanity to establish this equilibrium.
>
> Thus, these two poles—the luciferic and the ahrimanic—are continuously present within us. Viewed historically, we find that the influence of Lucifer dominated certain pre-Christian currents of cultural development and continued into the first centuries of our era. On the other hand, the influence of Ahriman

has been at work since the middle of the fifteenth century and will increase in strength until an actual incarnation of Ahriman takes place among Western humanity.

Now it is characteristic of such things that they are prepared long in advance. Ahrimanic powers prepare the evolution of mankind in such a way that it can fall prey to Ahriman when he appears in human form within Western civilization—hardly then to be called "civilization" in our sense—as once Lucifer appeared in human form in China, as once Christ appeared in human form in Asia Minor. It is no use harboring illusions today about these things, Ahriman will appear in human form and the only question is how he will find humanity prepared.[27]

It is essential that people identify the workings of Ahriman in the current events and trends that help prepare for his incarnation. It would benefit Ahriman greatly if human beings are not able to discern what types of trends and activities facilitate his incarnation. Such a situation would enable him to incarnate unnoticed.

An entity like Ahriman, who is seeking to incarnate in the Western world at a certain point after this current time of ours, is already preparing his incarnation. As he does so, he guides and governs particular forces in human evolution in such a way as to be very especially advantageous to him. It would be a bad thing indeed if human beings were to sleepwalk toward this and fail to recognize in certain phenomena occurring in human life these preparations for Ahriman's corporeal incarnation. People will only find the right outlook by perceiving in this or that sequence of events informing human evolution how Ahriman is preparing his earthly existence. It is high time that individuals should recognize which of the events and occurrences unfolding around them are the machinations of Ahriman and may be advantageous to him as he prepares his forthcoming incarnation on earth.

It would doubtless be most advantageous of all for him if the great majority of human beings had no inkling whatsoever of the

---

27   Rudolf Steiner, *The Incarnation of Ahriman*, lect. 10/27/1919.

things that favor and prepare his coming incarnation, if the great majority of people went about their lives with the view that these unfolding preparations for Ahriman's incarnation were good, progressive, of benefit to and appropriate for human evolution. If Ahriman could sneak into a slumbering humanity, this would give him the greatest pleasure. And this is why we must identify the events and occurrences within which Ahriman is working toward his coming incarnation.[28]

Our task is not to avoid ahrimanic tendencies or to oppose his incarnation. It is, however, imperative that we prepare for his incarnation by becoming aware of the forces and tendencies he is introducing into life and how we can offset them.

Nothing will help us to adopt the right stance regarding the part played by Ahriman in human evolution except an unprejudiced study of the forces through which Ahriman's influence works, as well as learning to know the forces through which we can arm ourselves against being tempted and led astray.[29]

We have entered a period in which humanity will be faced with perpetual warfare and strife. These upheavals will stimulate the growth of an "inventiveness in physical life," which will make possible "the bodily existence of a human individuality in whom Ahriman" can and will incarnate.[30]

Through the aid of spiritual science we can learn of the multiple ways that Ahriman will prepare for his incarnation and how to use his incarnation as a stimulus for greater spiritual development.

It is of the greatest importance that people should approach the coming incarnation of Ahriman with full consciousness of this

---

28   Rudolf Steiner, *Understanding Society*, lect. 11/1/1919.

29   Rudolf Steiner, *The Incarnation of Ahriman*, lect. 10/27/1919.

30   This is an apparent reference to an increase in destructive technology being developed to serve the demands of warfare and social upheaval. Such technologies will also be used to make it possible for Ahriman to incarnate in a physical body that will be prepared for him.

event. The incarnation of Lucifer could be recognized only by the prophetic insight of the priests of the mysteries. People were also very unconscious of what the incarnation of Christ and the event of Golgotha really signified. But they should await the incarnation of Ahriman with full consciousness amidst shattering events that will occur on the physical plane. Amidst the perpetual stresses of war and other tribulations of the immediate future, the human mind will become very inventive in the physical domain. And through this very growth of inventiveness in physical life—which cannot be averted in any way or by any means—the bodily exis-tence of a human individuality in whom Ahriman can incarnate will become possible and inevitable.[31]

Abstract, intellectual thinking

One of the most powerful and effective ways in which Ahriman pre-pares for his incarnation is through fostering and promoting abstract thinking. This is often employed to address social problems, whereby cold, indifferent, abstract theories are used instead of drawing upon direct experiences and observed phenomena.[32]

> *Everything that is developing as intellectual life without being suffused by warmth of soul, without being quickened by enthusi-asm, directly furthers the incarnation of Ahriman in a way that is after his own heart. It lulls people to sleep in the way I have described, so that its results are advantageous to Ahriman.*[33]
>
> *Among the most important means Ahriman has to work with from the other side is the furthering of abstract thinking in the human being. And because people cling so firmly today to this abstract thinking, they are working in the way most favorable for the coming of Ahriman. You must realize that there is no better way to prepare for Ahriman's cunning efforts to capture the whole earth for his own purposes than that human beings should con-tinue to live an abstract life, steeping themselves in abstractions,*

---

31 Rudolf Steiner, *The Incarnation of Ahriman*, lect. 11/4/1919.

32 More on this subject can be found in chapter 1.

33 Rudolf Steiner, *The Incarnation of Ahriman*, lect. 11/4/1919.

as they do in contemporary society. This is one of the ruses, one of the clever tricks, by which Ahriman prepares in his own way for his mastery and dominion over the earth. Instead of drawing on lived experience to show people what needs to happen, leaders offer them theories on every subject, including the social question. To those who expound these theories, knowledge gained from experience is abstract, because they have no inkling of what real life is. All this is preparation for Ahriman.[34]

If ever we let ourselves in for a discussion with Ahriman, we should inevitably be shattered by the logical conclusiveness, the magnificent certainty of aim with which he manipulates his arguments.

Every Ahriman-being is over-endowed with personal Intelligence in the way I have now described; critical to a degree in the repudiation of all things illogical; scornful and contemptuous in thought.[35]

Stirring up emotions that cause chaos and fragmentation of peoples

In our age of intellectualism and materialism, Ahriman stirs up emotions to separate people into small groups that attack one other. The intellect alone often cannot penetrate into full reality; it is limited to a domain in which opposing opinions can all be proved to be equally correct. Ahriman can make good use for his incarnation of the confusion that arises. This is particularly true when partisan groups are involved. Intellectualism that is devoid of warmth of soul provides fertile ground for the advancement of ahrimanic forces.

[Another] means that [Ahriman] employs is to stir up all the emotions that fragment people into small groups—groups that attack one another. You need only look at all the conflicting groups and interests that exist today, and if you are unprejudiced you will recognize that the explanation for this is not to be found in human nature alone....

---

34 Ibid., lect. 12/28/1919.
35 Rudolf Steiner, *Karmic Relationships,* vol. 3, lect. 8/1/1924.

These ahrimanic powers are working, in fact, wherever disharmonies arise between groups of people....

Present human thinking, the modern intellect, lies in a stratum of existence where it does not reach down to realities. One can therefore prove something quite strictly, and also prove its opposite. It is possible today to prove spiritualism, on the one hand, and materialism, on the other. And people may combat each other from equally good standpoints because modern intellectualism is in an upper layer of reality and does not plumb the depths of reality. And it is the same with partisan views. Someone who does not look deeper but simply lets himself be absorbed into a certain partisan group—by reason of his education, heredity, life circumstances, and nationality—quite honestly believes, or so he thinks, in the possibility of proving the tenets of the group into which he has slipped. And then—then he fights against someone else who has slipped into another partisan group! And the one is just as right as the other. This creates chaos and confusion in mankind that will gradually become ever greater unless people see through it. Ahriman makes use of this confusion in order to prepare the triumph of his incarnation and to drive people increasingly into something they find so difficult to be aware of: that intellectual or modern scientific reasoning can be used nowadays both to prove something, and equally well prove its opposite. The important point for us to recognize is that everything can be proved, and for that reason we must examine the proofs presented by modern science.[36]

Racism, nationalism, and corrupted patriotism

Stirring up strife among various peoples and groups through racism, chauvinism, and degenerate forms of patriotism and nationalism furthers the interests of Ahriman.

[A] tendency in modern life of benefit to Ahriman in preparing his incarnation is all that is so clearly in evidence in nationalism. Whatever can separate people into groups, whatever can alienate

---

36 Rudolf Steiner, *The Incarnation of Ahriman*, lect. 10/27/1919.

them from mutual understanding the whole world over and drive wedges between them, strengthens Ahriman's impulse.[37]

If an appeal is made today to national, racial, and similar relationships, to relationships not based on the spirit, then disharmony will increase amongst humanity. And it is this disharmony which the ahrimanic powers can put to special use. National chauvinism, perverted patriotism in every form, is the material from which Ahriman will build just what he needs.[38]

Using heredity differences to stir up conflicts

Ahriman also strives to use traditional forms of heredity, including family, races, and peoples, to stir up dissension and strife and further prepare for his incarnation.

Ahriman also makes use of everything arising from the old conditions of heredity which human beings have already outgrown in the fifth post-Atlantean epoch. The ahrimanic powers use everything that is derived from old circumstances of heredity in order to sow conflict between different groups. All that comes from old divisions of family, race, tribe, peoples is used by Ahriman to create confusion. "Freedom for every nation, even the smallest." ... These were fine-sounding words. But the powers hostile to man always use fine words in order to sow confusion and in order to attain the things that Ahriman wishes to attain for his incarnation.

If we ask who stirs up nations against each other, who raises issues that control and direct humanity today, the answer is: Ahriman and the ahrimanic deception which plays into human life. And in this sphere people very easily succumb to deception. They are not willing to descend to the lower strata where reality is to be found.[39]

---

37 Ibid., lect. 11/1/1919.
38 Ibid., lect. 11/4/1919.
39 Ibid., lect.10/27/1919.

Utilitarianism and emphasis on material needs

Ahriman supports and furthers the view that it is sufficient for people to simply be concerned with material and financial matters, thus devaluing the soul and spirit.[40] In such a thought climate there is little room for interest in anthroposophy or spiritual perspectives in general.

> *[Another of Ahriman's] endeavors is to preserve the already widespread attitude that public welfare depends only on providing for the economic and material needs of humanity....*
>
> *And now think of the consequences of this. What numbers of people there are today who no longer value the spirit for the sake of the spirit or the soul for the sake of the soul! They are out to absorb from cultural life only what is regarded as "useful." This is a significant and mysterious factor in the life of modern humanity and one we should be aware of. Average citizens who work assiduously in their offices from morning till evening and then go through their habitual evening routine, will not allow themselves to get mixed up with what they call the "twaddle" to be found in anthroposophy. It seems to them entirely redundant, for they think: that is something one cannot eat! It finally comes to this—although people will not admit it—that in ordinary life nothing in the way of knowledge is considered really useful unless it helps to put food in the mouth![41]*

Mechanical view of the cosmos

Another aspect of Ahriman's handiwork in preparation for his incarnation is promoting the view of the cosmos as if it were a large machine.

> *One of the developments in which Ahriman's impulse is clearly evident is the spread of the belief that the mechanistic, mathematical conceptions inaugurated by Galileo, Copernicus, and others explain what is happening in the cosmos. That is why anthroposophical spiritual science lays such stress upon the fact*

---

40 This tendency has a major influence on cultural life, especially through education reforms that focus on job skill preparation and material success over the development of social and spiritual values.

41 Rudolf Steiner, *The Incarnation of Ahriman*, lect. 11/1/1919.

*that **spirit** and **soul** must be discerned in the cosmos, not merely the mathematical, mechanistic laws put forward by Galileo and Copernicus as if the cosmos were some huge machine. It would augur success for Ahriman's temptations if human beings were to persist in merely calculating the revolutions of the heavenly bodies, in studying astrophysics for the sole purpose of ascertaining the material composition of the planets—an achievement of which the modern world is so proud.*[42]

Rejecting spiritual science and adhering solely to a literal interpretation of the Gospels

It furthers Ahriman's goals if a simple or literal interpretation of the Gospels prevails over a spiritual-scientific understanding of the Mystery of Golgotha—that is, the mystery of Christ's death and resurrection.

An exclusive adherence to what Christ said and did when he walked the earth is no longer sufficient. Rather, one should also take seriously His words, "I will be with you even until the end of the world," and listen to what the Christ is conveying now through His continued presence. Two things that Christ wishes to convey to us in this epoch are: 1) the necessity of changing our ways of thinking so that they reveal the threefold nature of the human being; and 2) the threefold nature of social life. More will be said about Ahriman's opposition to the threefold social organism later in this chapter.

The literal, word-for-word acceptance of the Gospels that is still so prevalent today, promotes ahrimanic culture. Even on external grounds it is obvious that a strictly literal acceptance of the Gospels is unjustified. For as you know, what is good and right for one time is not right for every other time.... The mere reading of the Gospel texts has had its day. What is essential now is to acquire a spiritual understanding of the Mystery of Golgotha in the light of the truths enshrined in the Gospels.[43]

---

42 Ibid.
43 Ibid., lect. 11/4/1919.

"I am with you always, even unto the end of the world." This means: Christ did not speak only during His time on earth; His utterance continues, and we must continue to listen for it. We should not wish merely to read the Gospels (though certainly they ought to be read over and over again); we should listen to the living revelation that springs from His continued presence among us. In this epoch He declares to us: "Make new your ways of thinking" (just as His forerunner, John the Baptist, said: "Change your thinking"), "so that they may reveal to you man's threefold nature which demands also that your social environment on earth shall have a threefold membering."[44]

Ahriman and the control of finance

Ahriman has been active in discreetly gaining the control of financial affairs. We must familiarize ourselves with the trends and tendencies he instills in human beings and social life (as described throughout this chapter) and consciously oppose him in these efforts.

It is not our task as human beings to hinder in any way this incarnation of Ahriman, but it is our task to prepare humanity in advance so that Ahriman can be weighed up in the right way. For Ahriman will have various tasks, and human beings must value rightly and make a right use of what enters the world through Ahriman. Humanity will be able to do this only if it is able to adjust in the right way now to what Ahriman is already sending to the earth from supersensible worlds in order to control financial affairs upon earth without being noticed. This must not happen. Ahriman must not control financial affairs and economics on the earth without being noticed.

We must thoroughly familiarize ourselves with his particular qualities and recognize what he does. We must be able to oppose him with full consciousness.[45]

---

44 Rudolf Steiner, *The Inner Aspect of the Social Question*, lect. 2/11/1919.
45 Rudolf Steiner, *The Incarnation of Ahriman*, lect. 12/25/1919.

Rulers as agents of financial and banking interests

The ruling types or classes have evolved over the ages from highly developed spiritual individuals or initiates, such as the Egyptian pharaohs, to leaders from the priestly class up to the Renaissance. Since then, rulers or political leaders have come under the influence, if not control, of bankers and financiers. This led to money itself becoming a primary means for Ahriman's machinations. This can only be overcome if government and cultural life can counterbalance these financial and economic forces.[46]

Ahriman skillfully prepares his goal beforehand; ever since the Reformation and the Renaissance, the economist has been emerging in modern civilization as the representative governing type. That is an actual historical fact. If you go back to ancient times, even to those that I have characterized today as the luciferic, who were the governing types then? Initiates—the Egyptian Pharaohs, the Babylonian rulers, the Asiatic rulers—they were initiates. Then the priest-type emerged as ruler and remained so right up to the Reformation and the Renaissance. Since that time, the economist has had the upper hand. Rulers are in fact merely the henchman and the enforcers of the economists. One must not imagine that the rulers of modern times are anything but the economists' agents. And all that has been enshrined as law and justice, if one scrutinizes it carefully, simply a consequence of thinking dictated by economics. In the nineteenth century, economics was, for the first time, replaced by a thinking based on finance and banking, and a financial system which swamps every other relation. One must only be able to examine these things and follow them up empirically and practically. . . .

But just because this dominion of the "mere" token for material goods (i.e. money) has arisen, Ahriman has been given another essential means of deceiving mankind. If people do not realize that the legislative state that safeguards human rights and

---

46 For more on money and the appropriate relations among and between the economy, government, and culture, see Gary Lamb and Sarah Hearn (ed.), *Steinerian Economics*, chapters 3, 9, and 11.

the organism of the spirit must balance and redress the economic order established by economists and the bankers, then again, through this lack of awareness, Ahriman will find an important instrument for preparing his incarnation. His incarnation is undoubtedly coming, and this lack of insight will smooth the way for his triumphant advance.[47]

The predominance of finance and money just mentioned also works back into the moral/ethical aspect of cultural life. Natural urges and wishes are transformed into a problem of happiness and wealth. Ahriman then links thoughts about happiness to the idea of goodness. In their desire to wrest control of cultural life, ahrimanic powers instill the idea in cultural life that truth can be found solely in material existence. And wealth and prosperity become the equivalent of goodness.

Let us think of the problem of natural urges and impulses.... The mind is directed to these impulses and a certain view of life gradually unfolds. The problem of natural urges and impulses transforms itself into the problem of happiness or prosperity, which assumes a definite character. Hence in the fifth post-Atlantean epoch, especially in the culture of the West, you find strivings in connection with the problem of prosperity, strivings directed to the creation of prosperity in life....

Thought about happiness and prosperity is, of course, quite justified. But under the influence of Ahriman it has assumed a certain character as a result of a really devilish tenet. This tenet defines the good in such a way that the good is said to manifest actually through happiness or prosperity.... Ahrimanic influences produced a mentality in humanity in the fifth post-Atlantean epoch that seeks for the good in prosperity, in happiness....

Side by side with the problem of natural urges and impulses is that of sensory existence, existence in the material world of the senses. In the fifth post-Atlantean epoch, the culture resulting from sensory existence ought, in reality, to be ennobled, but the ahrimanic powers desired to get this culture under their own control.

---

47   Rudolf Steiner, *The Incarnation of Ahriman*, lect. 10/27/1919.

Hence, their aim is to produce a mentality that considers truth to be found in sensory existence alone. To this extent ahrimanic impulses are active in all that is embraced in the problem of sensory existence, of existence in the world of the senses.[48]

Opposition to cultural freedom and social threefolding

Ahriman opposes an independent cultural life that is equal in importance to the realms of politics and economics. It is to his great advantage if cultural development is dominated by economic and political interests. Without the renewing forces of an independent and vibrant cultural life, modern civilization and culture will degenerate.

Ahriman experiences a free cultural life as a form of darkness, and an individual's enthusiasm for freedom as a blazing soul fire.

Consider for a moment something that relates to our reflections on society, in which we have now been engaging for several months. They aim to show the need to separate cultural and spiritual life, as well as the life of rights, or the state, from merely economic life. Above all they aim to establish conditions across the world, or at least—and we cannot presently do more than this—to see that conditions across the world will be right if they establish an autonomous life of spirit, one that is independent of the other structures in society, unlike our present cultural and spiritual life, which is fully entangled with economic life, on the one hand, and the political life of the state, on the other....

Ahriman's incarnation will benefit very especially from a refusal to establish an autonomous, free life of spirit, instead leaving this entangled in economic circulation or in the life of the state. This is because ahrimanic powers have the greatest interest in maintaining this merger of spiritual life with economic life and the state. Ahrimanic powers regard a free life of spirit as a kind of darkness; and they will experience human interest in this free life of spirit as a burning fire, a soul fire, but nevertheless a powerfully blazing fire. Therefore, in order to find the right

---

48 Rudolf Steiner, *Inner Impulses of Evolution*, lect. 9/24/1916.

stance toward the incarnation of Ahriman in the near future, we are obliged to establish this free life of spirit.[49]

A threefold social organism that views an independent spiritual-cultural life as being just as important as the economy provides a good foundation for meeting Ahriman's incarnation.

The more that people can be roused to conduct their affairs not for material ends alone but to regard a free and independent spiritual life as no less important than economic life, as an integral part of the social organism—the more they will be able to await Ahriman's incarnation with a stance and attitude worthy of humanity.[50]

Intellectualism and the use and abuse of statistics in science and politics

Statistics disconnected from the qualitative aspects of life are a useful means of deception that spread confusion. The same figures can easily be manipulated to support opposing points of view. This is particularly true for the social sciences, including politics and political parties.

Truth is beyond the reach of the kind of knowledge for which people aspire today. They feel on secure ground when they can reckon by means of figures, when they can prove things by statistics. But figures divorced from qualitative aspects are means whereby people are led astray in a direction favorable to Ahriman for his future incarnation in the third millennium AD.[51]

People love numbers and figures in science, but they also love figures in the social sphere as well. Social science consists almost entirely of statistics. And from statistics, that is to say from figures, the weightiest conclusions are reached. Well, figures can prove anything too, and back up any belief. Figures are not a means whereby the essential reality of things can be proved— they are simply a means of deception! Whenever one fails to look

---

49 Rudolf Steiner, *Understanding Society,* lect. 11/2/1919.
50 Rudolf Steiner, *The Incarnation of Ahriman,* lect. 11/1/1919.
51 Ibid.

beyond figures to qualitative aspects, these figures can be utterly deceptive.[52]

Abstract political party platforms

Political parties are based on abstract party platforms and programs. When politicians rely predominately on abstract thinking and statistics, opposing platforms can be presented as equally valid. Intellectual understanding alone remains at the surface of matters and cannot reach deeper layers where truth can be found.

Once it is realized that conflicting party programs can be proved equally correct, our attitude of soul will change from setting out to prove things to experiencing them. For to experience a thing is a very different matter from attempting to prove it intellectually.[53]

*Everywhere today we see parties being formed for one object or another. People nowadays have no discernment, nor do they have the desire to have it where party opinions and party programs are concerned. With intellectual ingenuity, proof can be furnished in support of the most radically opposed theories. Very clever arguments can be used to prove the soundness of Leninism—but the same applies to directly contrary principles and also to what lies between the two extremes. An excellent case can be made out for every party program; but the one who establishes the validity of the opposite program is equally right. The intellectualism prevailing among people today is not capable of demonstrating the **inner** potentialities and values of anything. It can furnish proofs; but what is intellectually proved should not be regarded as of real value or efficacy in life. People oppose one another in parties because the validity of every party opinion—at any rate the main party opinions—can be proved with equal justification. Our intellect penetrates no further than the surface of understanding and does not reach deeper layers where the truth actually lies.*[54]

---

52 Ibid., lect. 11/4/1919.
53 Ibid.
54 Ibid.

Part 7: Balancing and Redeeming Ahrimanic and Luciferic Forces with the Christ Force

Balance, not escapism

We should neither oppose nor try to flee from ahrimanic and luciferic influences. The correct attitude is that we acknowledge they are both necessary for evolution and that we must courageously find the correct balance between them in all aspects of life.

> *There is no question of saying that human beings must guard against ahrimanic and luciferic influences. What matters is for human beings to find the right attitude toward ahrimanic and luciferic influences, while maintaining always a balance between the two.*[55]
>
> *The human being's task is... to cultivate the position of balance and not to believe that he or she can simply escape from the clutches of Lucifer and Ahriman. Calmly and courageously, individuals must admit to themselves that both beings are necessary for world evolution, that in their own development they need both Lucifer and Ahriman in their active lives, but that the balance must be maintained in every sphere of life.*
>
> *Our activities, therefore, must be such that the balance is maintained between Lucifer and Ahriman. It was for this reason, too, that Lucifer and Ahriman had necessarily to play a part in earthly evolution.*[56]

The Christ as the balancing force: The sacredness of the number three

We must think of the world in terms of three or a triad rather than a duality such as God versus the devil. We can picture this triad in terms of a balance beam with luciferic and ahrimanic forces on each end of the beam. The beam can be represented as human life, and the fulcrum as the third element—divinely inspired humanity. Our human task in earthly life is to keep the beam in balance. In other words, to keep the

---

55   Rudolf Steiner, *Old and New Methods of Initiation,* lect. 1/1/1922.

56   Rudolf Steiner, *Memory and Habit,* lect. 8/26/1916.

forces of Lucifer and Ahriman in balance as divinely inspired human beings. Individual spiritual health depends on having a proper relationship to the cosmic principle of three.

> *The world can really be understood only in terms of a triad. On one side we have everything luciferic, on the other everything ahrimanic, and, in the third, central place, the point of balance between the two, humanity, with a sense of its relationship to the divine, of its divine essence. We can understand the world in the right way only when we see it based on this triad and are perfectly clear that human life is the beam of the scales. Here is the fulcrum: on one side is the luciferic element, actually pulling the pan upward; opposite is the ahrimanic element, pushing the pan downward. Our human task—our human essence—is to keep the beam balanced....*
>
> *Now, as you may well imagine, it lies in the deepest interests of the luciferic and ahrimanic powers to conceal this secret of the number three—after all, only the proper penetration of this secret would allow humanity to bring about the state of balance between these luciferic and ahrimanic powers. This means that we must make beneficial use of the luciferic tendency toward freedom, on the one hand, and of the ahrimanic tendency on the other. For human beings, the healthiest spiritual condition is to enter into a proper relationship with this cosmic trinity, this cosmic structure based on the principle of three....*
>
> *So, you see, we have to be clear that a realistic view of the structure of the cosmos requires us to recognize the role that the number three plays in it. We must acknowledge the opposing roles of luciferic and ahrimanic powers, while recognizing that the role of divine beings consists in holding a balance between the two. This needs to be contrasted with the illusion of the duality of God and the devil that has entered human spiritual evolution—the notion of divine spiritual powers above and diabolical powers below.*[57]

---

57   Rudolf Steiner, *The Incarnation of Ahriman,* lect. 11/21/1919.

We are at a point in human evolution when we must make a choice among three paths—luciferic, ahrimanic, or the path of Christ. The luciferic path is one of going through life in a musing, brooding state without clear ideas. The ahrimanic path is permeated with the intellect, combined with the desire to view everything from a mechanical perspective, devoid of imagination. The Christ path means to seek a balance, not to be overly drawn in the direction of one over the other in our journey through life. This balance can be achieved by using the forces of one to regulate the forces of the other.[58]

We are living in a decisive hour of earthly evolution in which humanity can choose one of three paths. [A luciferic path, which leads to] nebulous mysticism, in dreaming, in an infatuation for things of the physical senses, that is, in going along in a muse—for life in material nature is indeed only musing and brooding—in a sleep condition in which one passes through life without clear ideas. That is one of the tendencies to which man may incline.

[An ahrimanic path] would be for people to permeate themselves entirely with intellect and intelligence, to gather together as it were everything that intellect can gather together; to scorn all that poetry and phantasy can spread over earthly existence, to turn everywhere to the mechanical and to dried-up pedantry. Men stand today before the decision either to become spiritual voluptuaries entirely sunk in their own existence—for whether one submerges in one's own existence through nebulous mysticism or material desolation is ultimately only two sides of the same thing—or else to consider everything prosaically, to bring everything into a routine scheme, to classify and correlate everything. Those are two of the possibilities.

The third possibility, the path of Christ, is to seek for the balance, the equilibrium between the two. One cannot speak of the equilibrium in so definite a way as of the two extremes. One must strive for equilibrium by not being too strongly attracted by

---

58 The question of how to achieve balance by letting one be regulated by the other will be taken up further in volume 2.

either but pass through the two in a proper balance of life, letting the one be regulated and ordered by the other.[59]

Employing ahrimanic forces to counter and regulate luciferic forces, and vice versa

When considering Ahriman and Lucifer it is important to acknowledge we are dealing with two extremes: whenever we experience one of them overly strongly, we need to apply an equivalent amount of force from the other side. Ahriman, for instance, is greatly benefited when people respond with boredom to what can be viewed as tedious. In such situations, we should strive to find a point of engagement that ignites our interest and enthusiasm from Lucifer's side. And if we are overly preoccupied and inwardly troubled with something, we need to bring some cool, objective thoughts to the matter, inspired by Ahriman.

If we cannot do so in such situations, we should consider it as a weakness on our part, rather than as a fault in outer circumstances. Such circumstances should be a call to us to recognize the extent to which luciferic and ahrimanic forces are at play and then apply the appropriate counterbalancing measures.

*We should regard ahrimanic and luciferic impulses as two neces-
sary scales. The scale beam, balancing both, is what we ourselves
must be. That is the important thing.*

*How can we educate ourselves to do this? We can do so by
imbuing ourselves very strongly with a luciferic element to counter what arises in us as ahrimanic quality. What ahrimanic element arises very strongly in us today? Knowledge of the outer
world. The most ahrimanic element of all is our material perception of the outer world, for this is only a mirage. And if we can
develop keen, fervent, and enthusiastic interest in the mirage that
arises from chemistry, physics, astronomy, and so on, through*

---

59   Rudolf Steiner, "The Responsibility of Man For World-Evolution Through His Spiritual Connection with the Planet Earth and the World of the Stars" (Duplicated as manuscript by kind permission of the Rudolf Steiner-Nachlassverwaltung, Dornach, Switzerland) GA 203, lect. 1/30/1921; available from Rudolf Steiner Library, Hudson, NY.

our own luciferic interest, we detach from Ahriman something that should belong to him.

It is precisely this that people do not want; it seems very boring to them. And many who flee outward, material knowledge misjudge their task and prepare the best earthly conditions for Ahriman's incarnation. Likewise, what springs up inside people today has a very strong luciferic character. How can we educate ourselves properly in this respect? By taking our own ahrimanic element and drawing it into ourselves—that is, avoiding all illusions about our interiority, and regarding or observing ourselves as we otherwise regard the outer world. People today should really experience how needful they are of educating themselves in this way. Anyone with a certain capacity to observe these matters will frequently encounter the following fact of life.

Someone comes to you and relates something he feels indignant about in the behavior of person A, person B, person C, and countless others. He describes very precisely how indignant he is about this, that and the other person. And he has no idea that everything he relates are his own qualities or flaws! People have no sense at all of this! This idiosyncrasy has never been as widespread as it is today. And those who think this does not apply to them are the ones who do it most of all. What is involved here is to approach one's own interiority with ahrimanic coldness, ahrimanic sobriety. This interiority of ours will still be hot enough, even if cooled down a little! There is no need to fear that it will grow too cool. And it is true to say that modern humanity needs to find the right stance toward the forthcoming incarnation of Ahriman, to become more objective about inner life, at the same time bringing much subjective interest to bear on the surrounding world—not fantasy, though, but attentiveness, devotion, and especially interest.

You see, it is of great benefit to Ahriman and the path he is taking in order to shape his incarnation as favorably as possible if your education or other circumstances in life lead you to regard outward life as tedious. Just think how many people nowadays regard one thing or another as boring. For instance, I have met countless people who find it very boring indeed to acquaint themselves with the workings of banks or the stock exchange, or single and double bookkeeping. It is never right to regard such things as utterly boring. To find something boring simply means that you haven't yet discovered the point where it comes to be of burning interest. Every dry account book can, if you discover the angle on it that makes it of keen interest, be just as interesting as the Maid of Orleans by Schiller or Shakespeare's Hamlet, or anything else, say the Sistine Madonna by Raphael. It is just a question of discovering the point where everything in life turns out to be fascinating.

You might consider this very paradoxical. But it isn't. What is paradoxical is people's relationship to the truth nowadays. It is a far, far better stance to assume that we ourselves are flawed and unable to accomplish something than to ascribe this weakness to the world itself. Nothing better helps Ahriman prepare for his incarnation than for us to find something or other boring, to consider ourselves too good for something, to not want to have anything to do with whatever it is. We must always look for the point or angle that allows us to see the interest in something. Rather than subjectively rejecting or accepting things, it is important to objectively perceive the extent to which there is ahrimanic or luciferic quality in something, so that the balance beam sinks too low on one side or the other. Finding something interesting does not mean regarding it as right or justified, but only developing an inner strength to unite with the matter in hand and help send it in the right direction.[60]

Everything that is developing as intellectual life without being suffused by warmth of soul, without being quickened by enthusiasm, directly furthers the incarnation of Ahriman in a way that is after his own heart. It lulls people to sleep in the way I have described, so that its results are advantageous to Ahriman.[61]

---

60   Rudolf Steiner, *Understanding Society,* lect. 11/2/1919.
61   Rudolf Steiner, *The Incarnation of Ahriman,* lect. 11/4/1919.

Meeting Lucifer with morality and Ahriman with wholesome judgment

There are certain measures human beings can develop and employ to fend off temptations and intrigues aroused by Lucifer and Ahriman within our souls. Temptations, desires, passions, and self-delusions inspired by Lucifer can be met effectively with morality, decency, and humility, which cause him to retreat in a state of painful burning.

An effective means to counter Ahriman's cold, heartless intellectualism and delusions is through the development of well-rounded judgment schooled through spiritual science.

There is but one power before which Lucifer retreats, and that is morality which burns him like the most dreadful of fires. And there is no means by which to oppose Ahriman other than a power of judgment and discernment schooled by spiritual science. For Ahriman flees in terror from the wholesome power of judgment acquired upon earth. In the main there is nothing to which he has a greater aversion than the qualities we gain from a healthy education of our I-consciousness. For we shall see that Ahriman belongs to a very different region, far removed from that force of sound judgement which we develop in ourselves. The moment Ahriman encounters this, he receives a terrible shock, for this is something completely unknown to him, and he fears it. The more we apply ourselves in our life to develop this wholesome judgment, the more do we work in opposition to Ahriman. . . .

In fact, the best remedy against the particularly harmful diseases which result in visions and delusory voices induced by Ahriman is to make every effort to induce the person to acquire a wholesome and rational judgement. . . .

We now know what the luciferic and ahrimanic forces abhor. Lucifer has an aversion for humility and modesty in man and is repulsed if we have only such an opinion of ourselves as a wholesome judgement entitles us to hold. On the other hand, he is present, like the flies in the dirty room, whenever the qualities of vanity and ambition arise. All this and the illusions which we engender about ourselves, prepare us to receive Ahriman as well. Nothing can defend us against Ahriman unless we really make an effort to think wholesomely, as life between birth and death teaches us to do. And especially we, who stand on the rock of spiritual science, have every reason to emphasize again and again and as intensively as possible, the fact that it is not for us as earth-beings to disregard that which is to be given us through life upon earth.[62]

Finding the right relation to Lucifer, Christ, Ahriman, and the redemption of Ahriman

Finding a right relationship to and understanding of luciferic and ahrimanic forces and, consequently, the Christ impulse, is essential for humanity to work in harmony with the being of Christ toward achieving the goal of Earth existence.

There is a great deal in the spiritual and unspiritual currents of the present time of which men should be acutely aware, and determine their attitude of soul accordingly. People's ability and willingness to penetrate to the roots of such matters will determine the effect of Ahriman's incarnation on human beings, whether this incarnation will lead them to prevent the earth from reaching its goal, or bring home to them the very limited significance and scope of unspiritual intellectual life. If people adopt the right stance to tendencies leading toward Ahriman, then simply through his incarnation in earthly life they will recognize the ahrimanic influence on the one hand, and on the other its polar opposite—the luciferic influence. And then the very contrast between the ahrimanic and the luciferic will enable them to perceive the third reality. Human beings must consciously wrestle through to an understanding of this trinity of the Christ impulse, the ahrimanic, and the luciferic influences; for without this awareness, they will not be able to go forward into the future with the prospect of achieving the goal of Earth existence.[63]

---

62 Rudolf Steiner, *Manifestations of Karma*, lect. 5/22/1910.

63 Rudolf Steiner, *The Incarnation of Ahriman*, lect. 11/4/1919.

Rudolf Steiner portrayed the triad of Lucifer, Christ, and Ahriman, with Christ holding the other two in a state of balance, in a large wooden sculpture called the "Representative of Humanity." Representations of good and evil as a duality are no longer sufficient to correctly characterize life. Life must be portrayed in terms of a trinity of spiritual beings and related forces in which one component represents a state of balance between two opposite poles.

It is simply necessary that we should come to see clearly that man represents in his life a state of balance between conflicting powers. Every conception characterized by the idea of mere duality— a good and an evil principle—will always fail to illuminate life. Life can be illuminated only when we represent it from the point of view of a trinity, in which one element represents a state of balance and the two others represent the opposite poles, between which the state of balance tends to move continually like a pendulum. This is the reason for the Trinity we undertake to represent in our [sculptural] Group; the Representative of Humanity [Christ] balancing Ahriman and Lucifer.[64]

Redeeming Ahriman

In modern society, there is no way to evade Ahriman's influence and manifestations. Steiner uses the examples from his time of shorthand and typing as pervasive "ahrimanic arts." These types of activities can be counterbalanced, and Ahriman can be redeemed, by bringing a spiritual perspective to bear on them.

In these modern times we can hardly avoid carrying out ahrimanic activities, for instance shorthand and typing. These things are an ahrimanizing of our civilization to the highest degree. But if we bring spirituality into our civilization, we can even raise up into the sphere of the spirit things that are as obviously of a serious ahrimanic nature as shorthand and typing, and then Ahriman will be redeemed. This will only become possible if we are absolutely serious about the spirit. If people do shorthand

---

64   Rudolf Steiner, *The Challenge of the Times*, lect. 12/7/1918.

or actually use a typewriter whilst maintaining a materialistic attitude they will become deeply enmeshed in the ahrimanic element. You must realize that I am not encouraging a reaction against it. We should not start frowning on the demonology that has set in; for what has to happen is that the demons themselves must be redeemed.[65]

The importance of understanding technology, the mission of Christ, and the redemption of Ahriman

How the remainder of Earth evolution unfolds depends on an understanding of the mission of Christ and His ongoing activities. This knowledge is needed not only to re-spiritualize science, industry, and technology but also to redeem Ahriman. Otherwise, Earth evolution will be taken over by Ahriman.[66]

Everything that has arisen in recent times in the way of materialistic science and industrial technology is of an out-and-out ahrimanic nature, and if it were to spread without there being any Christ understanding, it would chain human beings to the earth. Human beings would not progress to the Jupiter evolution [a future stage of Earth evolution]. If, however, we bring an understanding of Christ, a new spiritual life, a newly activated imagination, inspiration, and intuition into what is merely a knowledge of the external world, then we redeem Ahriman. I have shown in all manner of ways in my mystery plays how this redemption can be put into the form of a picture. It would be allowing Ahriman to overcome human beings if an understanding of Christ could not undergo further development as a real spirit-filled understanding, freed from theology. If an understanding of Christ were not to re-spiritualize modern materialistic science and lifeless industrial mechanization, these things would deliver human beings up to death on earth—i.e., they

---

65   Rudolf Steiner, *Guardian Angels*, lect. 10/23/1921.

66   The mission of Christ will be investigated more thoroughly in relation to technology and social life in volume 2.

would construct a world in which human beings would more or less be fossils for the edification of ahrimanic beings.[67]

---

67 Rudolf Steiner, *Guardian Angels*, lect. 10/23/1921.

Thinking as a Spiritual Activity

[Thinking] takes place in the adjacent etheric and astral bodies and so on...thoughts do not enter the brain at all...they are reflected through the activity of the brain and thrown back again into etheric body, astral body, and I. (note 10)

The work of the brain has precisely the same significance as a mirror has for human beings who see themselves in it. (note 9)

NINE

Thinking as a Spiritual Activity

Introduction

In this chapter, the reader will find an array of statements made by Rudolf Steiner that make the case that thinking is an independent spiritual activity that takes place outside the brain. The brain's activity does not create thoughts, but instead it mirrors the results of the activity of thinking, thus enabling mental images to arise within human consciousness.

While there is more to add to what is contained in this chapter on the nature and dynamics of the thinking process, the contents here will be an invaluable aid to understanding key issues in relation to technology, especially the use and abuse of so-called artificial intelligence.

These issues include:

- *the nature of artificial intelligence and its relation to human thinking, consciousness, memory, and intelligence*
- *the question of what is taking place in any attempt to download the human brain with information (data) via computers using artificial intelligence*

So too, the contents are essential in determining:

- *the conditions under which the human being can claim freedom in thinking and willing, and*
- *whether there is a moral dimension to thinking as a spiritual activity.*

These issues and questions will be followed up more fully in volume two.

Chapter overview

As mentioned above, from a spiritual-scientific perspective, the brain does not produce thoughts. Rather, its solid parts, consisting of salt deposits that are continually forming and dissolving, act as a mirror that enables thought activity to become conscious in the human being in the form of mental pictures. In addition, the brain gathers intelligence that already exists everywhere in the perceptible world.

During waking hours, the brain is in a continual state of dying due to the presence of thinking. At night, when thinking is diminished or no longer active, the nervous system's life forces are replenished. Under normal conditions, thinking cannot observe itself while it is in a state of activity. It can only observe completed thoughts and existing images.

Electrical and magnetic forces entered the human organism during the evolutionary stage that Rudolf Steiner called Lemuria.[1] In the future, a connection will be established between the electrical and magnetic forces in the body with external electrical and mechanical forces. A significant challenge to human beings will arise because of these connections: how to bring together the forces in the human being with mechanical devices in the appropriate way that does not bring about undue harm to humanity.

An important task now and in the future will be to master thinking and control thought in a conscious and focused way. This will provide the foundation for developing imaginative or picture-forming cognition. This level of thinking will be necessary for overcoming abstract thinking and antisocial behavior that is so prevalent in modern life.

---

1   See Appendix A, figure A-2, for the location of Lemuria in Earth evolution. It precedes the historical Atlantis. In biblical lore, the story of Adam and Eve and the "Fall" took place during the time of Lemuria.

Part 1: THE NATURE OF THINKING

The essence of thinking as a spiritual activity

Thinking can be perceived as a self-enclosed activity that is a self-sustaining spiritual substance. If we do not understand and accept this fact, there arises the need to seek some type of metaphysical world beyond the world of thought activity modeled after the physical world. When observing or thinking about thinking, the spiritual substance or essence of thinking is grasped by the human being through the faculty of *intuition*, which Steiner describes as the conscious experience of a spiritual reality.

> *Those who find it necessary to explain thinking as such by appealing to something else—such as physical processes in the brain or unconscious mental processes lying behind observed, conscious thinking—misunderstand what the unprejudiced observation of thinking provides. To observe thinking is to live, during the observation, immediately within the weaving of a self-supporting spiritual entity. We could even say that whoever wants to grasp the essence of the spirit in the form in which it* first *presents itself to human beings can do so in the self-sustaining activity of thinking.*
>
> *In examining thinking itself, two things coincide that otherwise* **must** *always appear as separated: concepts and percepts [or perceptions]. If we do not understand this, the concepts developed in response to percepts will seem to us to be shadowy copies of these percepts, while the percepts themselves will seem to present us with a true reality. We will also build a metaphysical world for ourselves on the pattern of the perceived world. Following the style of our mental imagery, we will call this metaphysical world the atomic world, the world of the will, or of the unconscious spirit, and so forth. And we will fail to see how, in all of this, we have built up only a hypothetical metaphysical world on the pattern of our perceptual world. But, if we see what is really present in thinking, we will recognize that only one part of reality is present in the percept and that we experience the other part—which belongs to it and is necessary for it to appear as full reality—in*

the permeation of the percept by thinking. We shall then see, in what appears in consciousness as thinking, not a shadowy copy of reality, but a spiritual essence that sustains itself. Of this spiritual essence we can say that it becomes present to our consciousness through intuition. *Intuition is the conscious experience, within what is purely spiritual, of a purely spiritual content. The essence of thinking can be grasped only through intuition.*[2]

Living thinking and its corpse

It is important to make the distinction between the essence of living thinking, with its love-filled richness and mobility, and its reflection in normal consciousness, which appears as a dead abstraction or corpse by contrast. Thinking in its essence, however, is imbued with feeling and will. One of the great goals of spiritual development is to experience life within thinking.

The difficulty of grasping thinking in its essence by observing it consists in this: when the soul wants to bring it into the focus of attention, this essence has all too easily already slipped away from the observing soul. All that is left for the soul then is the dead abstraction, the corpse of living thinking. If we look only at this abstraction, we can easily feel drawn to the mysticism of feeling or the metaphysics of will, which seem so "full of life." We find it strange if anyone seeks to grasp the essence of reality in "mere thoughts." But whoever truly manages to experience life within thinking sees that dwelling in "mere feelings" or contemplating the element of will cannot even be compared with (let alone ranked above) the inner richness and the experience, the inner calmness and mobility, in the life of thinking. It is precisely the richness, the inner fullness of experience that makes its reflection in normal consciousness seem dead and abstract. . . . Yet this is only the sharply contoured shadow of the reality of thinking— a reality interwoven with light, [diving] down warmly into the phenomena of the world. This [diving] down occurs with a power that flows forth in the activity of thinking itself—the power of

---

2   Rudolf Steiner, *Intuitive Thinking as a Spiritual Path*, chap. 9.

love in spiritual form. One should not object that to speak of love in active thinking is to [project] a feeling, love, into thinking. This objection is actually a confirmation of what is being said here. For whoever turns toward essential *thinking finds within it both feeling and will, and both of these in the depths of their reality.*[3]

Thinking and the human organism

Even though thinking appears in and through the human organization, this organization does not affect the essential nature of thinking. Rather, thinking represses the human organization's activities and replaces them with its own. What is typically referred to as thinking is simply the reflection of thinking, not thinking itself.

In normal experience, human thinking appears only in and through the organization of body and soul. This organization makes itself felt so strongly in thinking that its true significance can only be seen by someone who has recognized that nothing of that organization plays a part in the essential nature of thinking. . . . For our organization has no effect on the essence of thinking but rather retreats when the activity of thinking appears. Our organization suspends its own activity—it makes room—and, in the space that has been made free, thinking appears. The effective essence in thinking has a double function. First, it represses the human organization's own activity and, second, it replaces that activity with itself. Even the first of these, the repression of the bodily organization, is a result of thinking activity, of the part of that activity that prepares the appearance of thinking. We can see from this in what sense thinking is reflected in the bodily organization. Once we see this, we will no longer be able to mistake the significance of that reflection and take it for thinking itself. If we walk over softened ground, our footsteps dig into the earth. We are not tempted to say that the footprints are driven upwards from below by forces in the ground. We will not attribute to **those** *forces any share in the origin of the footprints. Similarly, if we observe the essence of thinking without prejudice, we will not*

---

3   Ibid., chapter 8, "The Factors of Life," addendum to the new edition (1918).

attribute any part of this essence to traces in the bodily organism that arise because thinking prepares its appearance by means of the body.[4]

I-consciousness and the bodily organization

While the human organization has nothing to do with the content of thinking, it does enable the human being to have a sense of itself or its I, which lies in the essence of thinking. Once this I–consciousness is brought about through the bodily organization, it can then be taken up in one's own thinking and becomes a part of thinking's spiritual being.

*If the human organization plays no part in the **essence** of thinking, what significance does this organization play in the totality of the human being? The answer is that what happens in the human organization as a result of thinking has nothing to do with the essence of thinking, but it does have something to do with the origin of I-consciousness out of thinking. The real I certainly lies in thinking's own essence, but I-consciousness does not. Anyone who observes thinking without prejudice sees this is the case. The I is to be found in thinking; but I-consciousness appears because the traces of thinking activity are engraved in general consciousness, as characterized above. (I-consciousness therefore arises through the bodily organization. But let us not confuse this with the claim that I–consciousness, once arisen, remains dependent on the bodily organization. Once arisen, it is taken up into thinking, and thereafter shares in thinking's spiritual being.)*

I–consciousness is based on the human organization, from which our acts of will flow. Following the preceding discussion, insight into the connection between thinking, the conscious I, and acts of will can be achieved only if we first observe how an act of will proceeds from the human organization.[5]

---

4   Ibid., chap. 9.

5   Ibid.

The brain gathers intelligence from everywhere

The brain is not a machine that produces thoughts. Even so, it does gather already existing intelligence that is found everywhere in the manifest world. Thanks to our brain, we can then use this gathered intelligence for our own purposes.

> One is attacked from all sides today if one says, it is nonsense that the **brain** thinks, for it is agreed everywhere that the brain thinks and that where there is no brain, there can be no thinking, that there are no thoughts where no brain exists. Well, from my lectures you will have seen that the brain naturally plays its part in, and has a significance for, thinking. But if those people, who in fact make little use of their brains, claim that the brain is a sort of machine with which one thinks, then this is mere thoughtlessness....
>
> What works as intelligence through the human head is at work everywhere. Intelligence is at work everywhere; even in insects there is marvelous intelligence....
>
> Human beings simply gather this intelligence that is spread out in the world and put it to use. Owing to their well-developed brains, they can put to their own use what permeates the world. Thanks to their brains, human beings can utilize the intelligence contained in all things for their own benefit.
>
> Our brain is not given to us for the purpose of producing intelligence. It is sheer nonsense to believe that we produce intelligence. It is as stupid as saying, "I went to the pond with a water pitcher to fetch water. Look, it contains water now; a minute ago there was none; the water, therefore, materialized from the walls of the pitcher!" Everybody will say that is nonsense. The water came from the pond; it was not produced by the pitcher. The experts, however, point to the brain, which simply collects intelligence because it is present in everything, like the water, and claim that intelligence emerges from within it. It is as foolish as saying that water is produced by the pitcher. After all, intelligence is even present where there is no brain, just as the pond does not depend on the water pitcher. Intelligence exists everywhere,

and human beings can take hold of it. Just as the water from the pitcher can be put to use, so humans can make use of their brains when they gather the intelligence that is present everywhere in the world....

You cannot leave the brain to its own devices and expect it to function any more than the water pitcher. What must be present so that the brain can gather intelligence?... It is the soul-spiritual element of the human being that does the collecting.[6]

The brain as mirror of thinking and ideation

A true understanding of thinking or any aspect of the human being needs to take into consideration the fourfold human being, which consists of three bodies: physical, etheric, and astral, in addition to the I, or a person's individuality.[7] By taking such a multifaceted view of the human being, we can come to understand how the process of thinking and ideation takes place in the three higher members of the human being just referred to. However, the brain does play the role of a mirror that enables us to be aware of thinking activity, the essence of which takes place outside the physical brain.

So long as philosophy—the ordinary philosophy of the day—refuses to recognize the truth about the human being, that he consists of physical body, etheric body, astral body, and I, it can come to no viable theory of knowledge. For knowledge is bound up with the whole human being, and unless the true being of humans, their fourfold nature, is taken into account, the question as to what knowledge is will only be answered by the empty phrases which are so familiar in modern philosophy....[8]

You all know that human beings could never attain to knowledge if they did not think, if in their minds they did not carry on something akin to work in ideation or thinking. Knowledge does not come of itself. Human beings have to undertake work within

6   Rudolf Steiner, *Health and Illness*, lect. 1/5/1923.

7   Rudolf Steiner used the German word *ich* for a person's individuality.

8   For more on the production of thoughts and the human etheric body, see Rudolf Steiner, *Course for Young Doctors*, lect. 12/17/1920.

themselves, they have to allow ideas to pass through their minds if they want to know. As adherents of spiritual science, we have to ask ourselves where in human nature those processes take place which we designate as ideation, as mental representation, and which lead to knowledge.

According to the materialistic illusion, the typical philosophic fantasy of today, knowledge comes about as a result of work carried out by the brain. Admittedly, work does take place in the brain in the act of cognition, but if we bear in mind that the main thing in knowledge is the work within the soul in the life of ideation, the question must arise: "Has the content of the process of ideation anything to do with the work which goes on in the brain?" The brain is part of the physical body, and what constitutes the content of our life of ideation, what constitutes the work of our soul in ideation, in mental representation, which is what brings knowledge about, does not go as far as the physical body; that all takes place in the three higher members of the human being, takes place from the I through the astral body down to the etheric body. As far as its content goes, you will find nothing in any element of our process of ideation which takes place in the physical brain. Thus, if we are talking expressly of the content, or of the activity of mental representation, we must attribute that solely to the three higher supersensible members of the human being, and then we can ask ourselves what the brain has to do with all this that goes on supersensibly in the human being. The obvious truth upon which modern philosophy and psychology are based, that in the act of cognition processes do take place in the brain, has of course to be admitted, it cannot and should not be denied, but it is relatively unimportant. Nothing of the mental representation itself lives in the brain. What significance, then, has the brain, has the external bodily organization in general, for knowledge, or let us say to begin with, for the life of ideation?...

As regards what really happens in our souls in the forming of ideas and in thinking, the work of the brain has precisely the same significance as a mirror has for human beings who see themselves in it. When you with your personality move through space, you do not see yourself—unless you meet a mirror; then *you **do** see what you are, you see how you look. A person who claims that the brain thinks, a person who professes that the work of ideation, of representation, goes on in the brain, is just about as shrewd as the person who looks at a mirror and says: "I am not walking about out here, that is not me. I must get inside the mirror, that is where I am." One would soon become convinced that he or she was not in the mirror, but that the mirror was reflecting what was outside it. So, it is with the whole of the physical organization. What becomes evident through the work of the brain is the inward supersensible activity of the three higher members of the human organization. The mirror of the brain is needed in order that this activity may become evident to the human being himself, in order that through the mirror of the brain he may perceive what he is supersensibly; this is an inevitable result of our contemporary human organization. If, as an earthly being today, the human being had not this reflecting bodily organism, primarily the brain, he would still think his thoughts, but he would not be aware of them.*[9]

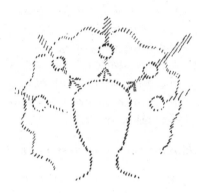

Figure 9.1: thinking taking place outside the physical body

Figure 9.1 illustrates the way thinking takes place in etheric and astral bodies, which are adjacent to the physical body. The circles represent the thoughts that are mirrored back into the etheric body, astral body, and the I and made visible to us by the brain.

Let us take [the above diagram] to represent the human physical bodily organization. If then we wish to express in correct diagrammatic form the human process of cognition, we have to

---

9   Rudolf Steiner, *Wonders of the World, Ordeals of the Soul, Revelations of the Spirit*, lect. 8/24/1911.

*say: "No part of what thinking is, nothing of the act of cogni-
tion, takes place anywhere within this external physical organism; it all takes place in the adjacent etheric and astral bodies
and so on." It is there that all the thoughts which I have indicated diagrammatically by these circles are to be found. These
thoughts do not enter the brain at all—it would be nonsense to
think that they do—they are reflected through the activity of
the brain and thrown back again into etheric body, astral body,
and I. And it is these images which we ourselves have first produced, and which are then made visible to us by the brain—it is
these mirrored images which we see when as earthly beings we
become aware of what actually goes on in our soul life. Within
the brain there is absolutely no thought; there is no more of
thought in the brain than there is of you in the mirror in which
you see yourself.*[10]

Thinking and the corresponding salt-depositing process in the body

The soul processes of thinking, feeling, and willing produce waves
that repeat themselves in the physical organism. In the case of thinking, whenever we focus on a thought, there is a crystallization process
that takes place in the body that results in the formation of salt deposits
between our blood and nervous systems.

*For every thought-process there is a corresponding process within
our organism; and the same is true in the case of every emotional
process, and every process which may be denoted as an "impulse
of will." We might put it in this way: whenever something takes
place in our soul life it produces a wave which repeats itself as
far down as the physical organism. Let us take first the process of
thinking, what occurs in thought. And here I wish to call attention
to the fact that it is best to fix our minds upon a thought process
that is either purely mathematical, or one which is equally objective, and which leaves our feeling and willing in a certain sense
uninfluenced; that is, we shall first consider thought processes in
pure and unalloyed form. What happens in our organism when*

---

10   Ibid.

such thought-processes go on within our soul life? Every time we fix upon a thought, there takes place in our organism a process which we may compare with another one of a different kind; by this I do not mean that what I am here stating is an analogy, for it is not an analogy, but an actual fact; and, when I say "we may compare" I mean that this comparison is to lead us to the facts of the matter. We may compare it with what takes place when we dissolve any kind of salt in a glass of water heated to a certain temperature, and by allowing this water to cool cause the salt to crystallize, thus bringing about the very opposite of the process of solution. When the salt is entirely dissolved the water is transparent; but when the water has cooled again, and the opposite process takes place in it, the salt separates itself from the water and crystallizes again. There comes about a reformation of the salt, a depositing of salt in the water. And when we observe water which at first was warm and then is brought to a state in which the salt recrystallizes in it, we see that there within the liquid a solid substance takes form. Something solid settles again, a salt-deposit. (As I said before, I have taken it for granted that these statements as to results of occult research will at first startle anyone who accepts quite pedantically, and in a purely conventional way, the facts recorded by external science.)

Now exactly the same process takes place within our organism when we think. *This corresponding process of thinking is a salt-depositing process, so to speak, which is caused by a certain activity in our blood and which irritates and reacts upon our nerve-system, a process, that is, which goes on in the "frontiers" between our blood- and nerve-systems. And just as we can look at the water in the glass and observe the formation of the salt as it separates and crystallizes, so we may see, when we observe a human being exercising thought, that just such a process, supersensibly perceptible in all its exactness to the clairvoyant eye, actually does take place. Thus, we have here brought before our minds the physical correlative of the process of thought.*[11]

---

11   Rudolf Steiner, *An Occult Physiology*, lect. 3/27/1911.

More on the brain as a mirror:
Salt deposits, mental images, and consciousness

As already mentioned in this chapter, the human being has four main members: I, astral body, etheric body, and physical body. The I, astral body, and etheric body respectively take hold of the warmth, gaseous, and fluid elements in the human being. The solid parts, which are mainly salt deposits, repel soul processes, including the soul process of thinking. These soul processes are reflected back in the form of mental pictures, which arise in one's consciousness.

> It can be said that the I takes hold of the inner warmth; the astral body of the gaseous; the ether body of the fluid and only the solid remains untouched; in the solid nothing enters. Picture to yourselves the way the human organism functions: You have the human brain that has fluid in it and solid parts into which, as I said, the soul does not enter. The solid parts are, in reality, salt deposits; whatever solid we have within us is always salt-like deposit. Our bones consist solely of such deposits. In the brain very fine deposits continually occur and again dissolve. There is always a tendency in our brain to bone formation. The brain has a tendency to become quite bony. But it does not become bony because everything is in movement and is continually dissolved. When we examine the organism, especially the brain, we first find within it a condition of warmth, and within the warmth the air, which is the bearer of the astral body and is continually playing into the cerebral fluid while being breathed in and out. We then have the cerebral fluid in which the ether body lives. Then we come to the solid into which the soul cannot enter because it consists of deposited salt. Because of this salt formation ... we have within us something into which the soul cannot enter.
>
> As human beings we have an organism; within this organism there are warmth, gaseous, and fluid elements, all of which the soul can penetrate. But there is something which the soul cannot penetrate. This is comparable to having objects on which light falls but cannot penetrate and is therefore thrown back. Let us say we have a mirror; light cannot go through it and is therefore

reflected. Similarly, the soul cannot penetrate the solid salt organism and is, therefore, continually reflected.

If this were not the case, there would be no consciousness at all. Your consciousness consists of soul experiences reflected from the salt organism. You are not aware of the soul life as it is absorbed by the warmth, gaseous, and fluid organism; you experience it only because the soul life within the warmth, gaseous, and fluid, is reflected everywhere by salt, just as sunbeams are reflected by a mirror. The outcome of this reflection is our mental pictures.[12]

Mirrored thoughts: Negative materiality in sun and brain

As previously mentioned in the chapter on electricity, Rudolf Steiner describes the sun in terms of a negative space. Similarly, the head has certain parts that are "emptier than empty." These make room for the soul-spiritual dimension of thinking to express itself. The active soul forms of thinking are everywhere pushing against the materiality of the brain and are thereby reflected. This reflection or mirroring of a soul activity that originates outside the brain is what we experience in our consciousness.

After death, consciousness can arise directly without the need for such a reflection process.

If one were fully to enter the place where physicists imagine the physical sun to be, one would initially find what one might identify as empty space. There is nothing there at all; there is absolutely nothing where the physical sun is supposed to be.... Nothing is there, only empty space. But what a strange empty space it is! When I say that nothing is there, I am not speaking altogether accurately; for there is less than nothing there. It is not merely an empty space but it contains less than nothing. An idea of this nature is extraordinarily difficult for modern Westerners to picture. Some people from the East would even today accept such an idea as a matter of course; for them there is nothing miraculous

---

12 Rudolf Steiner, *The Human Soul in Relation to World Evolution*, lect. 5/5/1922.

or difficult to understand if one were to say to them that less than nothing is there.... If you were to look through the Sun's corona, you would find the empty space that you would then enter most uncomfortably; for it would tear you apart. In this way it manifests its actual nature, that it is more—or, as I would rather say, less—than an empty space. You need only avail yourselves of the simplest mathematical concepts in order to cease finding what I am trying to say so puzzling: that an empty space is less than merely being empty. Let us suppose that you possess a property of some kind. It may also happen that you have given away what you possess and have nothing. But one can also have less than nothing; one can have debts, and then one truly has less than nothing. One can go from a space that is totally full to one that is ever less so, until one ends up with an empty space; and one can then go beyond mere emptiness in the same way that one can go from nothing to having debts.

That is the great misconception of the modern worldview, that it does not recognize this distinctive kind of negative materiality (if I may use such an expression), that it recognizes only emptiness and fullness and not what is less than emptiness.... There is also a place within the human being, I may say, which is emptier than empty; not in its totality but which has parts that are emptier than empty.... I am referring now to the physical human being who is as a whole a being who materially fills a space; but a certain member of human nature... does indeed have something about it, which is like the Sun, emptier than empty. This is... the head. It is just because man is organized in such a way that his head can become empty and in certain parts of it can be emptier than empty that the head has the possibility of making room for the spiritual dimension of life. Just picture the reality of this situation. Of course, this has to be done diagrammatically; but you may imagine that everything materially filling your head is indicated diagrammatically by what I am about to draw.

This would be your head [fig: 9.2]. But if I am going to draw it properly, I shall have to leave some empty spaces in this head. These are of course not so big, but there are empty spaces inside it; and into these empty spaces what I have over the course of these days referred to as the youthful spirit [young mind or spirit] can enter. This youthful spirit, in the form of its rays, is then incorporated in the drawing [yellow].

Now the materialists say that the brain is the instrument of the soul life, of the thinking. The opposite is true: the holes in the brain, what are more than holes (or, I could also say, less than holes), are the instrument of the soul life. And where there is no soul life, where the soul life is continually impinging, where the space in our skull is filled with the substance of the brain, nothing is thought, nothing is experienced by the soul. We need our physical brain not for our life of soul, we need it merely in order that we can take hold of our soul life, physically take hold of it. If the soul life that actually lives in the holes of the brain were not everywhere pushing against what is around it, it would vanish, it would never reach our consciousness. But it lives in the holes of the brain, which are emptier than empty.

Figure 9.2: spaces within the head

So, we must gradually correct our concepts. When we are standing in front of a mirror, we do not perceive ourselves but only our reflected image. We can forget ourselves: we see ourselves in the mirror. In the same way a person does not experience himself by assembling with his brain what lies in the holes of the brain; he experiences the way in which his soul life is reflected whenever it comes up against the substance of the brain. This reflective process takes place everywhere, and this is what a person experiences; he is actually experiencing the reflected image of his soul life. Whereas what slips through into the holes is that which then, once a person has passed through the gate of death, becomes conscious of itself without the resistance of the brain, because in that situation it is imbued with consciousness in a completely opposite sense.[13]

Life and death processes in white and red blood cells

Anatomically, brain cells are quite like the white corpuscles in the blood. However, they exhibit different dynamics. The white cells are full of life and in constant motion, while the brain cells are constantly dying and relatively immobile. In addition, white cells can reproduce and multiply, whereas the brain cells can do neither.[14]

The brain... consists of very small particles. When I draw these smallest parts, we realize that they... consist of some kind of lumpy, thick, and slimy substance [similar to white blood cells]. Several extensions consisting of the same substance radiate outward from this slime-like matter.

When we look at such a brain cell, we see that it stretches out its tiny feet or arms and touches those of the neighboring cells. These cells can be very long; some extend almost through half the body, and each one of them is again located next to others. When we study the human brain under a microscope, it appears like a number of dots in which the slime-like substance is more densely concentrated. Thick branches extend from there and intertwine. If you imagine a dense forest with thick tree crowns and big, interweaving branches, you get an idea of what the human brain looks like under a microscope.

Now you may say, all right, we have just heard a description of these white corpuscles living in our blood. The brain has been described as very similar; it, too, consists of many particles such as those we find in the blood. Thus, if we could remove all the white corpuscles from the blood without killing the person, and if we could put them neatly into the brain, after having removed that also, then we would have created a brain for that individual out of his or her own white blood cells.

---

13 Rudolf Steiner, *Human Evolution*, lect. 8/26/1918.
14 See the following note.

However, the strange thing is that before we could create a brain out of these white corpuscles, they would have to be almost dead. This is the difference between the white blood cells and the brain cells. The white corpuscles are full of life; they move around in our blood. I told you that they surge through the blood vessels just like the blood itself. Then they leave their original habitat. As I mentioned earlier, they become gourmets and even move all the way to the surface of the body. They move around everywhere in the human body.

In contrast to those cells, you will find that the brain cells always stay in one place. They are at rest. Each one merely extends its branches and thus touches the nearest neighbor. Whereas the white corpuscles are in constant motion, the brain cells are at rest and in fact are almost dead.... Our white corpuscles also have the ability to multiply. There are always some dying off and others being produced in this way....

The white blood cells are full of life, independent life, and they can reproduce. However, the intertwining brain cells cannot reproduce. One brain cell will never turn into two.[15] As the brain grows and increases in size, new, additional cells must move into the brain from the rest of the body. They must grow into the brain. The cells in the brain never multiply there, but merely accumulate. As long as we grow, new cells must constantly move into our head from the rest of the body, so that we have a sufficiently large brain when we are grown up.

The fact that the brain cells cannot multiply already tells us that they are almost dead. They are constantly in the process of dying. When we think about this in the right way, we discover a marvelous contrast in the human being: In the blood, we have cells, the white corpuscles, that are full of life, of a desire to live. In the brain, on the other hand, we have cells that actually have

---

15 There is some debate among researchers as to whether there are places in the brain where the brain can grow new cells (neurons). For instance, see Karen Weintraub, *Scientific American*, "The Adult Brain Does Grow New Neurons after All, Study Says," 3/25/2019 as found on 2/10/2021 at https://www.scientificamerican.com/article/the-adult-brain-does-grow-new-neurons-after-all-study-says/. There are also studies mentioned in the same article that cast doubt that such is the case.

a constant wish to die, that are constantly in the process of dying. Thus, it is true: as far as the brain is concerned, human beings are in a constant process of dying. The brain is constantly on the verge of dying.[16]

Electrical and magnetic forces in the human being

It is widely recognized that the human body is permeated with magnetic and electrical forces. According to Steiner, these forces entered the human organism for the first time several thousand years ago in the Lemuria epoch.[17]

Let us look back for a moment to an event of the Lemurian epoch.... There was a moment in evolution when what we today call magnetic and electric forces established themselves within the human being. For magnetic and electric forces live in us in a mysterious manner. Before this time, human beings lived on earth without the magnetic and electric forces that have developed ever since on a spiritual level between the workings of the nerves and the blood. They were incorporated into human beings at that time. The forces of magnetism we will leave out of consideration, and some forms of the forces of electricity. But the forces which I will distinguish as the electrical forces in galvanism, voltaism, etc., forces that have taken deep hold in the culture and civilization of our time, these forces entered the human organism in that far off time and combined with human life; and this very fact made it possible for them to remain for a long time unknown to human consciousness....

After humanity had passed the moment in the Lemurian age when it implanted into it the forces that pass through the wire today as electricity and work in an invisible manner in the human being, after this time had passed, electricity existed inside the human being.[18]

---

16   Rudolf Steiner, *The Human Being in Body, Soul, and Spirit*, lect. 8/5/1922.
17   See the position of Lemuria in Earth evolution in Appendix A, figure A:2.
18   Rudolf Steiner, *The Knights Templar*, lect. 10/2/1916.

Thoughts, electrical and magnetic forces, and the mastery of spiritual forces

The nervous system, like the brain, is in a continual process of dying and destruction. These death forces within the human being, which will become stronger in the future, are related to electrical and magnetic forces. Human beings will be faced with the challenge of directing their thoughts into outer mechanical forces. This should only be done at the right time by people who are suitably prepared.[19] This mastery of spiritual forces will need to extend to illnesses and death, including the spiritualization of medicine.

> *I have frequently made it a point, even in public lectures, to state that human consciousness is related to that of disintegration. Twice in public lectures in Basel, I said that we are in the process of dying within our nervous system. These forces of dying will become increasingly powerful, and a bond will be established between these forces, which are related to electromagnetism and external mechanistic forces. Human beings will, to a certain extent, "become their intentions," they will be able to direct thoughts into mechanical forces. Previously unknown forces in human nature will be discovered, forces that will be able to affect external electromagnetic forces.*
>
> *The first challenge related to this will be to unite human beings with technology, which must become an increasingly dominant factor in the future. The second problem involves calling for help from the spiritual situation. But this can be done only when the time is ripe and enough people have been prepared properly. Eventually, however, spiritual forces will be made flexible enough to master sickness and death; medicine will become intensely spiritualized. Caricatures of these facts come from certain sources, but they do show what must in fact happen.[20]*

---

19   See comments made by Rudolf Steiner to Ehrenfried Pfeiffer, mentioned in chapter 5, about the necessary conditions for the safe development of such technologies.

20   Rudolf Steiner, *The Reappearance of Christ in the Etheric*, lect. 11/25/1917.

Thinking and the brain in relation to generative and degenerative processes

In the nervous system, there is a continual process of the building up and breaking down of matter. This destroying or devolution of matter is what enables the human being to think. A fitting image of the relation of thinking to the brain is to imagine a dirt road that is filled with ruts after a rainstorm. The cause of the ruts does not lie in the earth but in the cars that drive over the road. In similar fashion, the brain is shaped from the outside by external etheric forces, not from the inside out.

In the human brain—we might even say, in the entire nervous system—matter is developed up to a certain point and then broken down. The depleted breakdown products are then reshaped in our nervous system. Breakdown and elimination, rather than synthesis and assimilation, underlie our conceptual activity. Our mental images depend on a constant atomistic dying process of sorts in our nervous system, a dying process that is constantly counteracted by reconstruction processes. We might say that the moment of death consolidates all the ongoing degenerative processes of the nervous system that are otherwise spread out over an entire earthly lifetime.

If we are capable of studying these activities, which involve the workings of material forces up to a certain point, followed by a degenerative process, we may ask ourselves what enables human beings to think. What forces enable us to be spiritual beings? Are they the same as the forces that allow us to enter earthly life through embryonic development? Not at all! Our physical system cannot be permitted to continue its linear development if we are to become human. After a certain point, devolution must set in. Devolution, not evolution, provides the basis for our mental activities.

Consider the consequences of the view I just formulated. People generally believe that the nerve process underlying thinking and conceptualizing is an ascending one like those of growth or nutrition. This is impossible. The basis of conceptualization is a degenerative process. *To provide a basis for our thoughts, for the functioning of spirit in us, matter must be destroyed and the products of destruction sculpturally reshaped. To be able to think, we must first destroy the material basis; we must punch holes in our brain, so to speak. Our ability to think is not based on organic growth forces. For the spirit to be able to move into the human body, our bodily organization must first undergo a process of degeneration, destruction, or partial death.*

Once you have understood this clearly, you will be able to express it in an image like this: We see a dirt road just after a rain. Cars must have been driving over the road, because it is rutted. But now let's assume that a being who has never seen cars comes down from Mars. The cars are gone, and the being from Mars sees only the ruts. So, it studies the ruts by going underground and then states that the forces that made the ruts exist below the surface of the Earth, in the Earth's interior, and that they worked upward from below to make the ruts. We cannot hold it against the being from Mars if it looks for the reason for the ruts in the wrong place, namely, in the soil, when in fact the ruts are due to cars driving over the dirt road.

Something similar is true of our brain. You may believe that it is shaped and organized from the inside out, but in fact the furrows in our brain are imprinted by soul-spiritual activity. At this point, we realize that our sensory-nervous system uses physical organs only to offer resistance to the spiritual or mental activities we carry out. We can draw conclusions about a car by tracing its tracks on a wet dirt road because everything the car did left a trace. Similarly, of course, we can also explain all thinking in terms of traces left in the brain. The materialistic view that explains thinking in terms of the brain is wonderfully deceptive. All thinking and conceptual activity can indeed be explained in terms of the brain, but only because spiritual activity has left its traces there.[21]

---

21   Rudolf Steiner, *The Healing Process*, lect. 9/3/1923.

Sculptural forces; Descending forces of the nerve sense system; Thinking as traces left in the brain

The nervous system, which is primarily in the head region, is the foundation for conceptualizing and thinking. There are two aspects of thinking. One is the mental images, thoughts, and conceptions present in our consciousness. The other is thought forces or etheric, sculptural forces, mentioned above, that work inwardly back into the body. These etheric, sculptural forces are especially active in forming the brain in small children.[22]

> If we look at the organization of the sensory-nervous system, which is primarily concentrated or localized in the human head, we will find, as I said before, that it supplies the foundations for our thinking and conceptualizing. But what is the human activity we call thinking? It is the reflection of the power of thoughts as such in our consciousness. Because of the way we perceive thinking, we say instinctively and involuntarily that a thought is not a reality. A thought as we experience it is powerless and is essentially present only in the form of an image.
>
> Thought activity, however, also has another, essentially different aspect. We can call this second aspect to mind quite easily if we simply consider how the conscious manifestation of thinking is still absent in a very small child, while this other aspect, the truly energizing, sculptural force of thought activity, is very much present. One aspect of thinking is revealed to ordinary consciousness in the form of mental images, thoughts, and concepts; the second is the force of thoughts that works back into the body. The latter aspect is identical to the sculptural force I mentioned earlier. Therefore, when we look at human mental activity in connection with the entire human organism, we must say that the aspect we perceive and experience directly is like a reflection of a real object. The reality of thought activity lies in its sculptural forces, which are directed inward. These inward-directed

---

22   And, therefore, these etheric forces should not be called away from this process of brain formation by premature exercise of conceptual thinking.

sculptural forces are evident in a very small child who has no conscious thought life as yet. In children, these forces work most strongly in shaping the brain, completing the organ that then forms the basis of true conceptual activity.

We do not hesitate to speak of latent warmth as opposed to manifest warmth. We know that certain processes release latent warmth, driving it out of the substance that binds it. Although we still hesitate to speak about it, a similar process takes place in children when conscious conceptual activity is consolidated out of the unconscious conceptual activity that is most active in shaping excreted matter to form the nervous system. This sculptural activity, which persists for the duration of a human life but is strongest in childhood, is the first suprasensible element in the human being.

Thoughts are suprasensible, but we experience only their reflections. The forces that shape our organs of thought, the forces that work on our nervous system, are also suprasensible.[23]

Waking and sleeping: Destruction and compensation

Two opposite processes take place in rhythmical alternation in the human body. They are 1) the destruction of delicate forms in our nervous system and brain while we are awake and engaged in thinking, and 2) reconstruction of delicate nerve structures in the nerves and brain while we are asleep. This is potentially an area for collaborative research that could include both natural and spiritual scientists.

To begin, we will consider a cycle familiar in everyday life, that of our waking and sleeping. What does it really signify? We can only understand the nature of sleep if we realize that in the present epoch the soul activity of human waking life brings about a continual destruction of delicate structures in the nervous system. With every thought and every impulse of will arising in us under the stimulus of the outside world, we are destroying delicate forms in our brain. In the near future, it will more and more be realized how sleep must supplement our waking day-life. We

---

23 Rudolf Steiner, *The Healing Process*, lect. 9/3/1923.

are approaching the point where natural science will join with spiritual science in these matters. Natural science has already produced more than one theory to the effect that our waking life operates in a kind of destructive way in the nerves and brain. Owing to this fact, we have to allow the corresponding reverse process—the compensation—to take place during sleep.

While we are asleep, forces of which we remain unconscious are at work in us that do not otherwise manifest themselves. They are busy reconstructing the finer nerve structures of our brain. Now, it is this very destruction that enables us to have processes of thought and to acquire knowledge. Ordinary knowledge would not be possible if processes of disintegration did not take place in us during our waking hours. Two opposite processes are at work in our nervous system—while we are awake a process of destruction, and during sleep a repairing process. Since it is to the destructive process that we owe our consciousness, it is that process we perceive. Our waking life consists in perceiving disintegrating processes. When we sleep, we are not conscious because no destructive process is at work in us. The force that at other times creates our consciousness is used up in constructive work when we sleep. There you have a cycle.[24]

When we are awake, the brain cells are really just about lifeless. And it is only because of this that we are able to think. If brain cells were more alive, we would not be able to think. We can see that this is so when we consider that the brain cells are more active when we are sleeping. It is precisely when we are not thinking but sleeping that they begin to live.[25]

Life and death forces, the nervous system, and consciousness

Consciousness arises through the interplay of the physical, etheric, and astral bodies.

The etheric or life body continually fends off the disintegration of the physical body until the moment of death. During waking life, the

24   Rudolf Steiner, *The Bhagavad Gita and the West*, lect. 6/1/1913.
25   Rudolf Steiner, *From Crystals to Crocodiles*, lect. discussion, 9/9/1922.

astral body suppresses the forces found in the ether body so that consciousness can arise. Consciousness cannot arise without this destruction of the life forces issuing from the etheric realm.

> *What is the function of the life body? At every moment it coun-
> teracts the destruction of the physical body, fights against this
> destruction; without the life body, the physical body would suc-
> cumb to the chemical and physical forces and disintegrate, as
> indeed it does as soon as the life body has abandoned it at death.
> While the two are united during life, the etheric body fights all
> the time against this disintegrating process.*
>
> *And what is the function of the astral body? It is very
> important to study this. In a certain sense the astral body is
> occupied during waking life—not during sleep—with killing the
> etheric body all the time, with suppressing the forces unfolded
> by the etheric body; hence the body becomes exhausted during
> the day. The astral body is all the time destroying the etheric
> body. But if this did not happen, no consciousness would arise.
> Consciousness is not possible without the gradual destruction
> of life. The spiritual activity of life which we are describing, the
> wonderful, scintillating life in the ether world and the constant
> suppression of this rhythm by the astral world, this is what
> gives rise to consciousness.*[26]

Part 2: INNER DEVELOPMENT
AND HIGHER LEVELS OF THINKING

Controlled thinking, imaginative cognition, and empathy

It is common today for people to allow thoughts to circulate undi-
rected in their heads. In the current age of the fifth post-Atlantean epoch,
it is essential to gain control over our thoughts to a similar degree as
we are able to control the movement of our limbs. The more that people
can consciously give direction to their thoughts the more they will be
able to think in pictures or imaginations. The capacity of thinking in

---

26   Rudolf Steiner, "Myths and Symbols," lect. 10/21/1907.

pictures will enable people to overcome antisocial instincts and to put themselves empathetically into the place of their fellow human beings, rather than remaining in their own viewpoints and opinions.[27]

> *It is necessary nowadays to learn quite concretely how to gain insight into supersensible worlds. We find ourselves in an age, for example, when a great, mighty transformation must come about, namely, that human beings [must change from being] thinking automatons into real, thinking human beings. Truly, it is shocking to say something like this. For it goes without saying that modern men and women consider themselves thinking beings. And if one demands of them that first of all they should become thinkers, they view that as more or less an insult. But nevertheless, it is so. Since the middle of the fifteenth century, people have been increasingly overcome by something that has turned them into thinking automatons.*
>
> *In a manner of speaking, we surrender nowadays to thoughts, we do not control them. Just imagine what it would mean if the same thing that happens to most of us these days in regard to the organ of thinking would happen in regard to other parts of the organism. Ask whether contemporary human beings can be inclined—I say, can be—to start intentionally with a thought and to conclude intentionally with a thought? Thoughts surge and seethe through people's heads nowadays. One cannot guard against them and submits to them automatically. Here, a thought arises, there, another is gone; images quiver and flash through the head. The best way to describe how people think would be to say: It thinks in human beings.*
>
> *Imagine if the same thing were to happen to us in regard to our arms and legs, and if we could not control them any more than we control our thinking! Just imagine that you would behave in public in regard to your arms the same as you behave in regard to your organ of thinking! Imagine all the different kinds of thoughts that flash through your head when you cross a*

---

27 This capacity of empathy will be addressed further in volume 2 when considering the necessary conditions for developing moral technologies or any form of sacred creation.

street. Now picture that you would constantly wave yours arms and hands around in the same way your thoughts flit hither and thither, not to mention your legs! Furthermore, we now face an epoch when we will have to learn to gain control over our thoughts, meaning specifically, to gain control over our thinking organs, just as we have control over our arms and legs. Human-ity is entering such an age. A certain inner discipline of thinking must take effect, but people today are still far from acquiring such a faculty.

Since the middle of the fifteenth century, humanity has entered the fifth post-Atlantean epoch [1413–3573 A.D.]. Before this epoch is over, human beings will actually have to learn to control their thinking, as they do their arms and legs. The true mission of this fifth post-Atlantean epoch will be fulfilled for those who will be able to do that. You can see that we deal with a serious matter if we try to consider what is, in a manner of speaking, arising on the horizon of humanity's evolution at the present time.

Now, something essentially different will be linked with the control of thinking that I have just mentioned. The more that human beings begin to control their thinking, the more will they be in a position to imagine pictorially again, to have imagi-nations. And imaginations will be required by human beings, for only through them will the antisocial impulses, so rampant today, develop into social impulses. Thus, through imaginations, human beings will acquire the faculty to put themselves in the place of other persons.... You cannot put yourself in the place of your fellows merely through abstract thinking. Abstract thinking makes you stubborn; abstract thinking causes you to be attentive only to your own opinion. Above all, abstract thinking generally leads us to close ourselves off more or less from the mobility that is needed for us to live with the spiritual world.[28]

---

28 Rudolf Steiner, *The Time-Sequence and Spiritual Foundation of Threefolding*, lect. 3/23/1919.

Imaginative cognition as sense-free thinking

Spiritual science refers to three levels of spiritual cognition or thinking, with imaginative cognition being the first level followed by inspiration and intuition.[29] Already at the level of imaginative cognition, the thinking process is freed from sense impressions and intellectual knowledge connected to the physical body. Thus, the human being attains a state of being independent of the physical body in his or her thinking, while still being within the body.

> It has often been said, even in public lectures, that at the stage of imaginative cognition a tableau of the present earthly life spreads out before man. A vista of his life lies before him in mighty pictures, and he is able to behold things that cannot be yielded by memory in the ordinary sense.
>
> In this vista which opens out as a result of the striving for imaginative knowledge, man is, to begin with, entirely within his physical and etheric bodies, but through the appropriate exercises he makes himself completely independent of everything by which impressions are transmitted to him from his physical body. In the activity of imaginative cognition man is therefore independent of his sense-impressions, and also of his intellectual knowledge. He lives entirely in the etheric body and the memory-tableau lies outspread before him.
>
> We can therefore say: man is now living in the supersensible, inwardly detached from his physical body. . . .
>
> It is necessary to bear in mind the difference between the condition of being bound up with the physical body and thus living within it, and the condition of being independent of the physical body but for all that remaining within it. There is a real difference, and it is the latter condition that obtains in the activity of

---

29 The path of inner development and exercises, which can lead to spiritual perception starting with imaginative cognition, can be found in the following books by Rudolf Steiner: *How to Know Higher Worlds: A Modern Path of Initiation, Theosophy,* and *An Outline of Esoteric Science,* from SteinerBooks / Anthroposophic Press.

imaginative knowledge. We remain within the physical body, we do not leave it, but we are nevertheless independent of it.[30]

Sense-free thinking: The intermediate path

In addition to achieving a state of sense-free thinking though working assiduously with the inner exercises that are contained in several of Rudolf Steiner's books, there is another way to achieve sense-free thinking, which Rudolf Steiner refers to as the *intermediate path*.[31] It requires a study of two of his epistemological works, *The Science of Knowing* and *Intuitive Thinking as a Spiritual Path*, both of which require rigorous thought control and enhanced memory.[32]

> *The path that leads us to sense-free thinking by means of information conveyed by spiritual science is absolutely reliable. However, there is another one that is even more reliable and, above all, more exact. It is presented in my books* The Science of Knowing: Outline of an Epistemology Implicit in the Goethean Worldview *and* Intuitive Thinking as a Spiritual Path. *These books present the knowledge human thinking can gain when it does not devote itself to the impressions of the external physical world of the senses, but only to itself. What is then at work is not the thinking that indulges only in memories of sense-perceptible things. It is pure thinking, which acts like a living entity within the human being. Although these books include none of the information conveyed by spiritual science, they demonstrate that pure thinking, working only within itself, is capable of unlocking the secrets of the universe, life, and the human being. These works constitute an important intermediate level between knowing the world of the senses and knowing the spiritual world. They present*

---

30 Rudolf Steiner, *Karmic Relationships,* vol. 2, lect. 5/30/1924.

31 For more on the topic of the intermediate path, See Ronald Milito's article, "Rudolf Steiner's Intermediate Path: A Road Less Traveled," at http://mathsciencehelp .com/intermediatepath2.pdf.

32 Rudolf Steiner, *The Science of Knowing*; and *Intuitive Thinking as a Spiritual Path: A Philosophy of Freedom* (also published as *The Philosophy of Spiritual Activity* and *The Philosophy of Freedom*.)

what thinking can gain by rising above sensory observation while not yet becoming involved in spiritual research.[33]

Individuals can go very far in this matter of catharsis [cleansing or purification of the soul] if, for example, they have gone through and inwardly experienced all that is in my book Intuitive Thinking as a Spiritual Path *and feels that this book was for them a stimulation and that now that they have reached the point where they themselves can actually reproduce the thoughts just as they are there presented. If a person holds the same relation to this book that a virtuoso, in playing a selection on the piano holds to the composer of that piece, that is, he reproduces the whole within himself—naturally according to his ability to do so—then through the strictly built up sequence of thought of this book—for it is written in this manner—catharsis will be developed to a high degree... [but if] a person has not been successful... one should not think what has been said is untrue, but rather that he or she has not studied it properly or with sufficient energy [and] thoroughness.*[34]

---

33 *An Outline of Esoteric Science*, chapter 5.
34 Rudolf Steiner, *The Gospel of St. John*, lect. 5/31/1908.

Appendix A: Earth Evolution Illustrations

Note: there are two phases of Earth evolution between "Conditions of Consciousness" and "Seven Evolutionary Epochs" not shown here: Seven Conditions of Life and Seven Conditions of Form.

Source: *Apocalypse of St. John* (London, Rudolf Steiner Press, 1977), CW 104, pullout illustration.

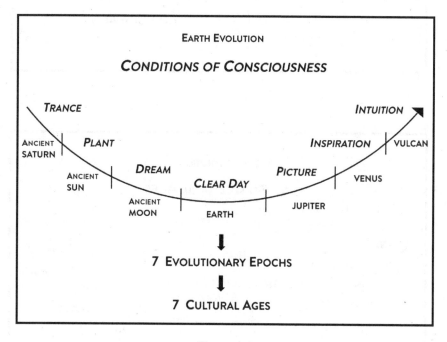

Figure: A-1

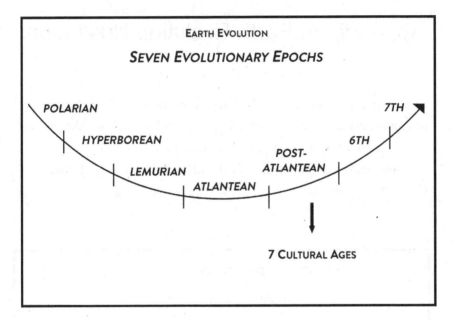

Figure: A-2

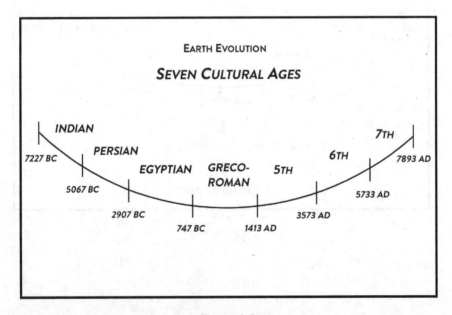

Figure: A-3

Appendix B: Publishers Referenced in this Volume

PRIMARY SOURCES

SteinerBooks / Anthroposophic Press

P.O. Box 58, Hudson, NY 12534, USA
Contact through website: https://steinerbooks.org/contact-us-1
Orders:
Phone: 703-661-1594
Email: steinermail@presswarehouse.com
Online: https://steinerbooks.org/

Rudolf Steiner Press: Editorial office

Hillside House, The Square
Forest Row, East Sussex, RH18 5ES UK
Phone: 01342 824433 / Fax: 01342 826437
Orders: https://rudolfsteinerpress.com
Telephone: 0845 370 0063
International: 0044 141 642 9192

Mercury Press

241 Hungry Hollow Road
Chestnut Ridge, NY 10977 USA
Orders: http://www.mercurypress.org/
Phone: 845-425-9357
Email: mercurypress@fellowshipcommunity.org
Fax: 845-356-8468

ADDITIONAL SOURCES

Adonis Press
Hillsdale, NY USA
http://www.adonispress.org/
Books available through SteinerBooks

Anthroposophical Society in Germany
Rudolf Steiner Haus
Zur Uhlandshöhe 10
70188 Stuttgart
Tel 0711 / 164 31 21
Fax 0711 / 164 31 30
info@anthroposophische-gesellschaft.org

(Publisher of Die «Mitteilungen aus der anthroposophischen Arbeit in Deutschland» sind Bestandteil der Zeitschrift «Anthroposophie weltweit» as referenced in chapter 5.)

Biodynamic Farming and Gardening Association
See SteinerBooks.

Association of Waldorf Schools of North America (AWSNA)
See Waldorf Publications.

Completion Press
M.S. 905
Lower Beechmont
QLD 4211, Australia
http://www.completionpress.com.au
Phone: +61 7 5533 1177
Email: info@completionpress.com.au

Perseus Verlag Basel

Postfach 611, CH-4144, Arlesheim, Switzerland

Phone: 0041 (0)79 343 74 31

Fax: 0041 (0)61 261 68 36

Email: kontakt@perseus.ch

(Publisher of Der Europäer)

Research Institute for Waldorf Education

351 Fairview Avenue, Suite 625

Hudson, NY 12534 USA

https://www.waldorfresearchinstitute.org

Email: patrice@waldorf-research.org

Phone: 518-828-9999

Rudolf Steiner Verlag

Sankt-Johanns-Vorstadt 19

4056 Basel, Switzerland

https://www.steinerverlag.com

Phone: +41 61 706 91 30

Verlag am Goetheanum

Hügelweg 53

CH—4143 Dornach, Switzerland

https://goetheanum-verlag.ch

Phone: +41 61 706 42 00

Fax: +41 61 706 42 01

Email: info@goetheanum-verlag.ch

Waldorf Publications

351 Fairview Ave. Suite 625

Hudson, NY 12534 USA

https://www.waldorfpublications.org

Phone: 518-828-9999

Email: publications@waldorf-research.org

Fax: 518-684-1588

Bibliography

Barnes, John Michael. *The Third Culture: Participatory Science as the Basis for a Healing Culture*. Hillsdale, NY: Adonis Press, 2009.

Fels, Alice. *Studien zur Einfuhrung in die Mysteriendramen Rudolf Steiners*. Dornach: Philosophicher Verlag, 1961.

Furst, Branko. *The Heart and Circulation: An Integrative Model*. New York: Springer, 2014.

Holdrege, Craig (ed.). *The Dynamic Heart and Circulation*. (Fair Oaks, CA. AWSNA Publications, 2002.

Lamb, Gary. *The Social Mission of Waldorf Education*. Hudson, NY: Waldorf Publications, 2017.

Lamb, Gary, and Sarah Hearn (eds.). *Steinerian Economics: A Compendium*. Hillsdale, NY: Adonis Press, 2014.

Langley, Janet, and Jennifer Militzer-Kopperl. *The Roadmap to Literacy: A Guide to Teaching Language Arts in Waldorf Schools Grades 1 through 3*. Maitland, FL: Mill City Press, 2019.

Meyer, Thomas (ed.), *Ehrenfried Pfeiffer: A Modern Quest for the Spirit*. Chestnut Ridge, NY: Mercury Press, 2010.

Pfeiffer, Ehrenfried. *On Rudolf Steiner's Mystery Dramas*. Spring Valley, NY: Mercury Press, 1988.

Savoldelli, Reto Andrea. *The Future Art of Cinema: Rudolf Steiner's Vision*. Forest Row, UK: Temple Lodge, 2020.

Steiner, Rudolf. *Alchemy of the Everyday*. Weil am Rhein, Germany: Vitra Design Museum and Authors, 2010.

———. *Anthroposophical Leading Thoughts: Anthroposophy as a Path of Knowledge: The Michael Mystery*. Forest Row, UK: Rudolf Steiner Press, 2007 (CW 26).

———. *Anthroposophy and the Social Question*. Spring Valley, NY: Mercury Press, 1982; also, *Conscious Society: Anthroposophy and the Social Question*. Forest Row, UK: Rudolf Steiner Press, 2018 (CW 34).

———. *Anthroposophy in Everyday Life: Practical Training in Thought–Overcoming Nervousness–Facing Karma–The Four Temperaments*. Hudson, NY: Anthroposophic Press, 1995 (collection).

———. *The Apocalypse of St. John*. Hudson, NY: Anthroposophic Press, 1993 (CW 104).

———. *Approaching the Mystery of Golgotha*. Great Barrington, MA: SteinerBooks, 2006 (CW 152).

———. *Art as Seen in the Light of Mystery Wisdom*. Forest Row, UK: Rudolf Steiner Press, 2010 (GA 275).

————. "Atomism and Its Refutation." Spring Valley, NY: Mercury Press, 1975 (CW 38).

————. *Awake! For the Sake of the Future*. Great Barrington, MA: Steiner Books, 2015 (CW 220).

————. *Becoming the Archangel Michael's Companions: Rudolf Steiner's Challenge to the Younger Generation*. Great Barrington, MA: SteinerBooks, 2007 (CW 217).

————. *The Bhagavad Gita and the West: The Esoteric Significance of the Bhagavad Gita and Its Relation to the Epistles of Paul*. Great Barrington, MA: SteinerBooks, 2009 (CW 146).

————. *The Boundaries of Natural Science*. Spring Valley, NY: Anthroposophic Press, 1983 (CW 322).

————. *Building Stones for an Understanding of the Mystery of Golgotha: Human Life in a Cosmic Context*. Forest Row, UK: Rudolf Steiner Press, 2015 (CW 175).

————. *The Challenge of the Times*. Spring Valley, NY: Anthroposophic Press, 1941 (CW 186).

————. *The Child's Changing Consciousness: As the Basis of Pedagogical Practice*. Hudson, NY: Anthroposophic Press, 1996 (CW 306).

————. *Christ and the Human Soul*. London, UK: Rudolf Steiner Press, 1984 (CW 155).

————. *The Christian Mystery: Early Lectures*. Hudson, NY: Anthroposophic Press, 1998 (collection).

————. *Conscious Society: Anthroposophy and the Social Question*. Forest Row, UK: Rudolf Steiner Press, 2018 (CW 34).

————. *Course for Young Doctors*. Spring Valley, NY: Mercury Press, 1997 (CW 316); newer translation, see *Understanding Healing*.

————. *Death as Metamorphosis of Life: Including "What Does the Angel Do in Our Astral Body?" and "How Do I Find Christ?"* Great Barrington, MA: SteinerBooks, 2008 (CW 182).

————. *The Destinies of Individuals and of Nations*. Forest Row, UK: Rudolf Steiner Press, 1987 (CW 157).

————. *Earthly Knowledge and Heavenly Wisdom*. Hudson, NY: Anthroposophic Press, 1991 (CW 221).

————. *Education as a Force for Social Change*. Hudson, NY: Anthroposophic Press, 1997 (CW 296, 192, 330/331).

————. *The Education of the Child: And Early Lectures on Education*. Hudson, NY: Anthroposophic Press, 1996 (CW 293, 66).

————. *Education, Teaching, and Practical Life*. Ghent, NY: AWSNA, 2007 (CW 297a).

————. *Esoteric Christianity and the Mission of Christian Rosenkreutz*. Forest Row, UK: Rudolf Steiner Press, 2000 (CW 130).

————. *The Essence of the Active Word: Course for the Priests of the Christian Community*. Dornach, Switzerland: Rudolf Steiner Publications, 1994 (CW 345).

———. *The Essentials of Education*. Great Barrington, MA: Anthroposophic Press, 1997 (CW 308).

———. *The Evolution of Consciousness: As Revealed through Initiation Knowledge*. Forest Row, UK: Rudolf Steiner Press, 2006 (CW 227).

———. *Faculty Meetings with Rudolf Steiner*. Hudson, NY: Anthroposophic Press, 1998 (2 vols., CW 300a/b).

———. *The Fall of the Spirits of Darkness*. Bristol, UK: Rudolf Steiner Press, 1993 (CW 177).

———. *Four Mystery Dramas*. Great Barrington, MA: SteinerBooks, 2014 (CW 14).

———. *Freedom of Thought and Societal Forces: Implementing the Demands of Modern Society*. Great Barrington, MA: SteinerBooks, 2008 (CW 333).

———. *From Crystals to Crocodiles...: Answers to Questions*. Forest Row, UK: Rudolf Steiner Press, 2002 (CW 347).

———. *From Beetroot to Buddhism...: Answers to Questions*. Forest Row, UK: Rudolf Steiner Press, 1999 (CW 353).

———. *Goethe's Faust in the Light of Anthroposophy: Volume Two of Spiritual-Scientific Commentaries on Goethe's* Faust. Great Barrington, MA: SteinerBooks, 2016 (CW 273).

———. *Goethe's Theory of Knowledge: An Outline of the Epistemology of His Worldview*. Great Barrington, MA: SteinerBooks, 2008 (CW 2)

———. *Goethean Science*. Spring Valley, NY: Mercury Press, 1988 (CW 1).

———. *Good Health: Self-education and the Secret of Wellbeing*. Forest Row, UK: Rudolf Steiner Press, 2017 (collection).

———. *The Gospel of St. John*. Spring Valley, NY: Anthroposophic Press, 1984 (CW 103).

———. *Guardian Angels: Connecting with Our Spiritual Guides and Helpers*. Forest Row, UK: Rudolf Steiner Press, 2004 (collection).

———. *Guidance in Esoteric Training: From the Esoteric School*. Forest Row, UK: Rudolf Steiner Press, 2001 (CW 267/268)

———. *Harmony of the Creative Word: The Human Being and the Elemental, Animal, Plant, and Mineral Kingdoms*. Forest Row, UK: Rudolf Steiner Press, 2001 (CW 230).

———. *The Healing Process: Spirit, Nature, and Our Bodies*. Great Barrington, MA: SteinerBooks, 2009 (CW 319).

———. *Health and Illness*. Spring Valley, NY: Anthroposophic Press, 1983 (CW 348).

———. *Health Care as a Social Issue*. Spring Valley, NY: Mercury Press, 1984 (CW 314).

———. *How the Spiritual World Projects into Physical Existence: The Influence of the Dead*. Forest Row, UK: Rudolf Steiner Press, 2014 (CW 150).

———. *How to Know Higher Worlds: A Modern Path of Initiation*. Hudson, NY: Anthroposophic Press, 1994 (CW 10).

———. *The Human Being in Body, Soul, and Spirit*. Hudson, NY: Anthroposophic Press, 1989 (CW 347).

————. *Human Evolution: A Spiritual-Scientific Quest.* Forest Row, UK: Rudolf Steiner Press, 2014 (CW 183).

————. *The Human Soul in Relation to World Evolution.* Spring Valley, NY: Anthroposophic Press, 1985 (CW 212).

————. *The Human Spirit: Past and Present—Occult Fraternities and the Mystery of Golgotha.* Forest Row, UK: Rudolf Steiner Press, 2015 (CW 167).

————. *Human Values in Education.* Great Barrington, MA: Anthroposophic Press, 2004 (CW 310).

————. *Illness and Therapy: Spiritual-Scientific Aspects of Healing.* Forest Row, UK: Rudolf Steiner Press, 2013 (CW 313).

————. *The Incarnation of Ahriman: The Embodiment of Evil on Earth.* Forest Row, UK: Rudolf Steiner Press, 2009 (collection).

————. *The Inner Aspect of the Social Question.* London: Rudolf Steiner Press, 1974 (CW 193); see also *Problems of Society.*

————. *Inner Impulses of Evolution: The Mexican Mysteries, the Knights Templar.* Hudson, NY: Anthroposophic Press, 1984 (CW 171).

————. *The Inner Nature of Man: And Our Life between Death and Rebirth.* Forest Row, UK: Rudolf Steiner Press, 2013 (CW 153).

————. *Intuitive Thinking as a Spiritual Path: A Philosophy of Freedom.* Hudson, NY: Anthroposophic Press, 1995 (CW 4).

————. *The Karma of Materialism.* Spring Valley, NY: Anthroposophic Press, 1985 (CW 176).

————. *The Karma of Untruthfulness: Secret Societies, the Media, and Preparations for the Great War* (2 vols.). Forest Row, UK: Rudolf Steiner Press, 2005 (CW 173/174).

————. *The Karma of Vocation.* Spring Valley, NY: Anthroposophic Press, 1984 (CW 172).

————. *Karmic Relationships: Esoteric Studies,* vol. 2. Forest Row, UK: Rudolf Steiner Press, 1974 (CW 236).

————. *Karmic Relationships: Esoteric Studies,* vol. 3. Forest Row, UK: Rudolf Steiner Press, 2002 (CW 237).

————. *The Knights Templar: The Mystery of the Warrior Monks.* Forest Row, UK: Rudolf Steiner Press, 2007 (collection).

————. *Lebendiges Naturerkennen, Intellektueller Sündenfall, und Spirituelle Sündenerhebung.* Dornach: Rudolf Steiner Verlag, 1982 (tr. T. O'Keefe and C. Venho); English: *Awake! For the Sake of the Future* (CW 220).

————. *The Light Course: First Course in Natural Science: Light, Color, Sound— Mass, Electricity, Magnetism.* Great Barrington, MA: Anthroposophic Press, 2001 (CW 320).

————. *Man and the Earth in Northern and Southern Regions.* Hudson, NY: Rudolf Steiner Library, unpublished ms. (CW 351).

————. *Man and the World of Stars: The Spiritual Communion of Mankind.* New York: Anthroposophic Press, 1963 (CW 219).

————. *Manifestations of Karma.* Forest Row, UK: Rudolf Steiner Press, 2011 (CW 120).

———. *Memory and Habit: The Sense for Truth, The Phenomenon of Metamorphosis in Life.* London: Anthroposophic Publishing, 1948 (CW 170); see also *The Riddle of Humanity.*

———. *A Modern Art of Education.* Great Barrington, MA: Anthroposophic Press, 2004 (CW 307).

———. *Mystery of the Universe: The Human Being, Model of Creation.* Forest Row, UK: Rudolf Steiner Press, 2001 (CW 201).

———. *Natural Science at the Crossroads.* Chestnut Ridge, NY: Mercury Press, 2020 (CW 56).

———. *The New Spirituality and the Christ Experience of the Twentieth Century.* Hudson, NY: Anthroposophic Press, 1988 (CW 200).

———. *The Occult Movement in the Nineteenth Century and Its Relation to Modern Culture.* London, UK: Rudolf Steiner Press, 1973 (CW 254).

———. *An Occult Physiology.* Forest Row, UK: Rudolf Steiner Press, 2005 (CW 128).

———. *Old and New Methods of Initiation.* Forest Row, UK: Rudolf Steiner Press, 1991 (CW 210)

———. *Original Impulses for the Science of the Spirit.* Lower Beechmont, Australia: Completion Press, 2001 (CW 96).

———. *On the Play of the Child.* Spring Valley, NY: WECAN, 2012 (ed. F. Jaffke).

———. *The Origins of Natural Science.* Spring Valley, NY: Anthroposophic Press, 1985 (CW 326).

———. *An Outline of Esoteric Science.* Hudson, NY: Anthroposophic Press, 1997 (CW 13).

———. "Overcoming Nervousness." Spring Valley, NY: Anthroposophic Press 1969; see *Anthroposophy in Everyday Life.*

———. *Polarities in the Evolution of Mankind: West and East; Materialism and Mysticism; Knowledge and Belief.* New York: Anthroposophic Press, 1987 (CW 197).

———. *Practical Advice to Teachers.* Hudson, NY: Anthroposophic Press, 2000 (CW 294).

———. *The Problems of Our Times.* New York: Anthroposophic Press, 1943 (CW 193); new translation available as *Problems of Society.*

———. *Problems of Society: An Esoteric View, from Luciferic Past to Ahrimanic Future.* Forest Row, UK: Rudolf Steiner Press, 2016 (CW 193)

———. *The Reappearance of Christ in the Etheric* (Great Barrington, MA: SteinerBooks, 2003 (collection).

———. *Reimagining Academic Studies: Science, Philosophy, Education, Social Science, Theology, Theory of Language.* Great Barrington MA: SteinerBooks, 2015 (CW 8).

———. *The Renewal of Education.* Great Barrington, MA: Anthroposophic Press, 2001 (CW 301).

———. *The Renewal of the Social Organism.* Spring Valley, NY: Anthroposophic Press, 1985 (CW 24).

————. *Rethinking Economics: Lectures and Seminars on World Economics.* Great Barrington, MA: Steiner Books, 2013 (CW 340, 341).

————. *The Riddle of Humanity: Spiritual Background of Human History.* Forest Row, UK: Rudolf Steiner Press, 1990 (CW 170).

————. *Rudolf Steiner in the Waldorf School: Lectures and Addresses to Children, Parents, and Teachers.* Hudson, NY: Anthroposophic Press, 1996 (CW 298).

————. *The Science of Knowing: Outline of an Epistemology Implicit in the Goethean World View.* Chestnut Ridge, NY: Mercury Press, 1988 (CW 2); see also newer translation, *Goethe's Theory of Knowledge.*

————. *The Schiller File: Supplements to the Collected Works of Rudolf Steiner: Scientific Research Suggested by Dr. Rudolf Steiner.* Great Barrington, MA: SteinerBooks, 2010.

————. *Secret Brotherhoods: And the Mystery of the Human Double.* Forest Row, UK: Rudolf Steiner Press, 2004 (CW 178).

————. *Secrets of the Threshold.* Hudson, NY: Anthroposophic Press, 1987 (CW 147).

————. *Social and Antisocial Forces in the Human Being.* Spring Valley, NY: Mercury Press, 1982 (CW 186).

————. *The Social Future: Culture, Equality, and the Economy.* Great Barrington, MA: SteinerBooks, 2013 (CW 332a).

————. *Soul Economy: Body, Soul, and Spirit in Waldorf Education.* Great Barrington, MA: Anthroposophic Press 2003 (CW 303).

————. *The Spiritual Foundations for the Renewal of Agriculture.* Kimberton, PA: Biodynamic Farming and Gardening Association, 1993 (CW 327).

————. *The Spiritual Ground of Education.* Great Barrington, MA: Anthroposophic Press, 2004 (CW 305).

————. *Spiritual Science as a Foundation for Social Forms.* Hudson, NY: Anthroposophic Press, 1986 (GA 199).

————. *St. John's Tide.* Spring Valley, NY: Mercury Press, 1984 (CW 224).

————. *The Temple Legend: Freemasonry and Related Occult Movements: From the Contents of the Esoteric School.* Forest Row, UK: Rudolf Steiner Press, 2014 (CW 93).

————. *The Tension between East and West.* Spring Valley, NY: Anthroposophic Press, 1983 (CW 83).

————. *Theosophy: An Introduction to the Spiritual Processes in Human Life and in the Cosmos.* Hudson, NY: Anthroposophic Press, 1994 (CW 9).

————. *Three Streams in Human Evolution.* Forest Row, UK: Rudolf Steiner Press, 1985 (CW 184).

————. *The Time-Sequence and Spiritual Foundations for Threefolding.* Spring Valley, NY: Mercury Press, 1998 (CW 190).

————. *Toward Imagination: Culture and the Individual.* Hudson, NY: Anthroposophic Press, 1990 (CW 169).

————. *Towards Social Renewal: Rethinking the Basis of Society.* Forest Row, UK: Rudolf Steiner Press, 2009 (CW 23).

————. *Understanding Healing: Meditative Reflections on Deepening Medicine through Spiritual Science*. Forest Row, UK: Rudolf Steiner Press (CW 316).

————. *Understanding Society through Spiritual-Scientific Knowledge: Social Threefolding, Christ, Lucifer, and Ahriman*. Forest Row, UK: Rudolf Steiner Press, 2017 (CW 191).

————. *Unifying Humanity Spiritually: Through the Christ Impulse*. Forest Row, UK: Rudolf Steiner Press, 2014 (CW 165).

————. *Waldorf Education and Anthroposophy 2*. Hudson, NY: Anthroposophic Press, 1996 (CW 304a).

————. *Warmth Course*. Chestnut Ridge, NY: Mercury Press, 2016 (CW 321).

————. *Wonders of the World, Ordeals of the Soul, Revelations of the Spirit*. London: Rudolf Steiner Press, 1963 (CW 129).

Veit, Wolfgang. *Bewegte Bilder: Der Zyklus "Metamorphosen der Furcht" von Jan Stuten—Entwurf zu einer neuen Licht-Spiel-Kunst nach einer Idee von Rudolf Steiner*. Stuttgart: Urachhaus, 1993.

Wachsmuth, Guenther. *The Life and Work of Rudolf Steiner: From the Turn of the Century to His Death*. Blauvelt, NY: Spiritual Science Library, 1989.

Acknowledgements

Firstly, I must express my deep appreciation to Virginia Hermann and Martin "Marty" Miller for their devoted work toward the completion of this book. They contributed in untold ways, including materials research, proofreading, sorting and sequencing passages, transcribing passages, and offering their abiding support and friendship. This book would never have reached completion without their help.

In addition to Virginia and Marty, five other people read through all the chapters at various stages of our research, which included proofing, editing, fact checking, and suggestions: Sherry Wildfeuer, Gopi Krishna Vijaya, Ronald Milito, Rachel Schneider, and Judith Soleil. Several people with impeccable timing jumped in to help to proofread or edit a chapter or two, including Magdalena Bermudez, Charlotte Hoppe, Emily Jones, Cameron MacArthur, and Jane Ried.

Additionally, numerous people reviewed one or more chapters, sharing their personal and professional perspectives and insights. These include David Adams, John Barnes, John Bloom, Harlan Gilbert, Michael Howard, Snetu Karania, Kevin Kilb, Patrice Maynard, Robert Oelhaf, Daniel Perez, Nicanor Perlas, Janene Ping, Martin Ping, Barbara Reynolds, Christopher Schaefer, David Schwartz, Stephen Usher, and Charles Weems. An additional thanks goes to Michael Howard for creating artistic renderings for each chapter, the cover seal, various atomic perspectives, and central and cosmic forces. Thanks also go to Tara Bowers for her general support that kept the editor focused on his work.

Our materials research resulted in several hundred potential references, which needed to be sorted, catalogued, and transcribed. My thanks to Michael Lapointe, Peter Buckbee, and Nadia Bedard who set up what eventually became a thirty-five-page spreadsheet, logged in reference information, and helped with transcribing passages.

Much of the research for this book took place at the Rudolf Steiner Library with its vast collection of Rudolf Steiner and related works in Hudson, New York. Library workers Kathleen Bradley and Martin Miller were ever ready to assist us to track down even the most elusive citations. Also, the Rudolf Steiner Archive & e.Lib was a valuable aid in researching references.

I also want to thank our grassroots supporters who responded to our annual appeals with donations and pledged monthly payments and attended our presentations on ethical technology over the last three years.

And a special thanks goes to the following organizations and people who provided grants in support of Volume 1: Foundation for Cultural Renewal, Foundation for Rudolf Steiner Books, RSF Social Finance, Rudolf Steiner Charitable Trust, Triodos Foundation, Gordon Edwards, Alice Groh, and Don Jamison and Christina M. Root.

We relied on the works of several publishers to obtain the appropriate perspectives of Rudolf Steiner for Volume 1, especially SteinerBooks and Rudolf Steiner Press. There is a complete list and contact information at the end of the book for all the publishers whose works we accessed.

Also, I need to acknowledge the many friends and colleagues who have departed this world whose support and guidance I have felt throughout the process of preparing Volume 1 of *A Road to Sacred Creation*.

And ultimately, I would like to acknowledge and thank the spiritual leader and initiate, Rudolf Steiner, whose illuminating insights flow through every page of this volume.

About the Editor

Gary Lamb is a director of the Hawthorne Valley Center for Social Research and its Ethical Technology Initiative, located in the Hudson Valley region of Upstate New York. His technical background includes a degree in civil technology and mathematics, and employment in the fields of building construction, medical technology, and manufacturing. Prior to working on *A Road to Sacred Creation,* he edited *Steinerian Economics* (2014) with Sarah Hearn, a compendium of Rudolf Steiner's perspectives on economics, published by Adonis Press, and he has authored books on Waldorf education and associative economics: *Social Mission of Waldorf Education* (2017); *Wellsprings of the Spirit* (2007); and *Associative Economics* (2016), all published by AWSNA Publications (now Waldorf Publications). Gary was also the managing editor of *The Threefold Review,* a journal based on Rudolf Steiner's ideas on a threefold social organism.